The Unofficial Adult Coloring & Picture Book:

Coping Skills via Trauma Recovery

By Brian D. Satterfield

The Unofficial Adult Coloring & Picture Book: Coping Skills via Trauma Recovery
by Brian D. Satterfield
ISBN-13: 9780999471739

Published by Brian D. Satterfield®, Pa (USA)

Please enjoy this project! And, try to allow the flow within and among us from the spirit in each of us humans being. ~Brian

For my best four-legged companions waiting patiently for the gods, rebirth, or myself… Till we meet again, I miss and love everyone one of you. In loving memory of Tuesday, Buttons, Elmer, Wacey, Keria, Boba and Rylee. Painfully, Boba and Rylee died while editing books number one and four. I'm a domesticated animal person. I've been living with some feline(s) and canine(s) since 1994. Pets are great companions and an even better positive life coping skill for me…

And, the fur-babies keeping me going via big mouths, porch time, farts and belches: Rylee's presence (Roo/Smiley Rylee) Voodoo (Hell Beast/Kinky Boots) and Vulcan (Handsome Rob/Mr. Annoying), and adjusting to our home front as of FEB 2020 – the rescued baby "Athena"...

A few humans also: Gram (Margaret Willard), Mum (Janice Marie) and the father seed who allowed the gods to form within my mum, Kimberly…

To the best human partner, "Mrs. Right-For-Me" to grow old with and beyond: Stacey Lynn

Everyone else, Not sure that I didn't forget you!

Agencies I thank for keeping my sanity and pain train manageable:
Mechanicsburg Chiropractic, UPMC Family Practice, UPMC Pain Management Clinic, Kakari Eye Institute, Mechanicsburg Veterinary Center, NAMI, MHA, US Pain Connection, Male Survivor, Disabilities Rights of Pa, the Appalachian Trail, Cumberland/Perry County MH/IDD Office, PRO-A, OMHSAS, SAMHSA, Blink Health (discount generic prescription drug program), Philadelphia professional franchisee sports teams, Planet Fitness, Drayer Physical Therapy, International Pain Foundation… Plus a few I'm sure I've missed!

Folks I thank: you know who you are…

Support open source - Developed on Kubuntu 18.04 using LibreOffice 6.0 and GIMP 2.8

Also from the author...

The Mental Health Survival Guide: Managing the Severities of Multi-Mental Health Diagnosis
ISBN: 9780999471708

Napkin Notes Volume One: Hand Drawn Expressions
ISBN: 9780999471715

Hawaiian Shorts Volume One: Rants & Raves via Trauma Recovery
ISBN: 9780999471722

A-Z 95 Positive Life Coping Skills
@ www.brianstraumaproject.org

Free Health & Free Legal Resources
Free on social media, also all of Brian's books
And, www.brianstraumaproject.org

Connect with Brian here:

www.brianstraumaproject.org

twitter.com/bdsatterfield

pinterest.com/
brianstraumaproject

facebook.com/briandsatterfield

linkedin.com/in/brian-d-
satterfield

youtube/decide2evolve

brianstraumaproject@gmail.com

D2E

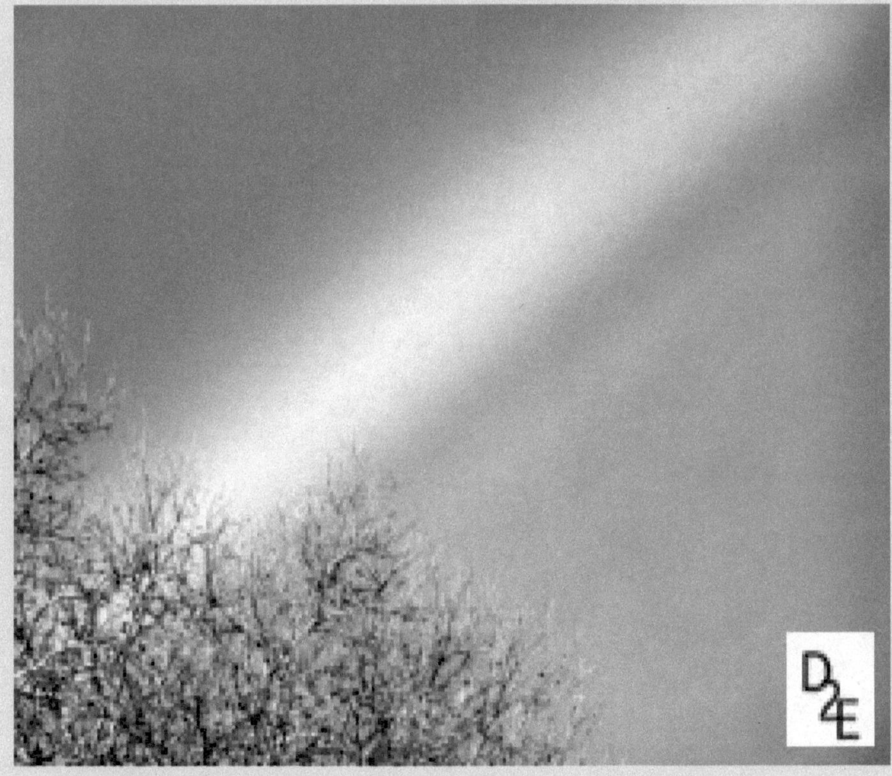
D4E

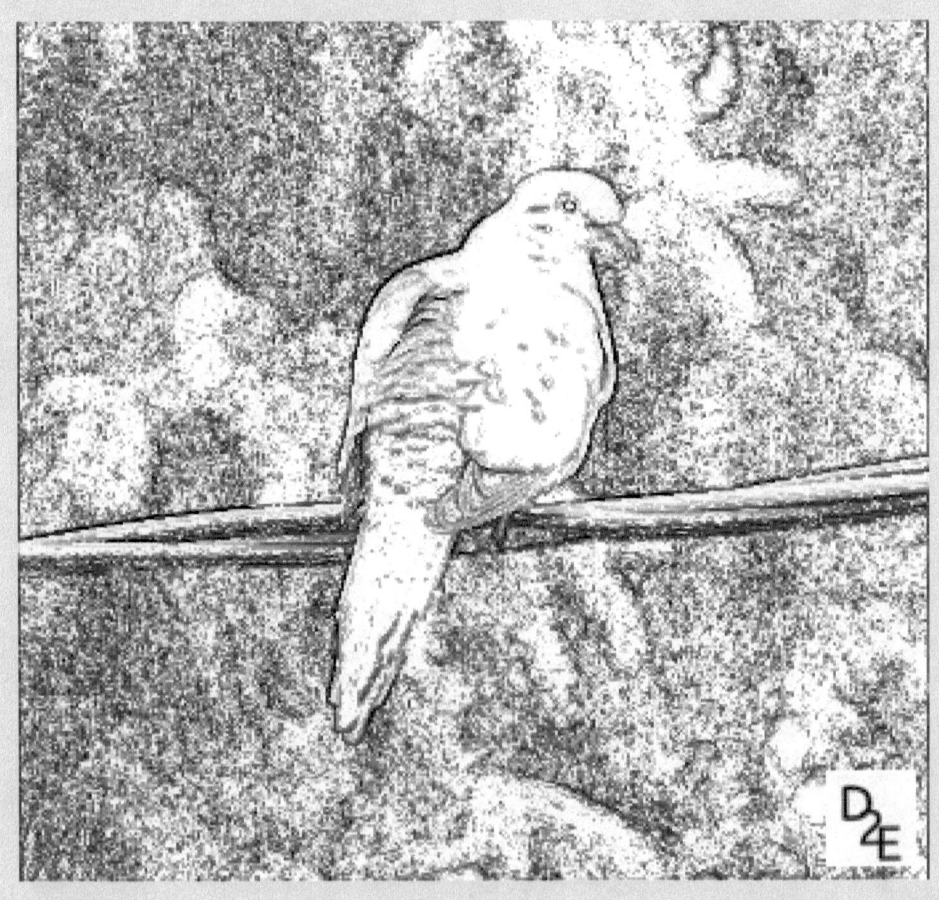
D2E

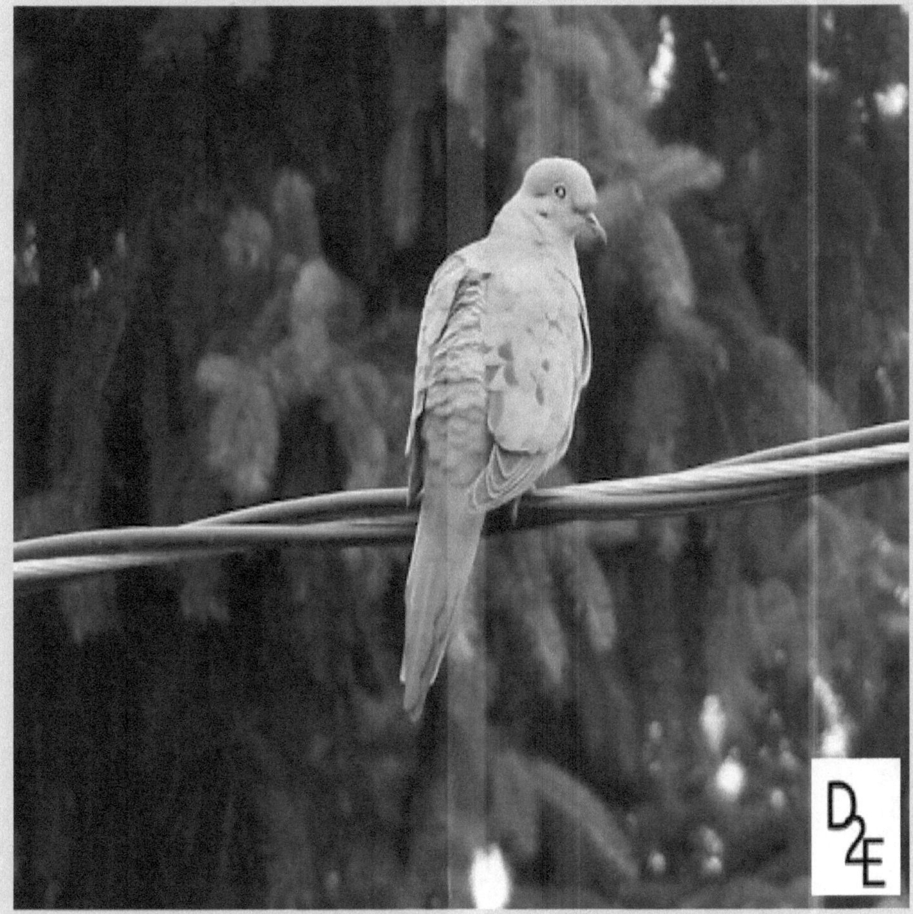

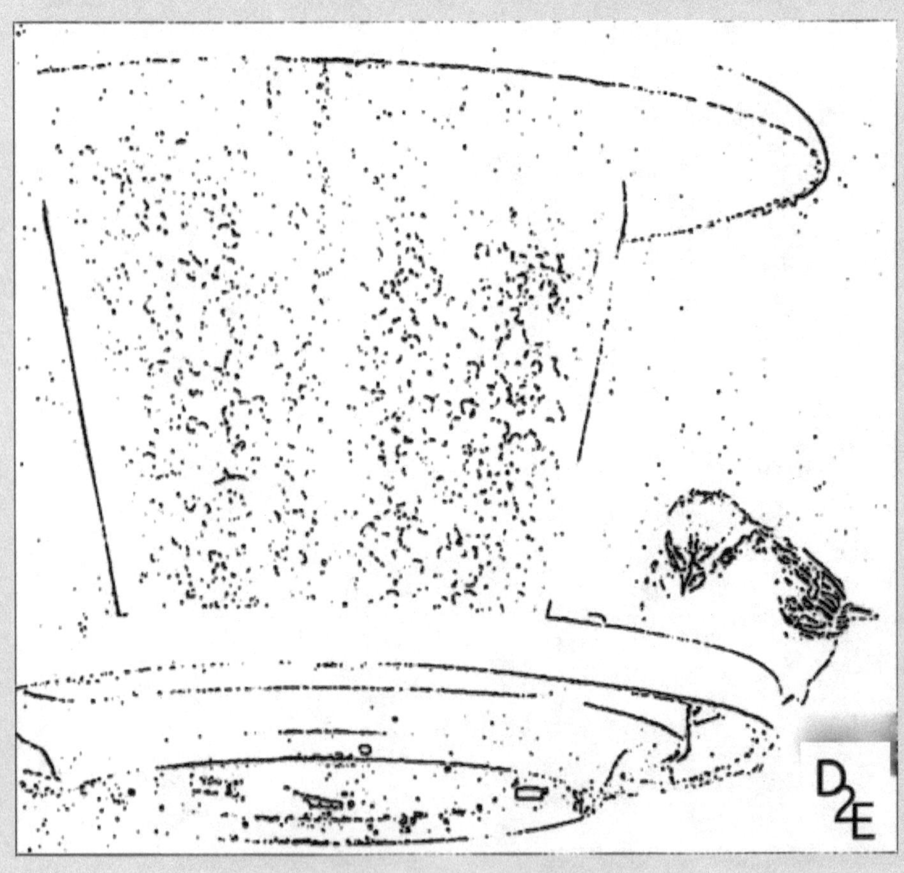
D2E

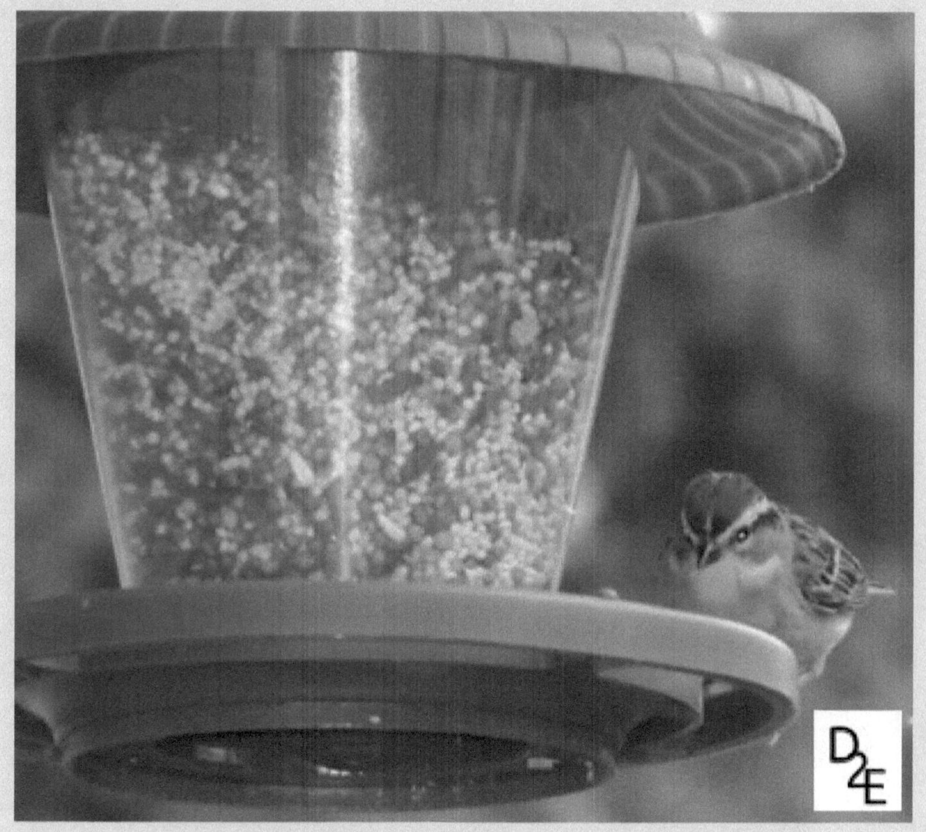

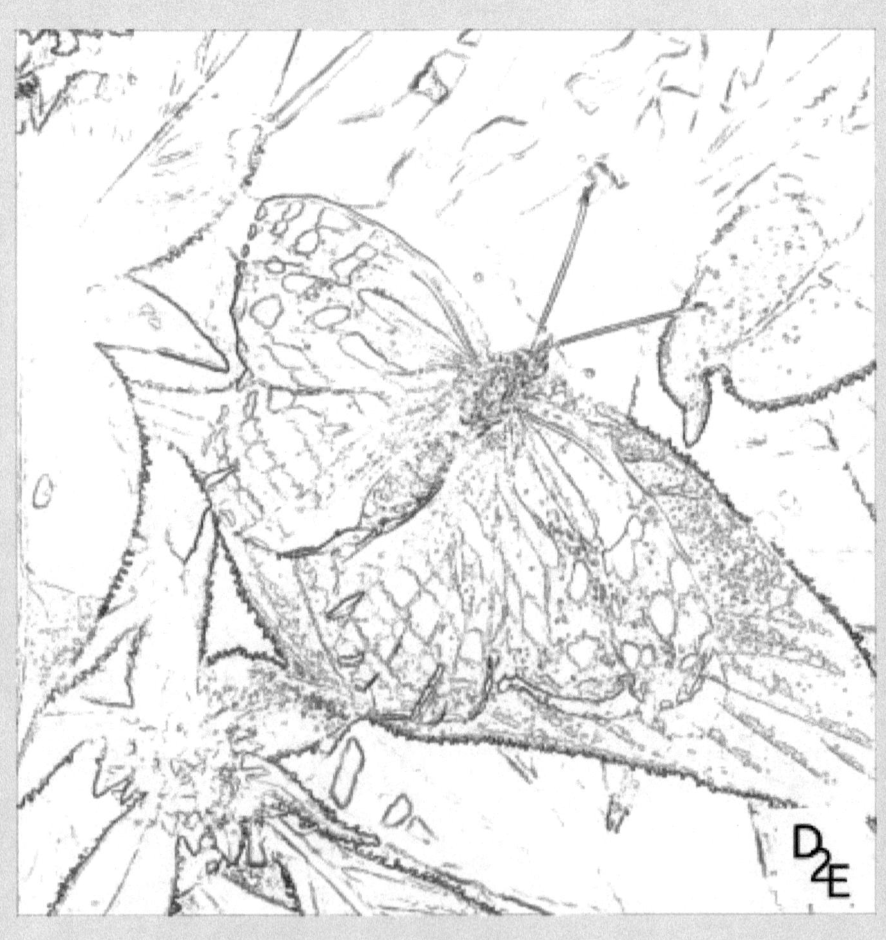
D2E

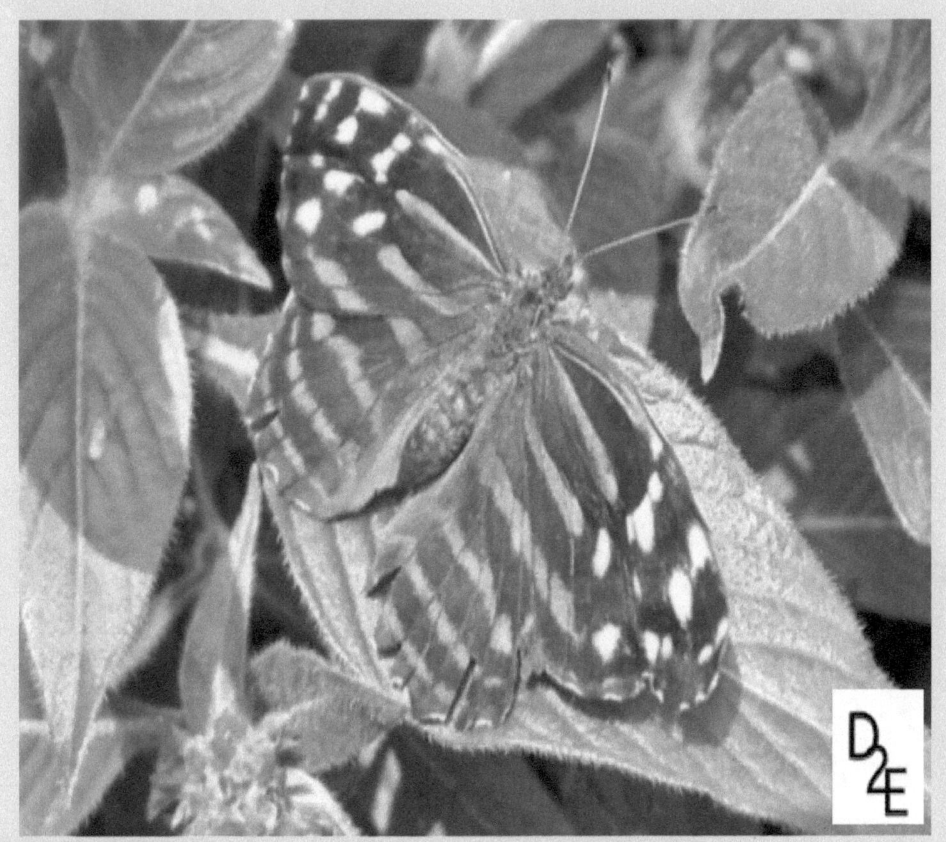

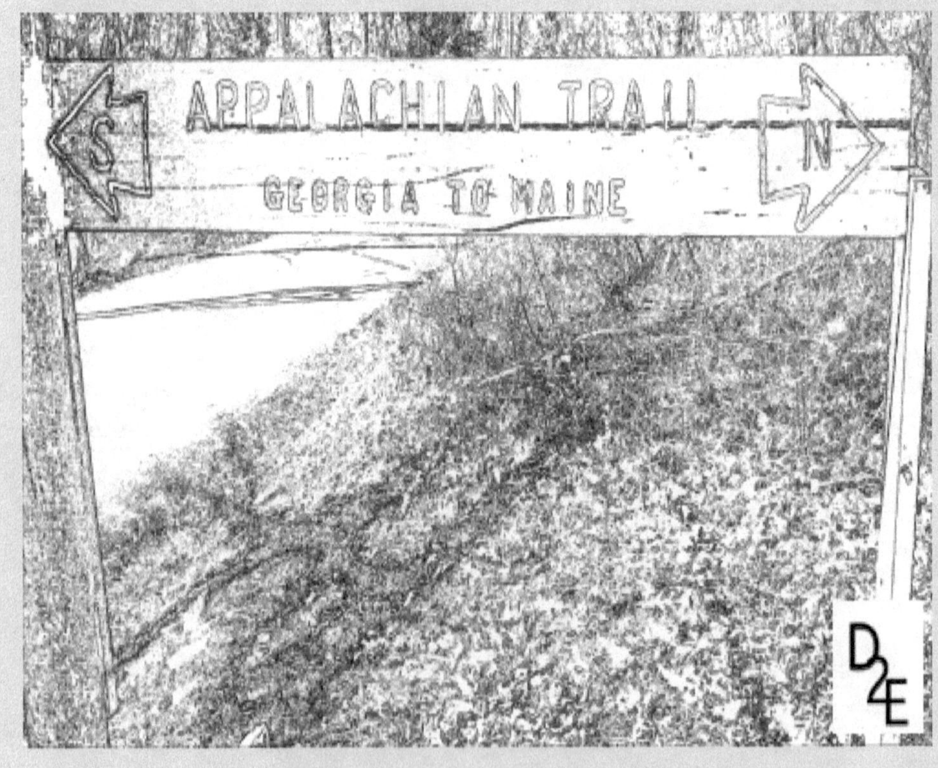
S
APPALACHIAN TRAIL
N
GEORGIA TO MAINE
D2E

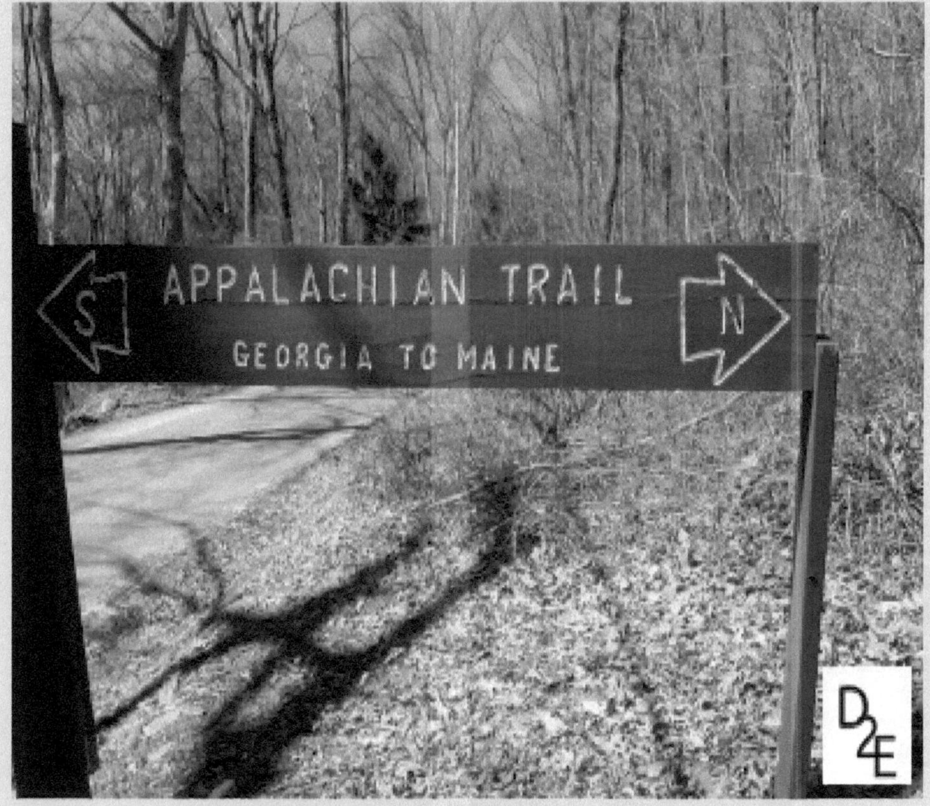
APPALACHIAN TRAIL
GEORGIA TO MAINE
S
N
D2E

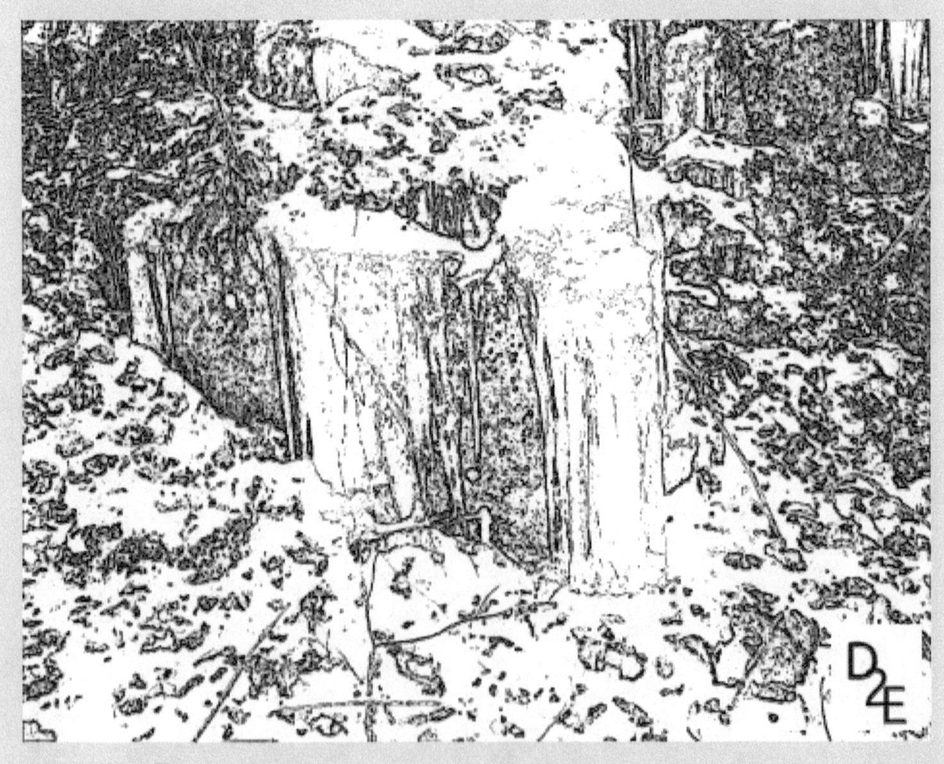
D2E

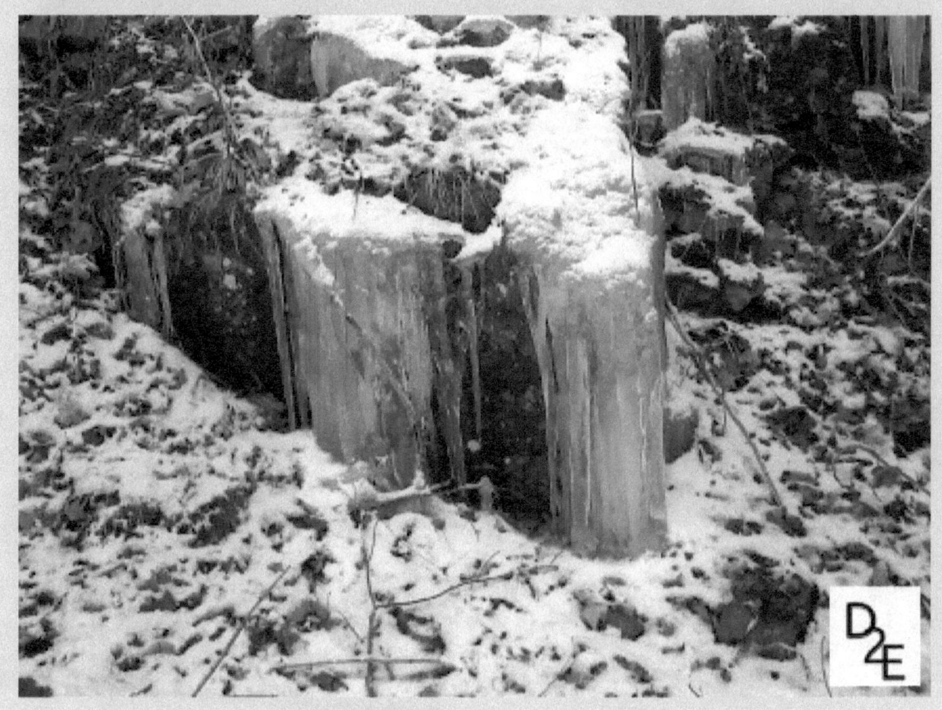
D2E

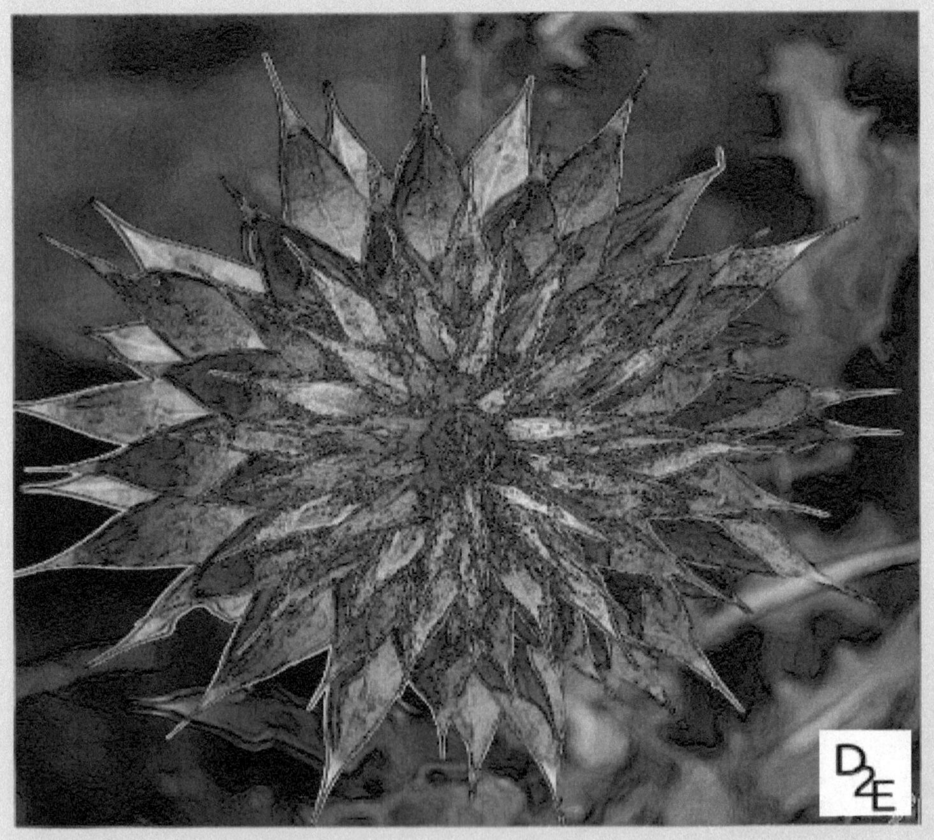
D2E

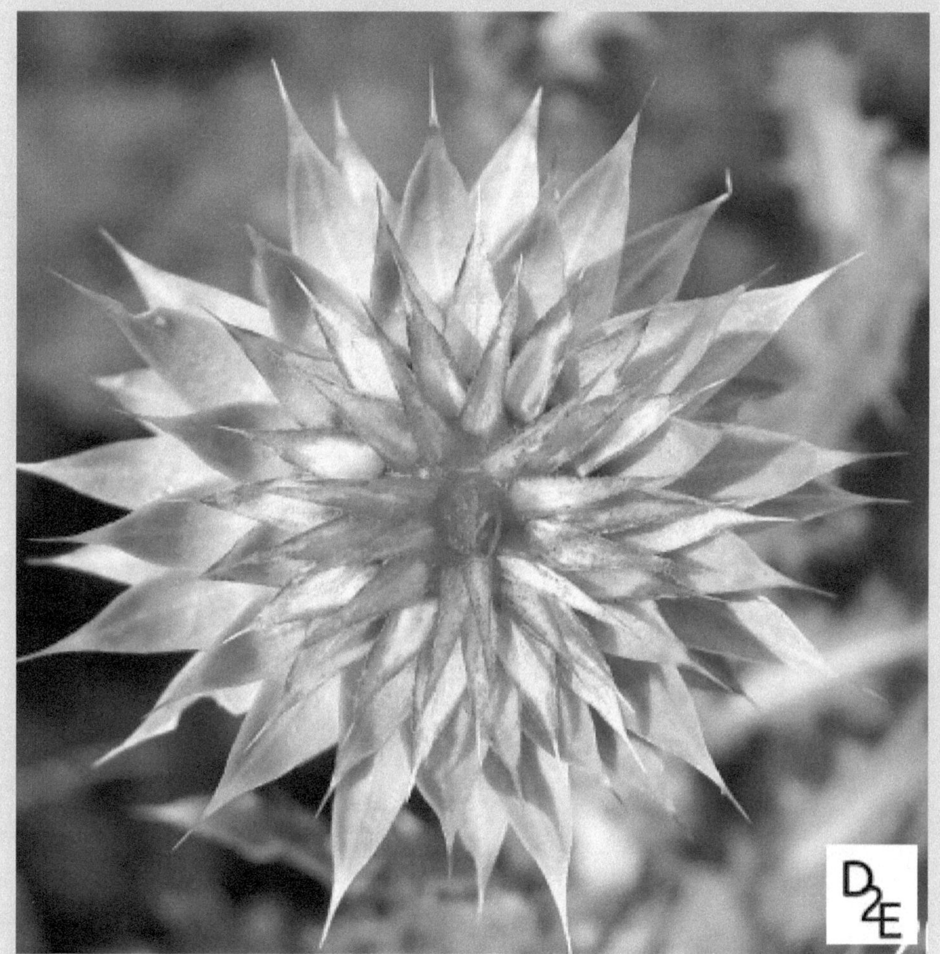
D2E

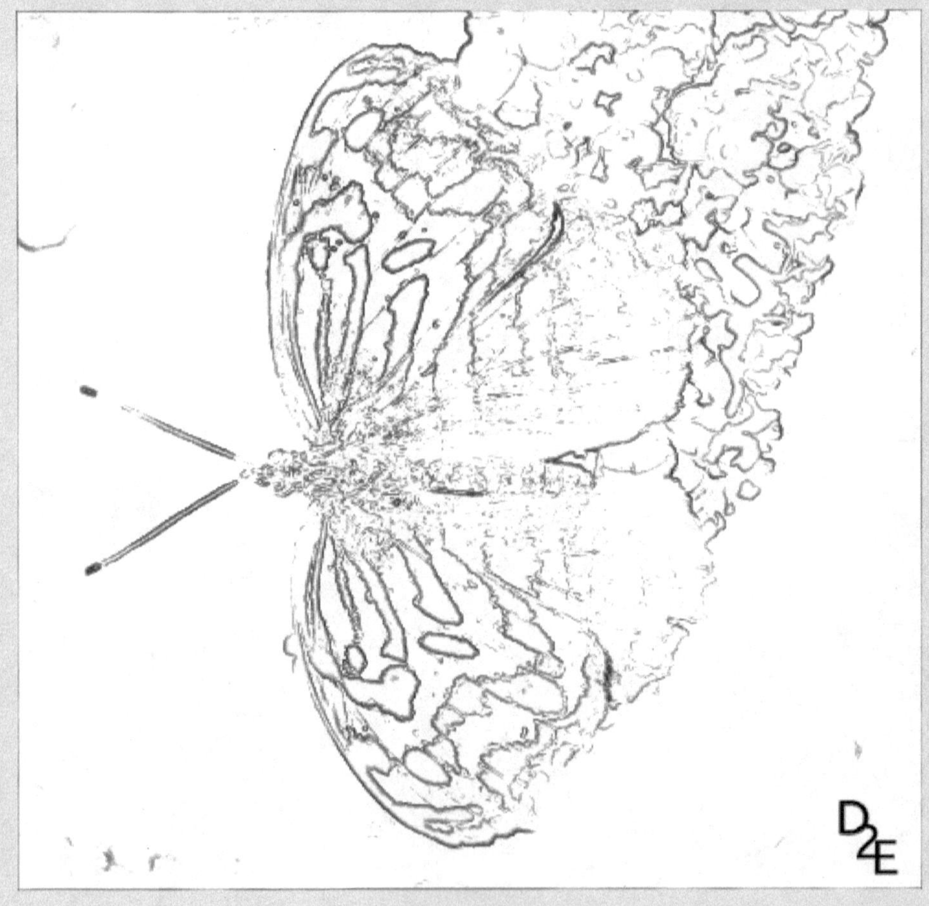

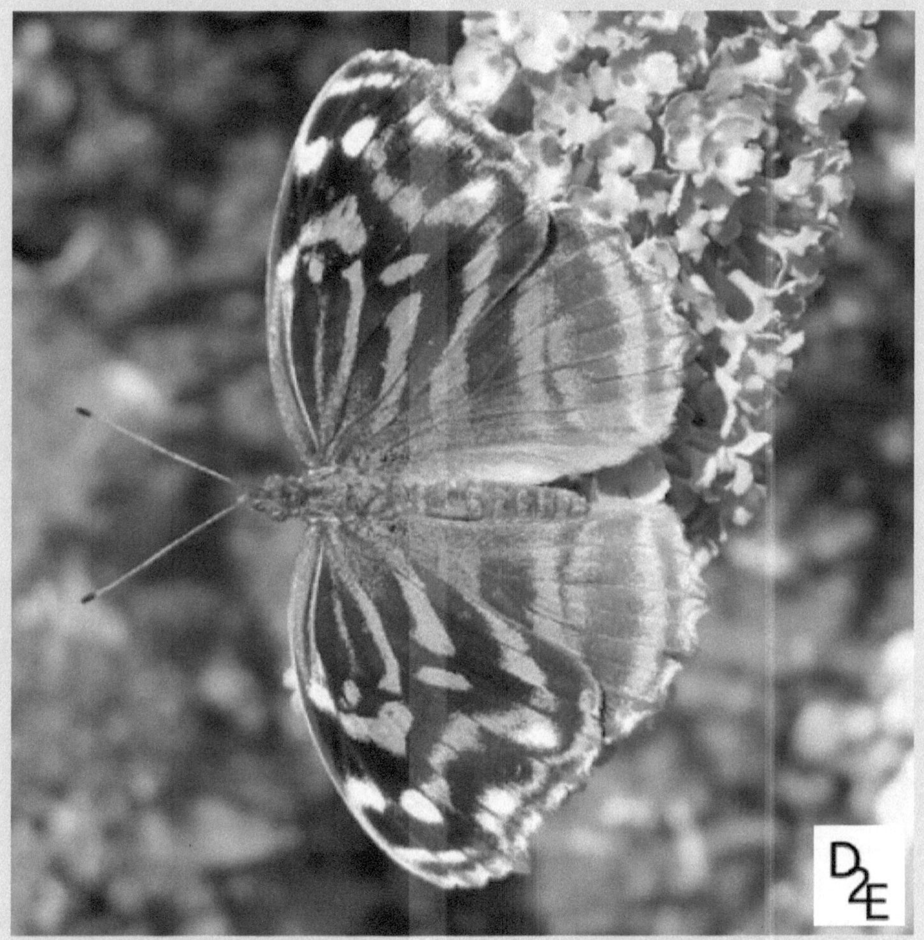

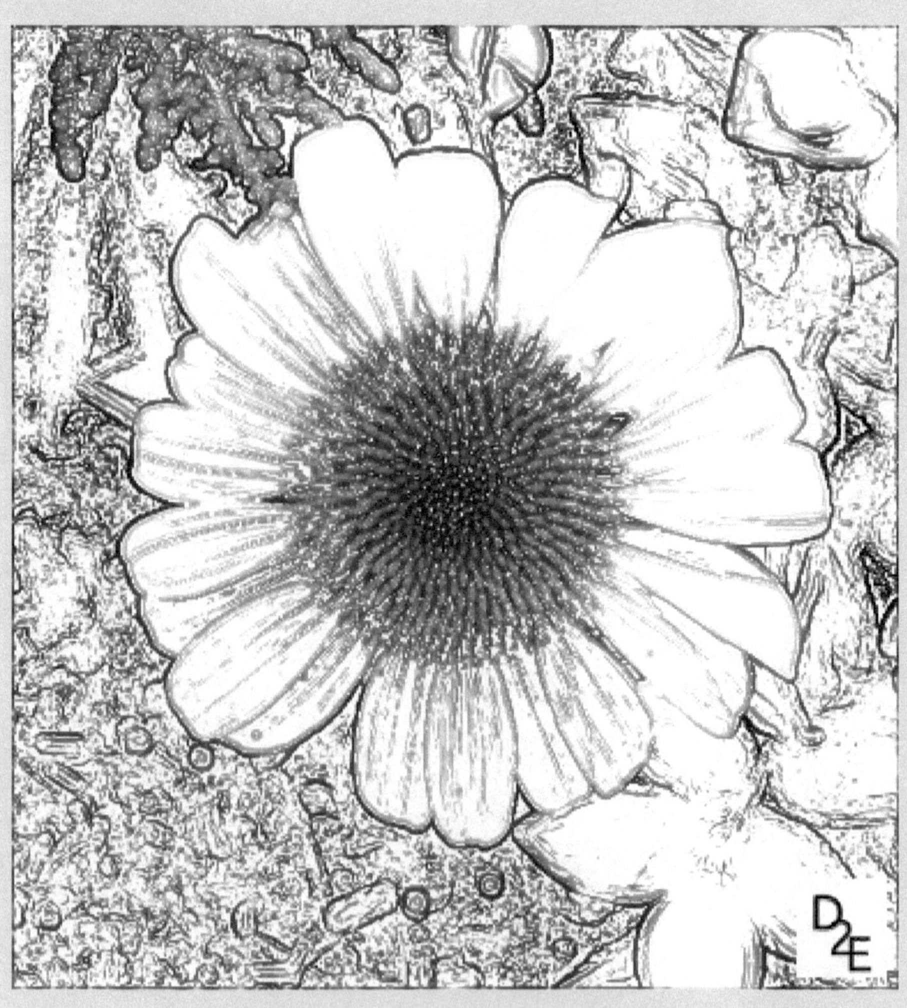
D2E

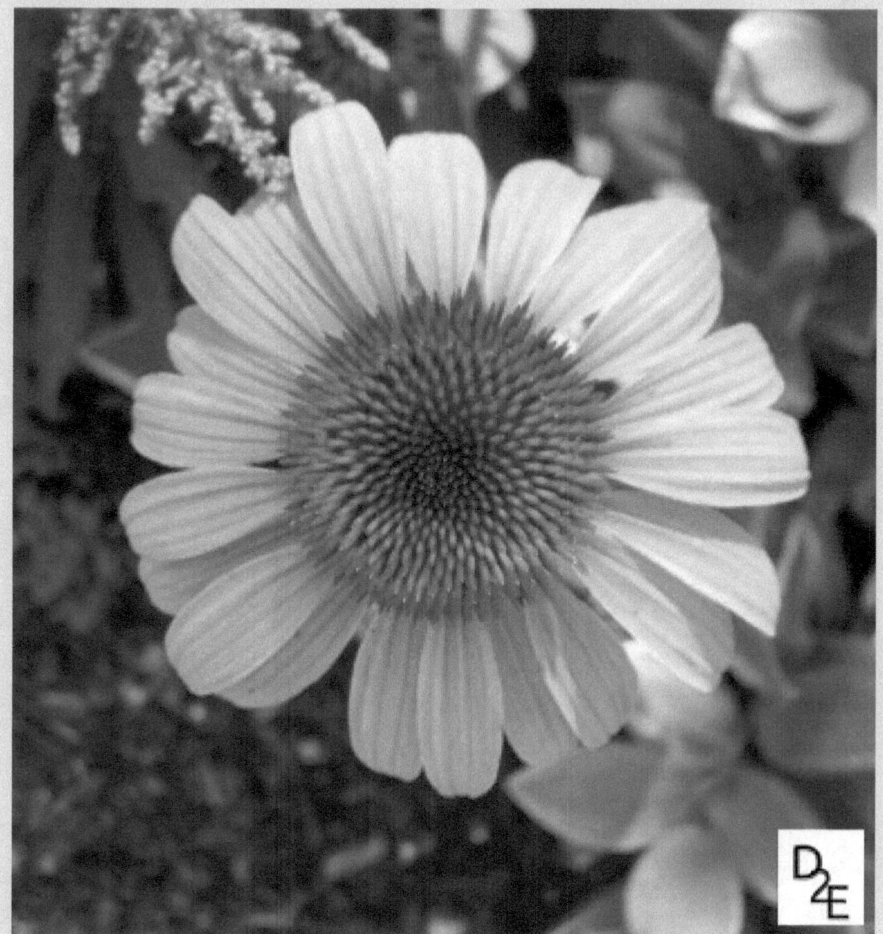
D2E

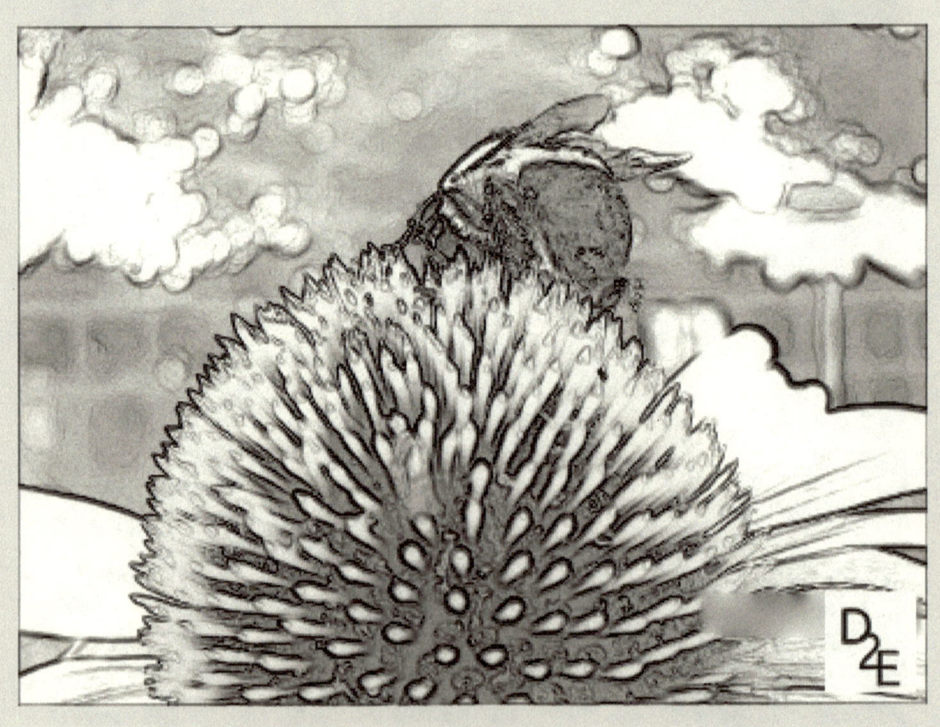
D2E

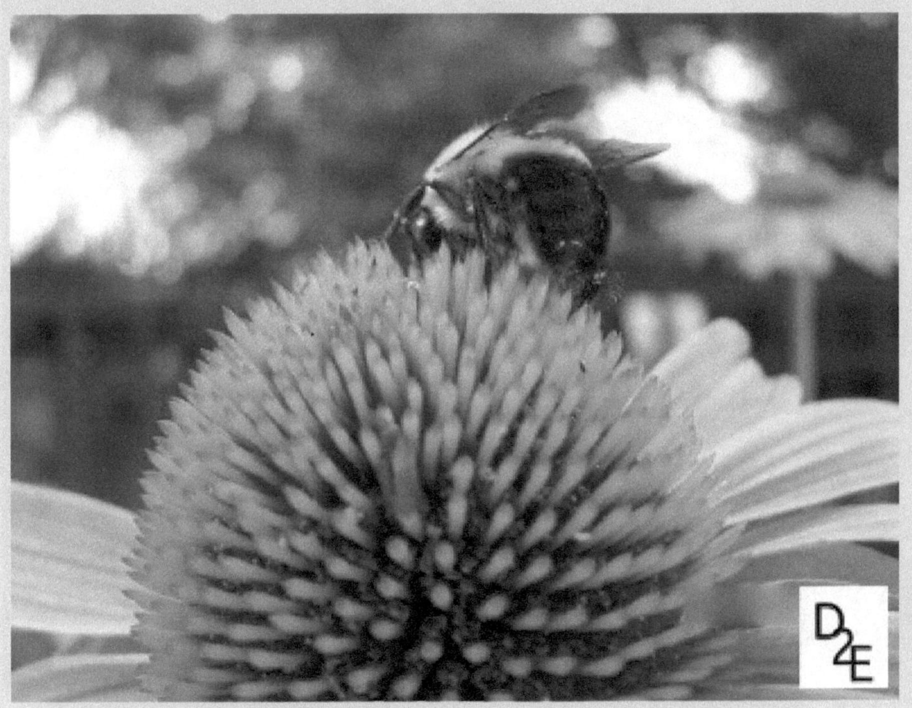
D2E

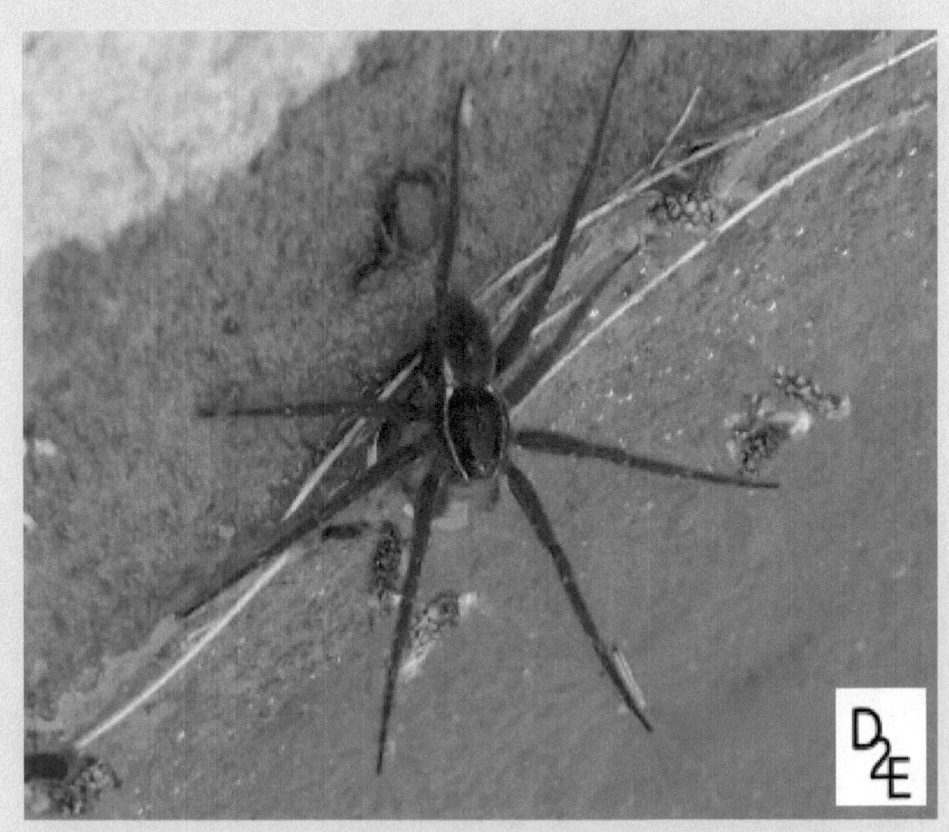

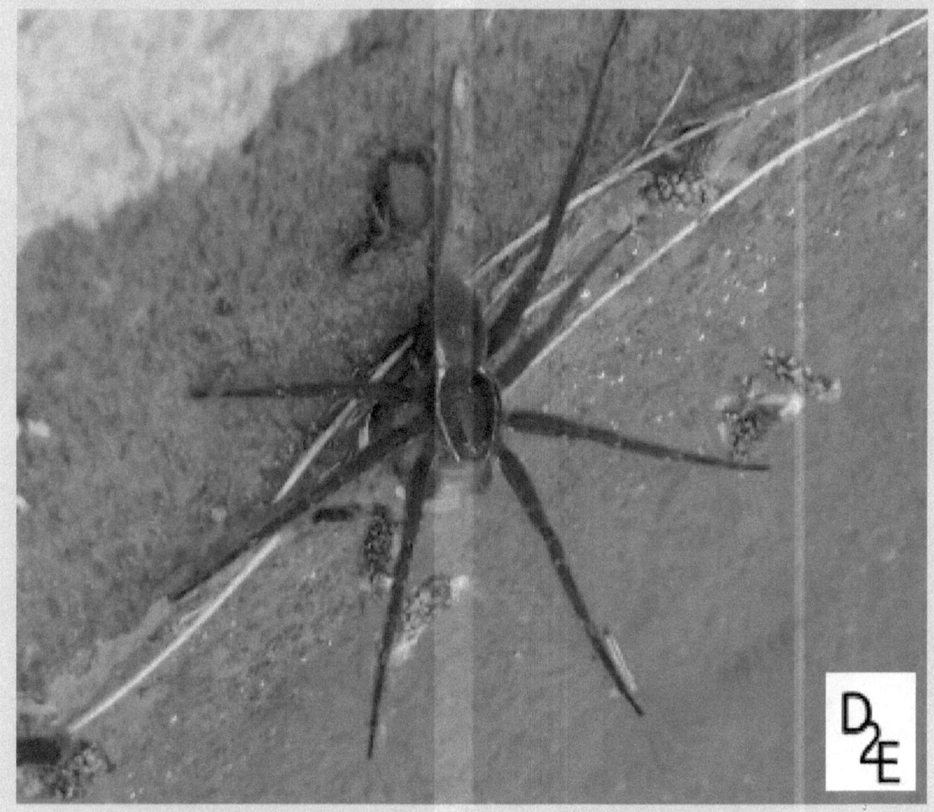
D4E

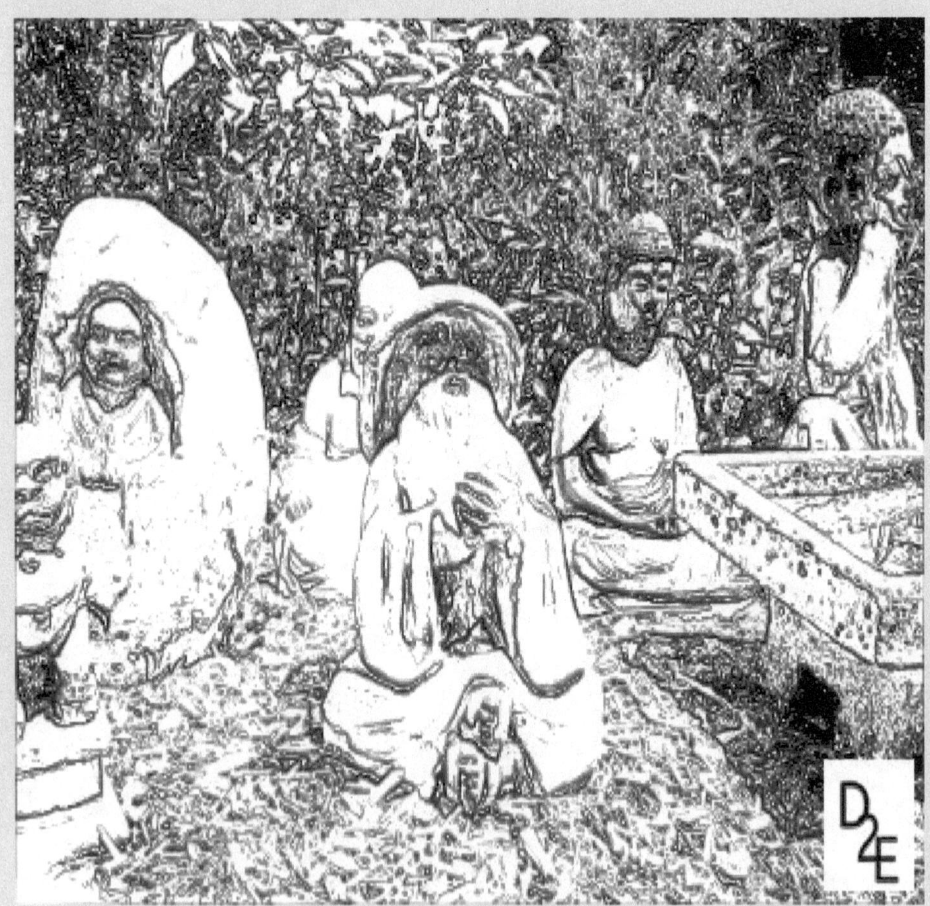
D2E

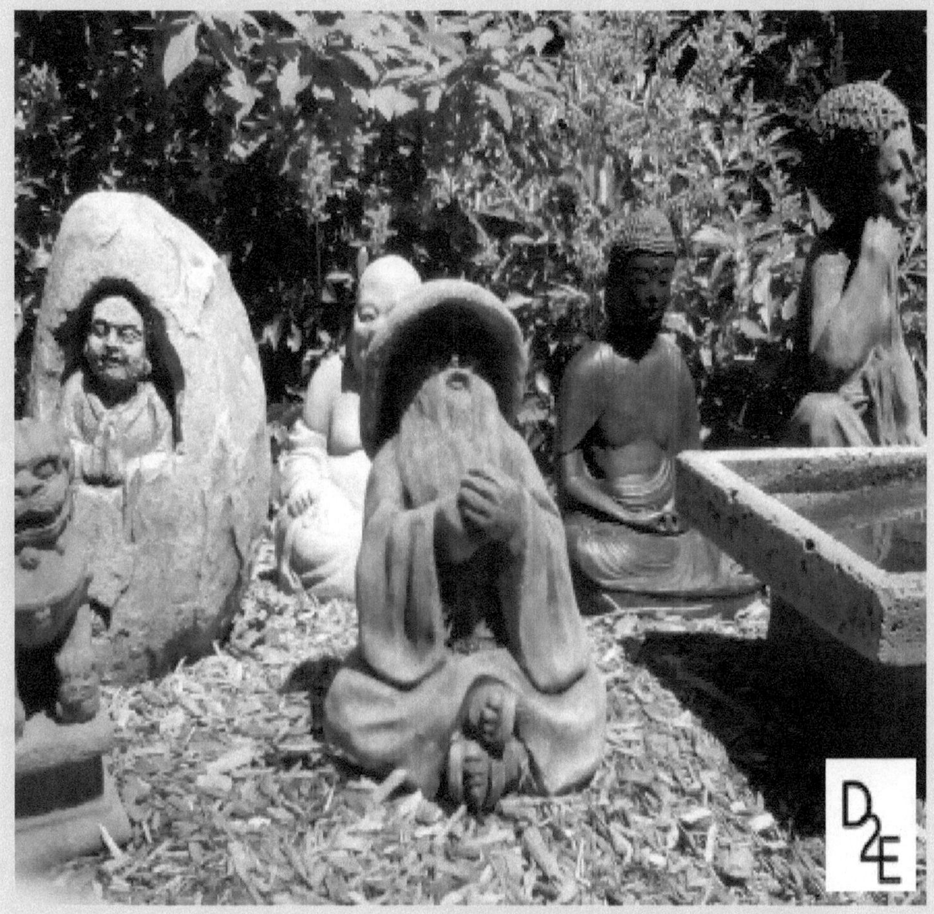
D2E

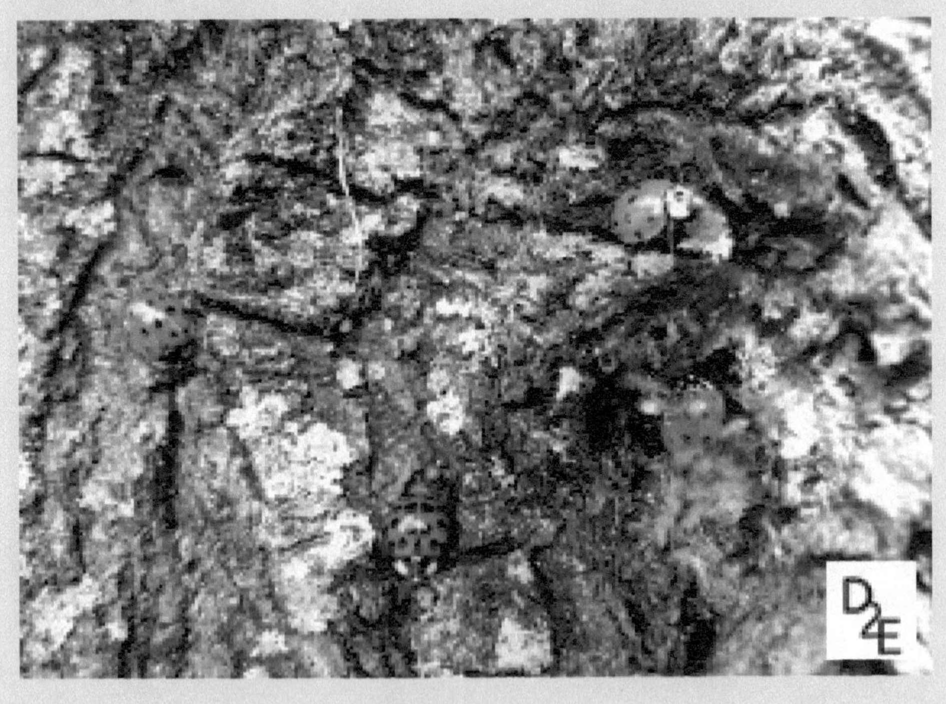

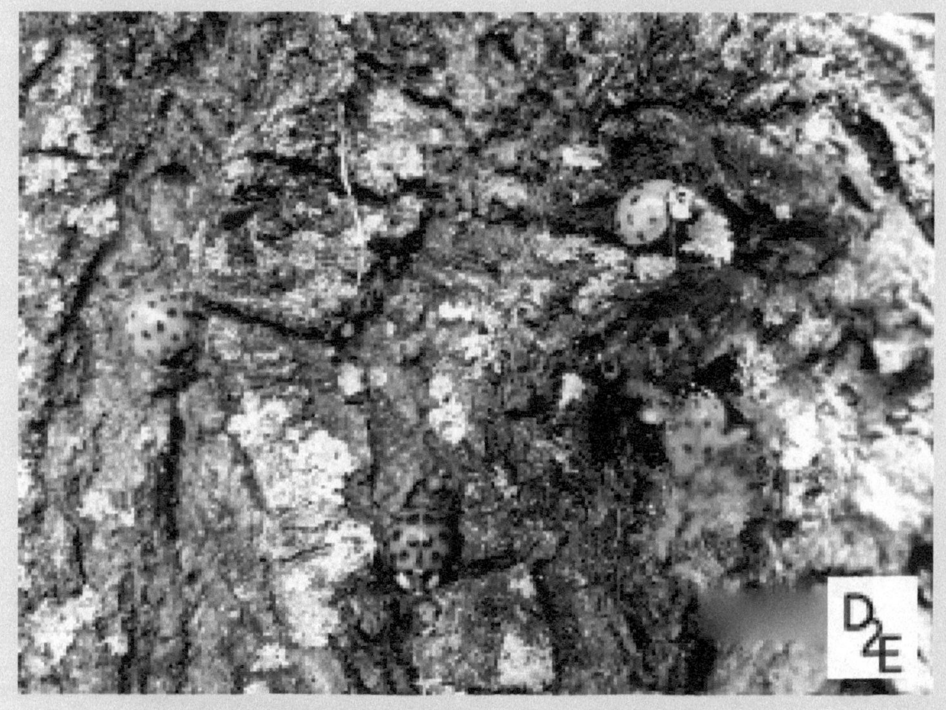
D2E

D2E

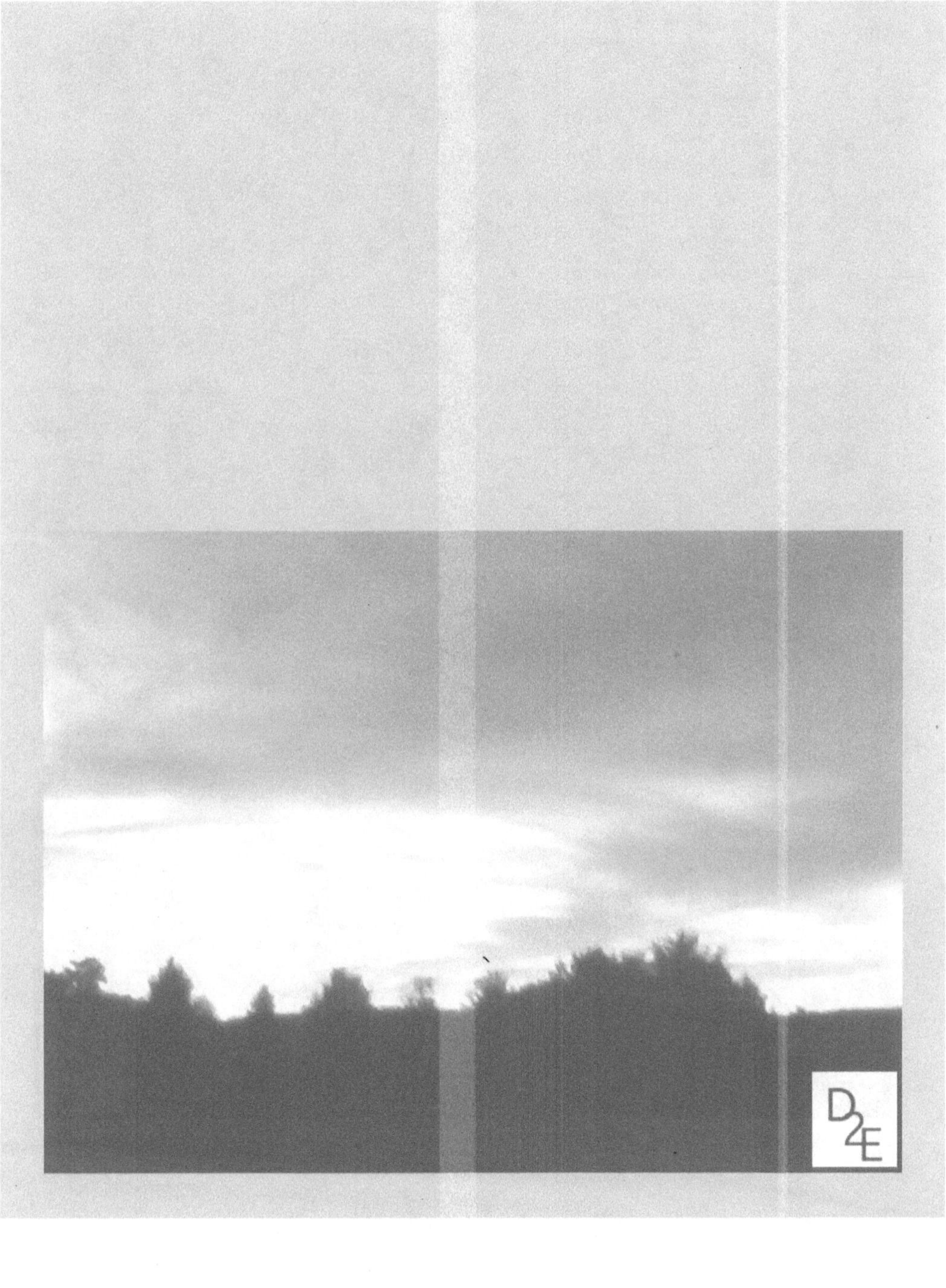

D2E

D2E

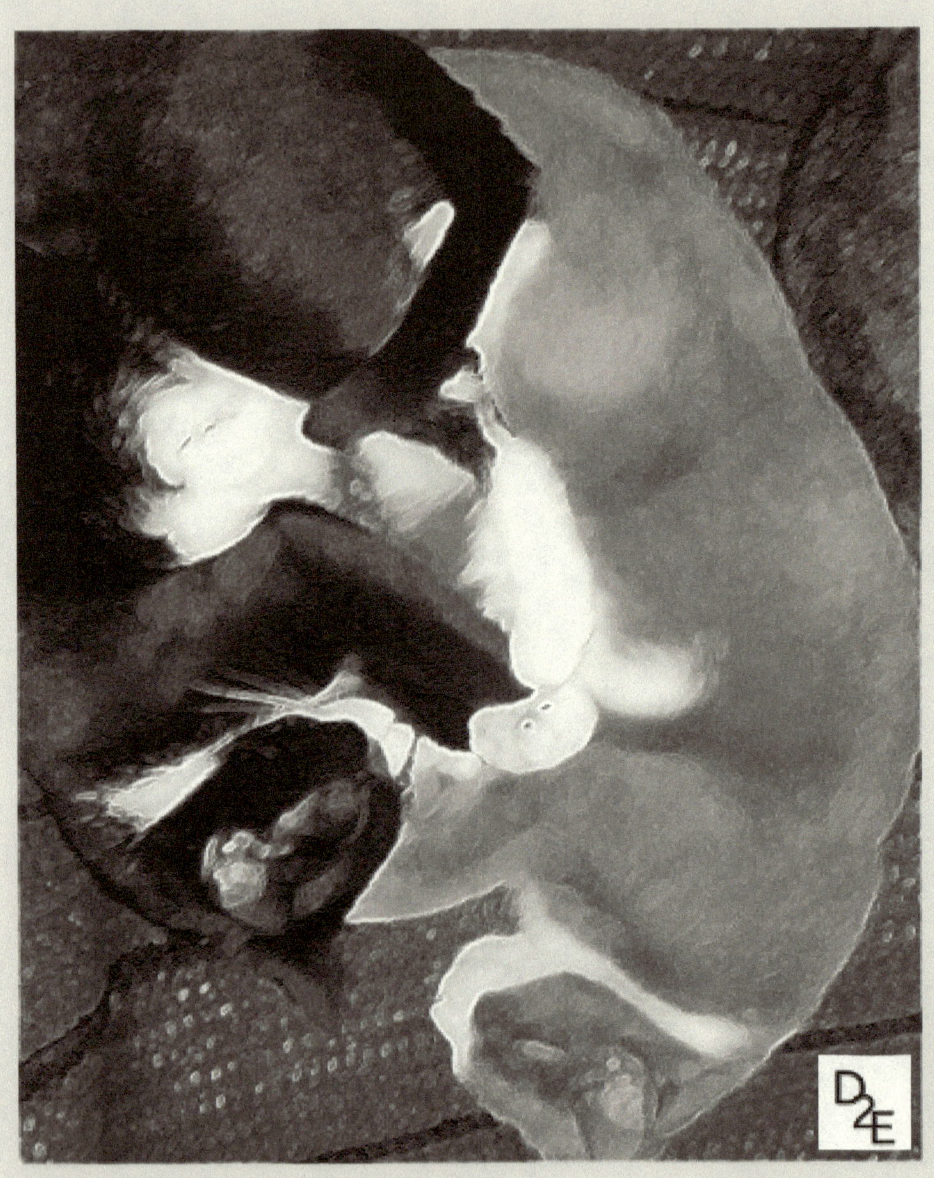
D2E

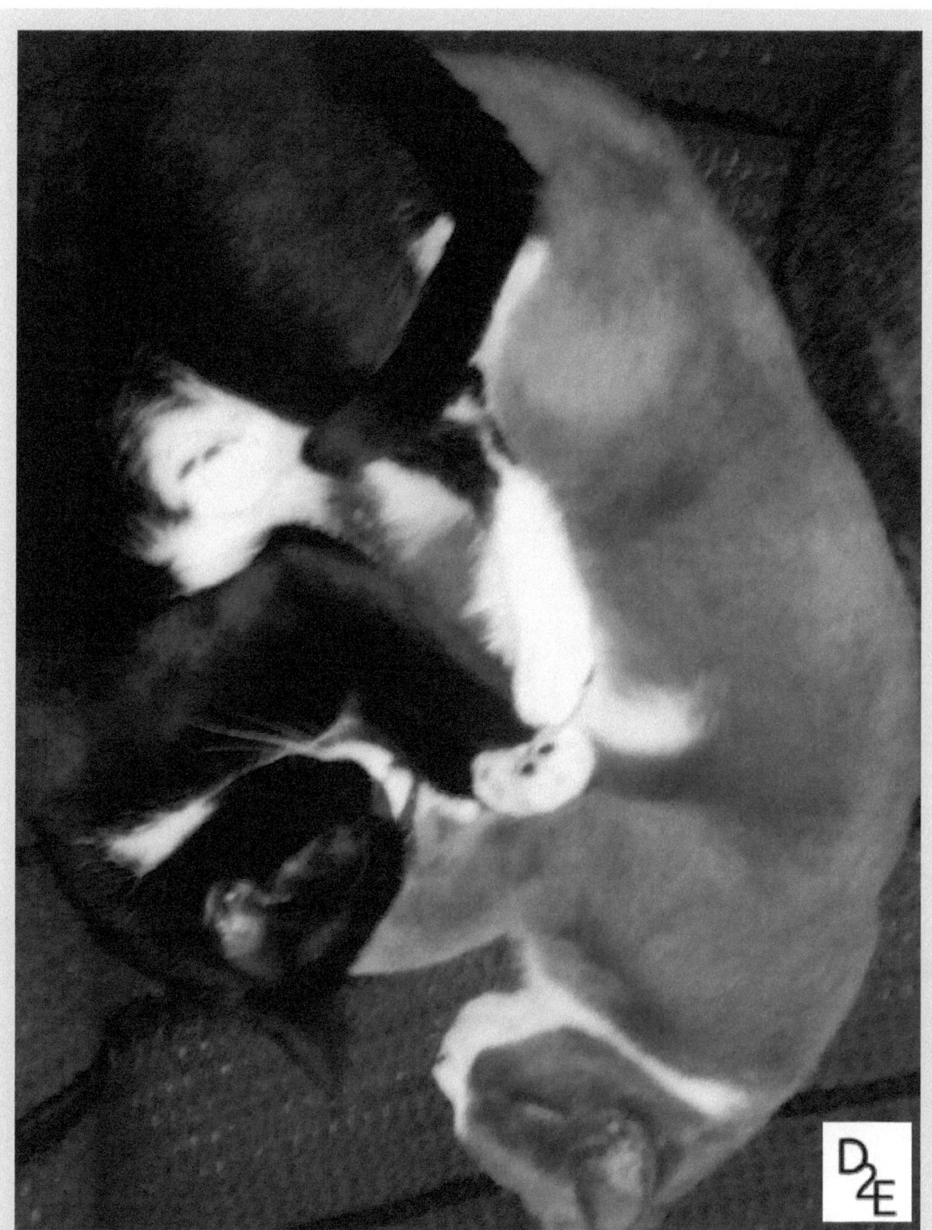
D2E

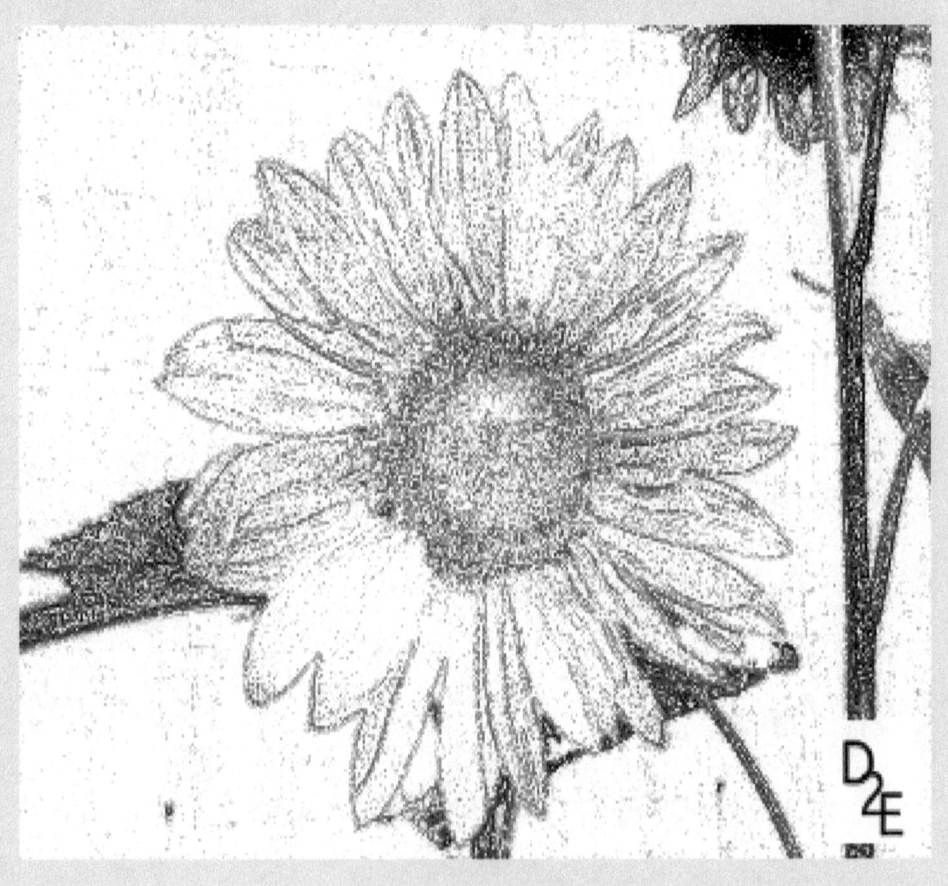
D2E

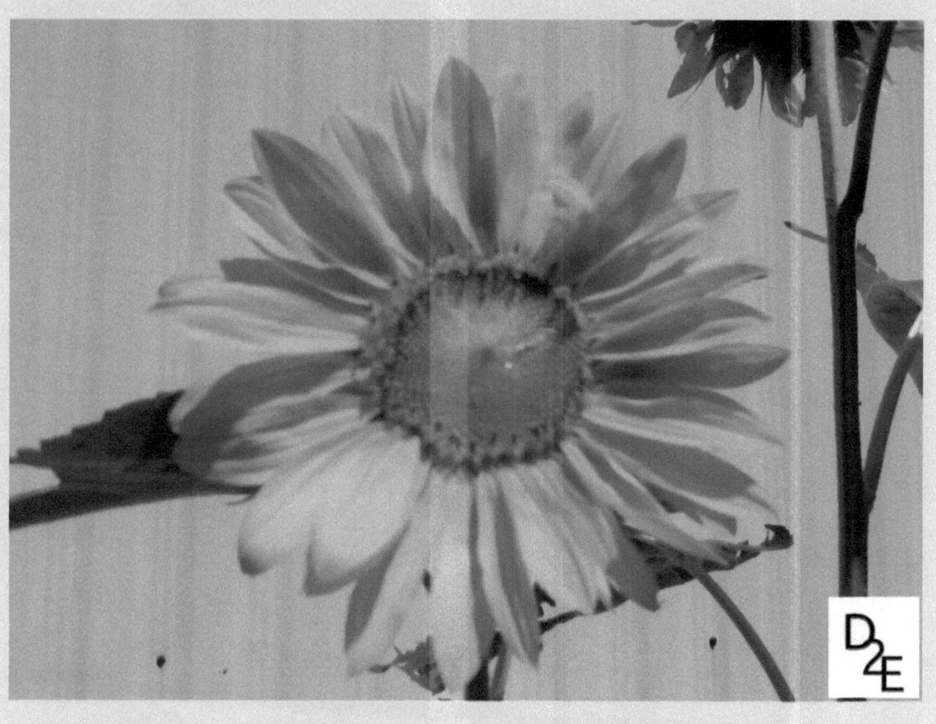

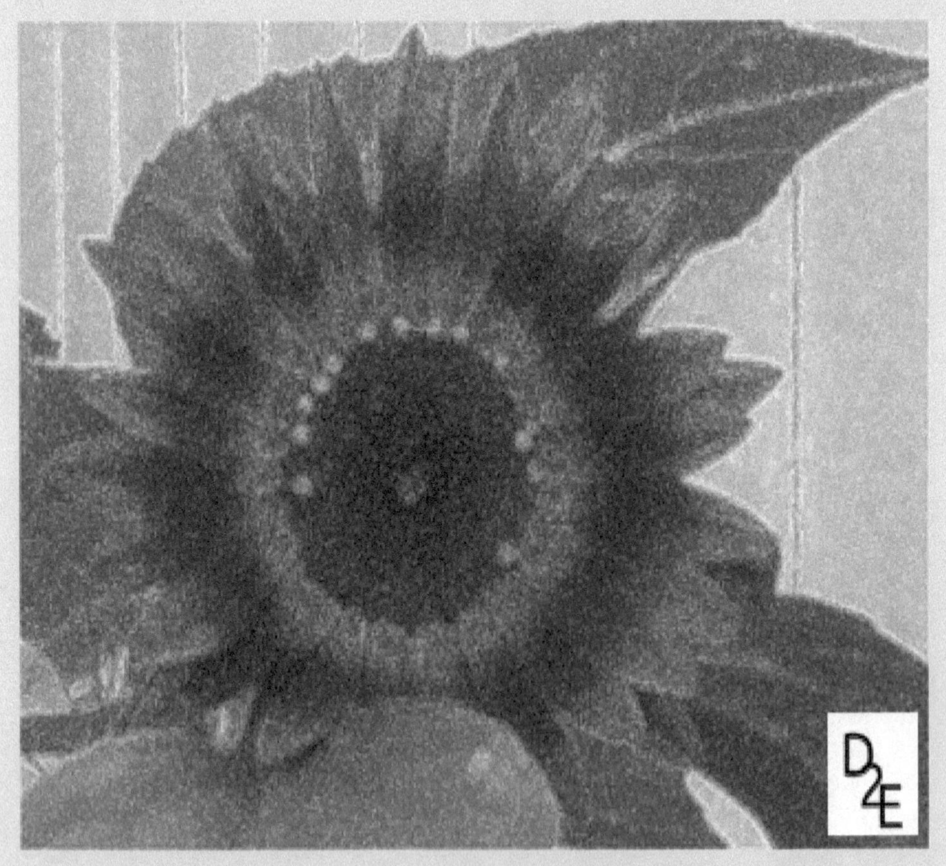

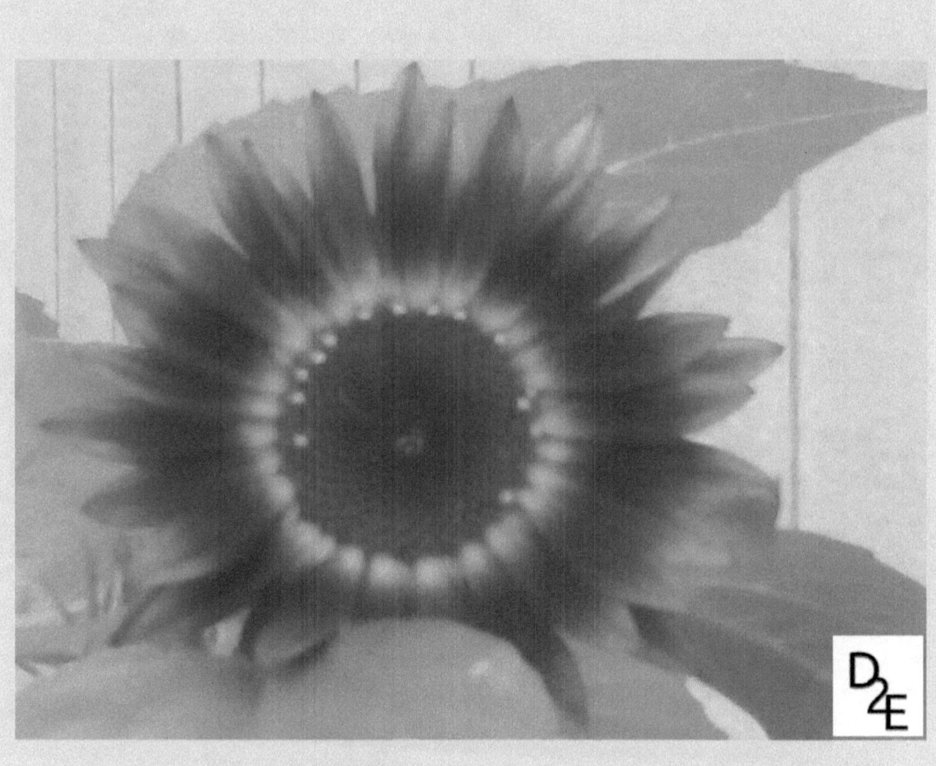
D2E

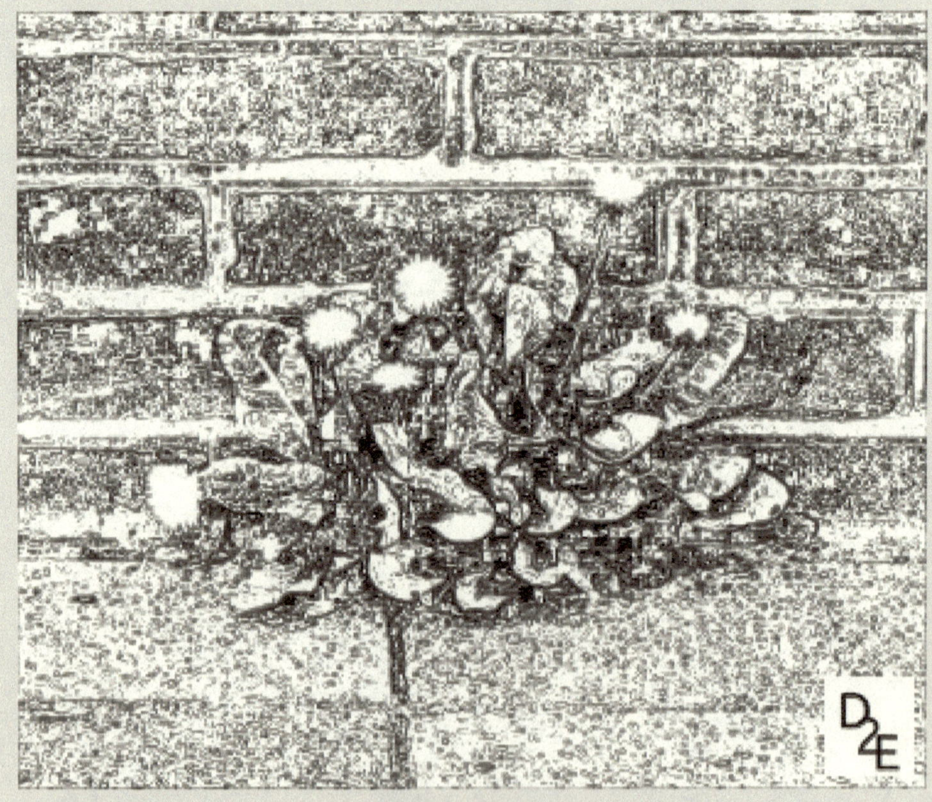
D2E

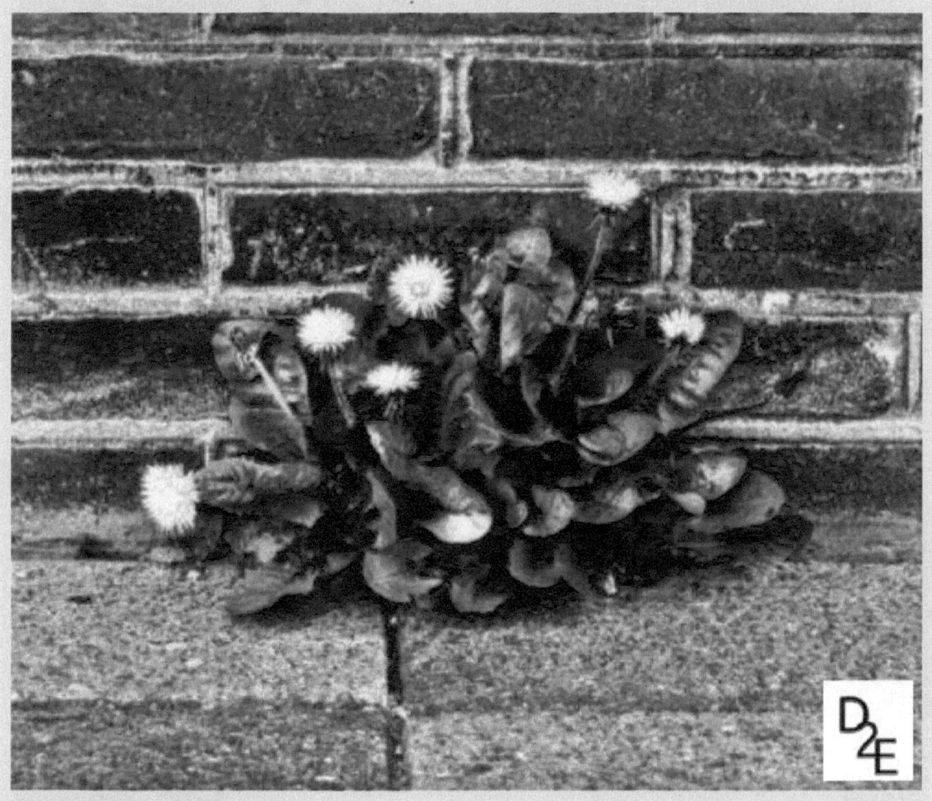
D2E

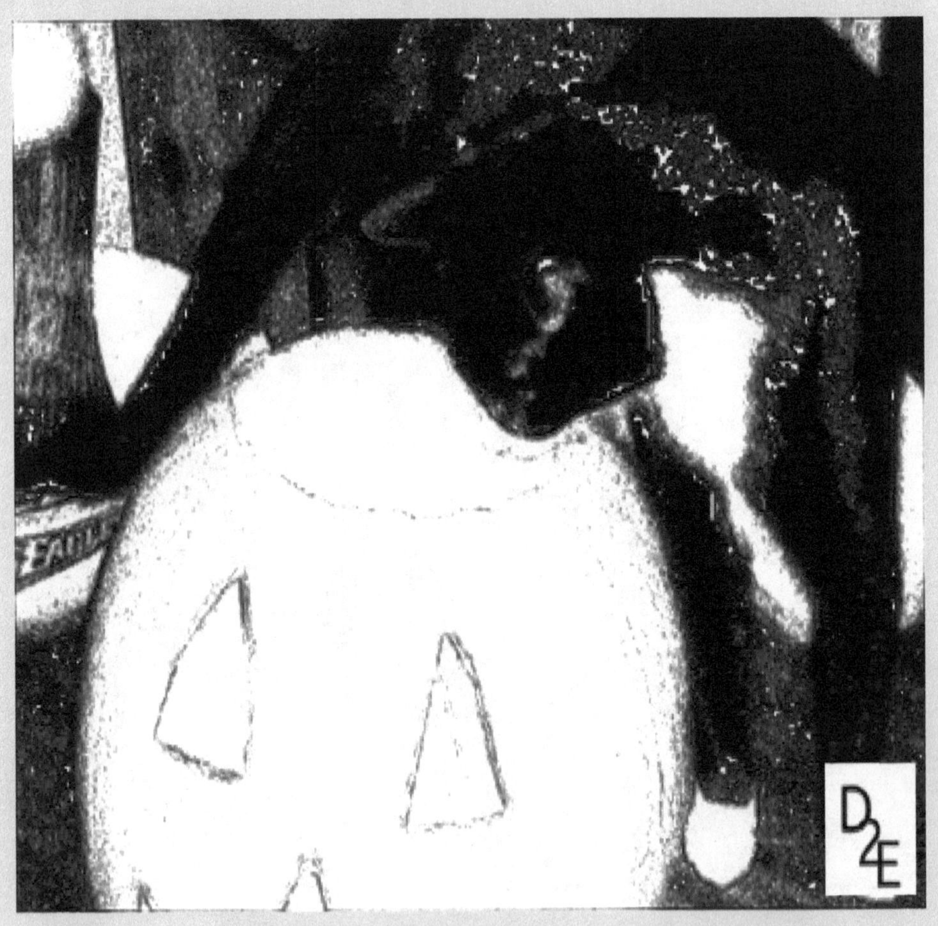
D2E

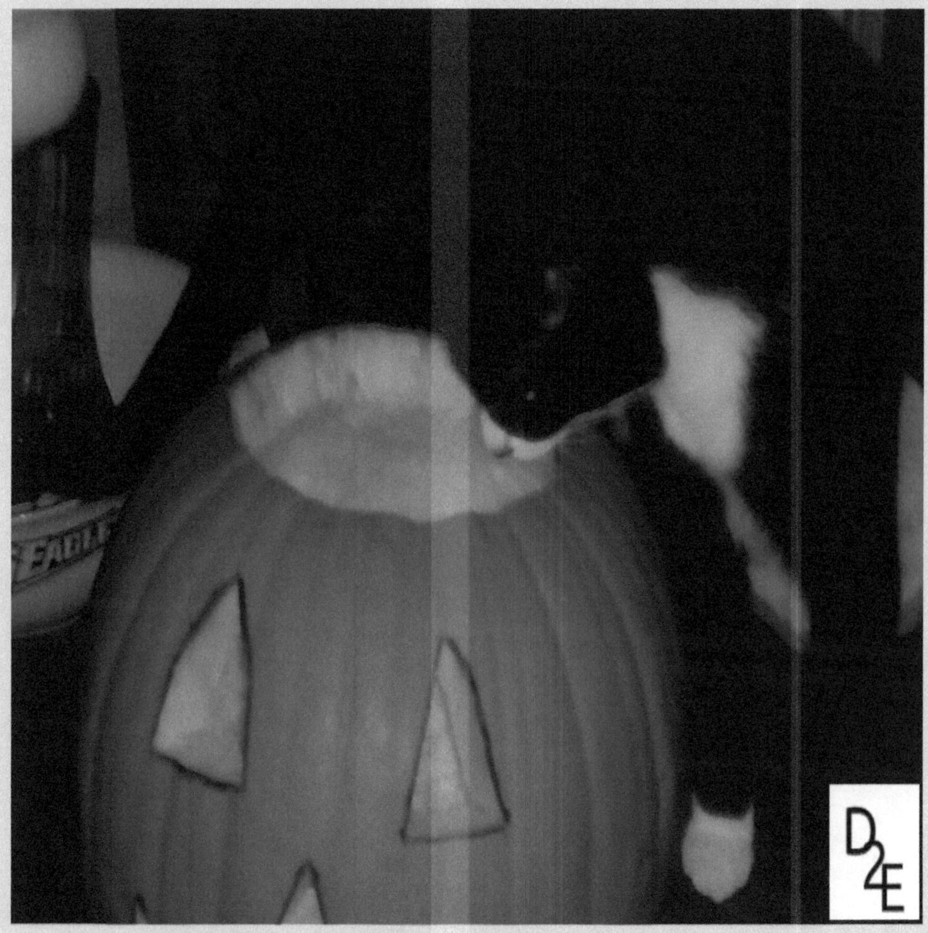
D2E

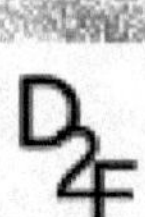
D2E

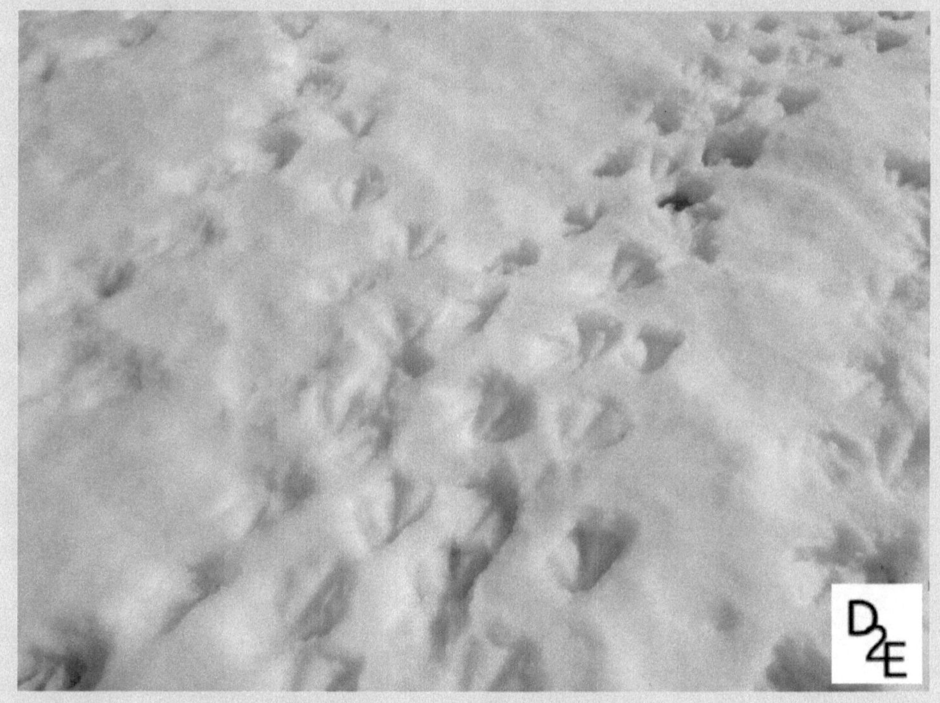
D2E

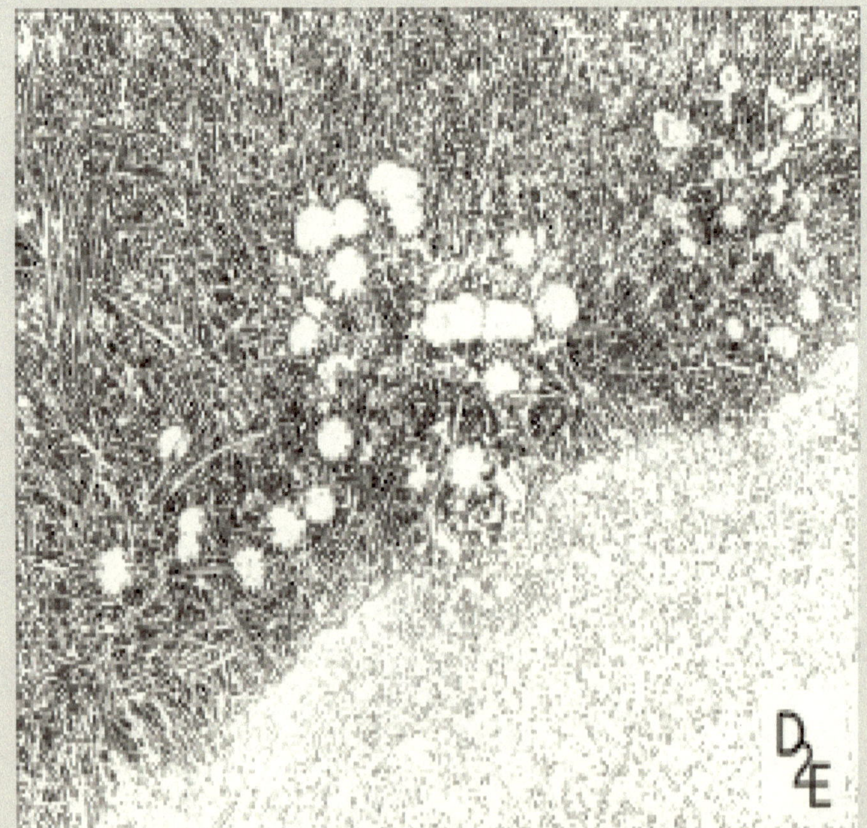
D4E

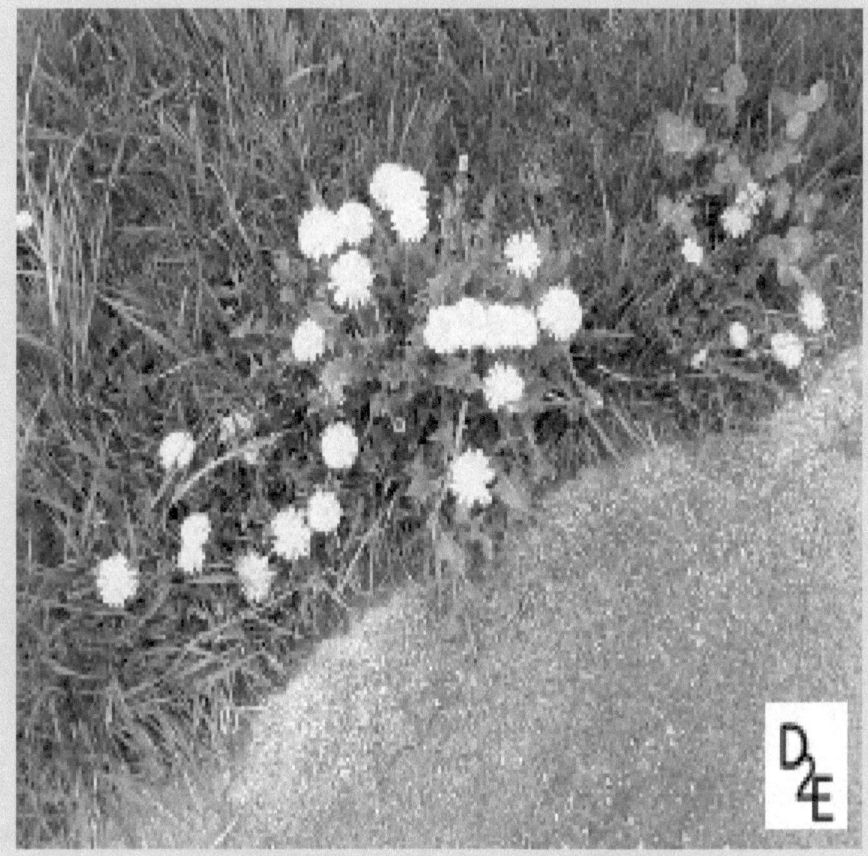

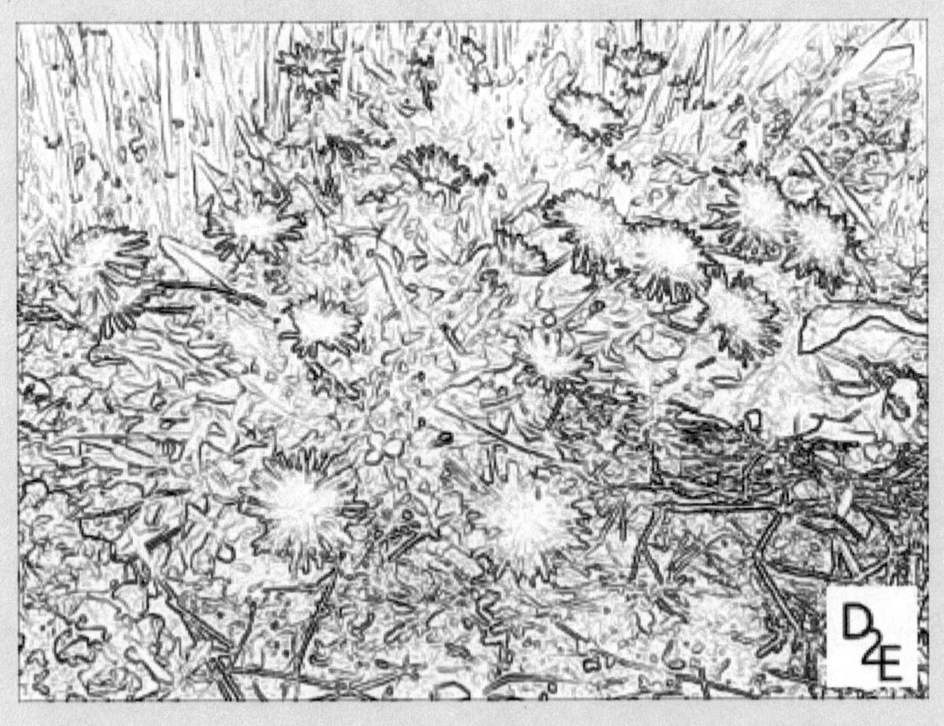
D2E

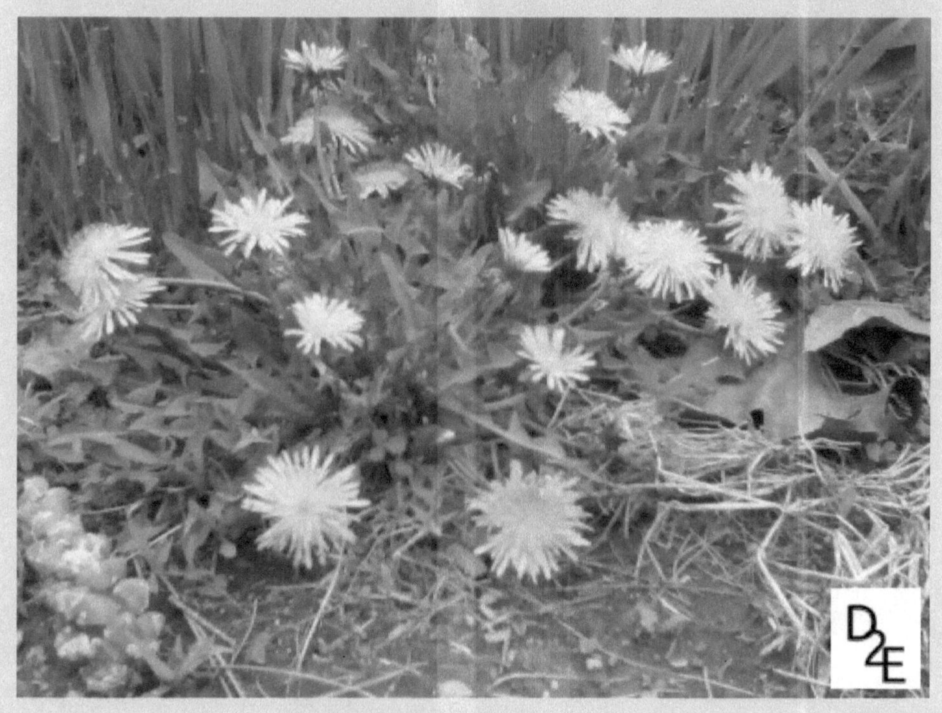
D2E

D2E

D2E

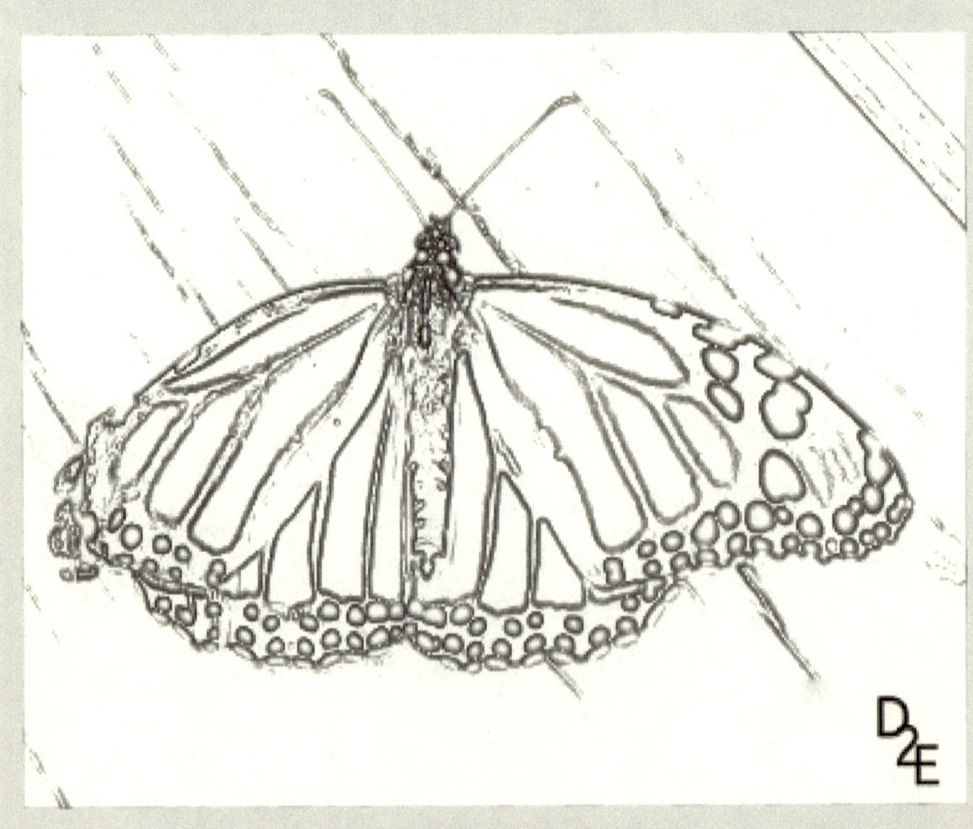
D4E

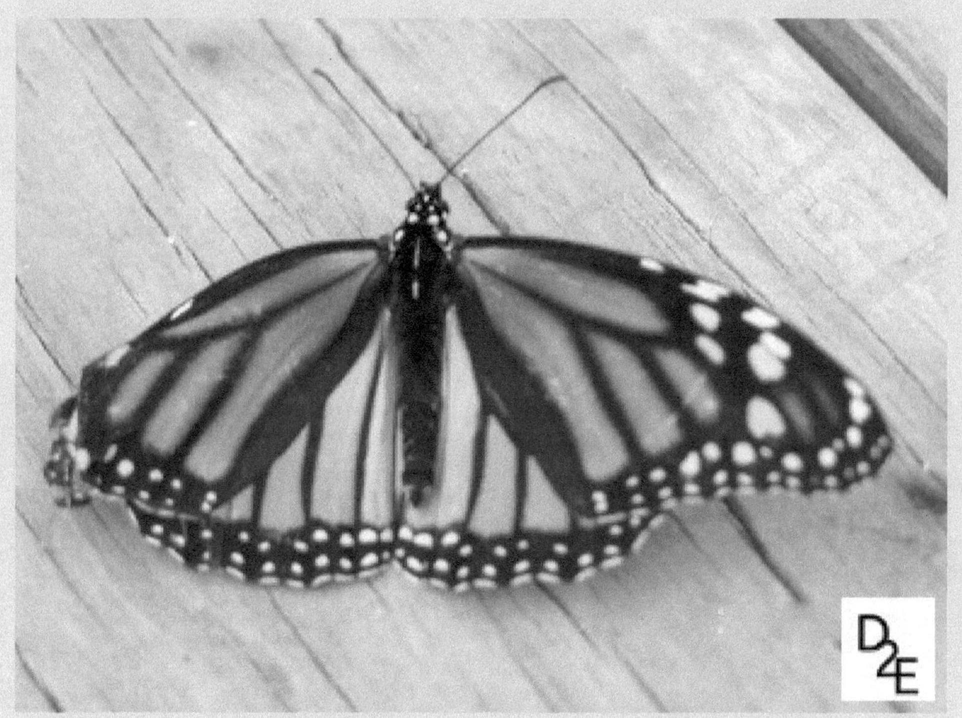
D2E

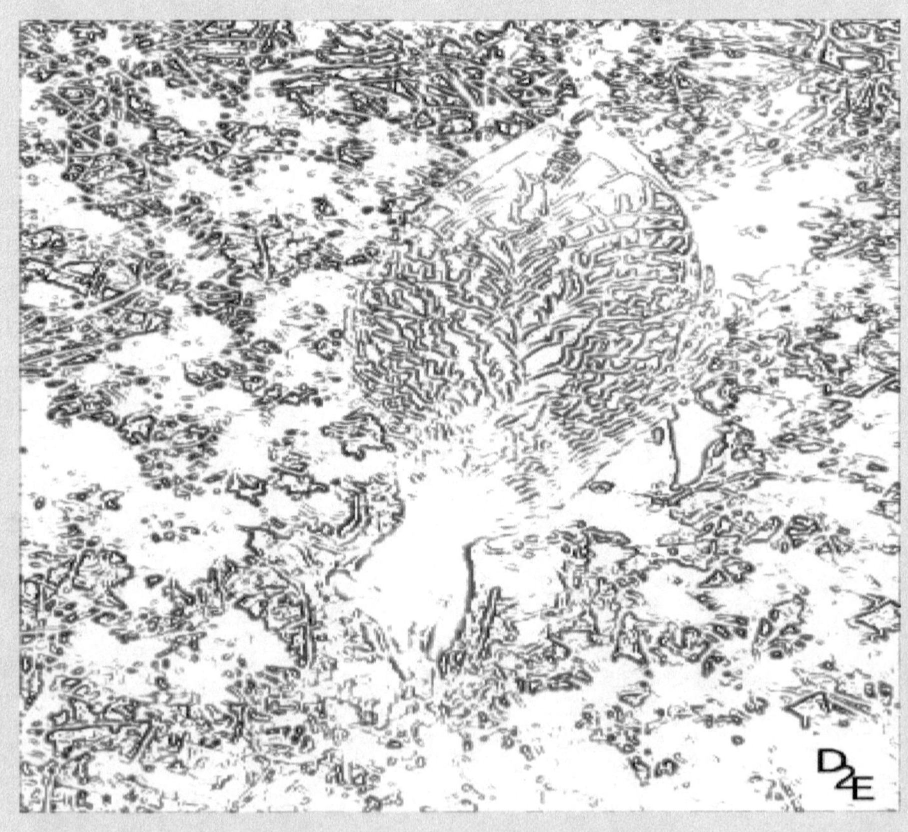
D2E

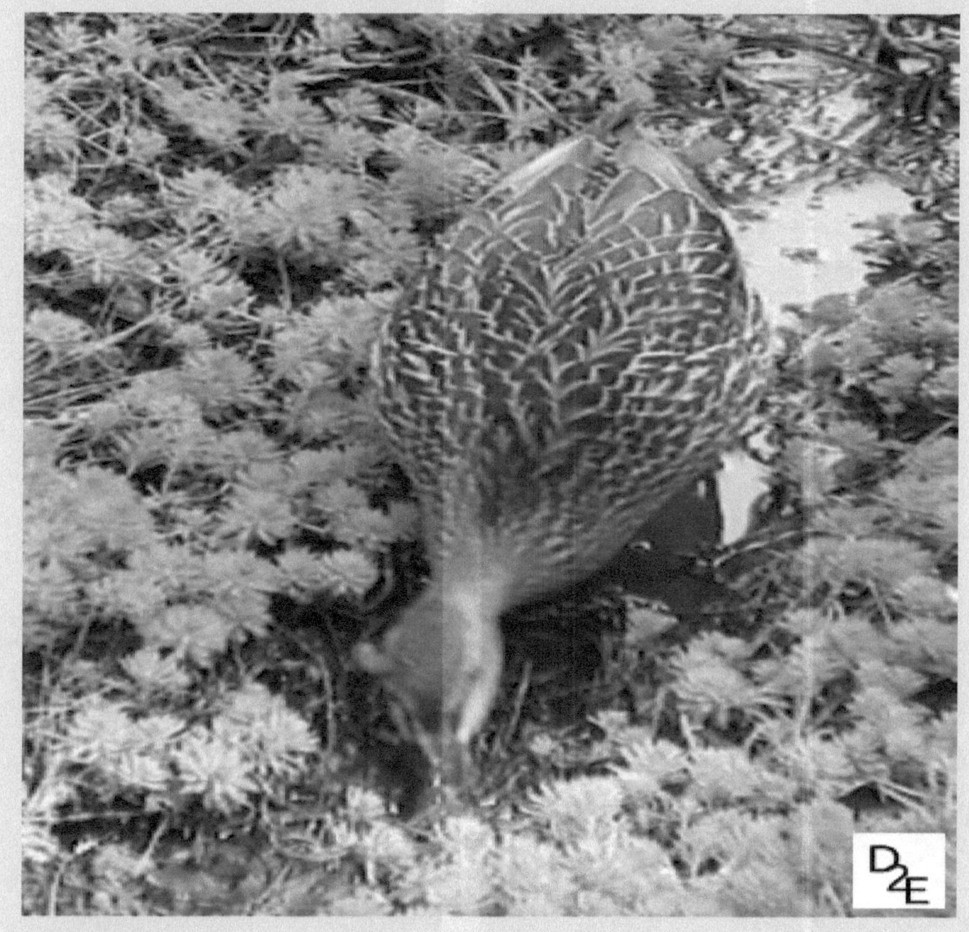
D2E

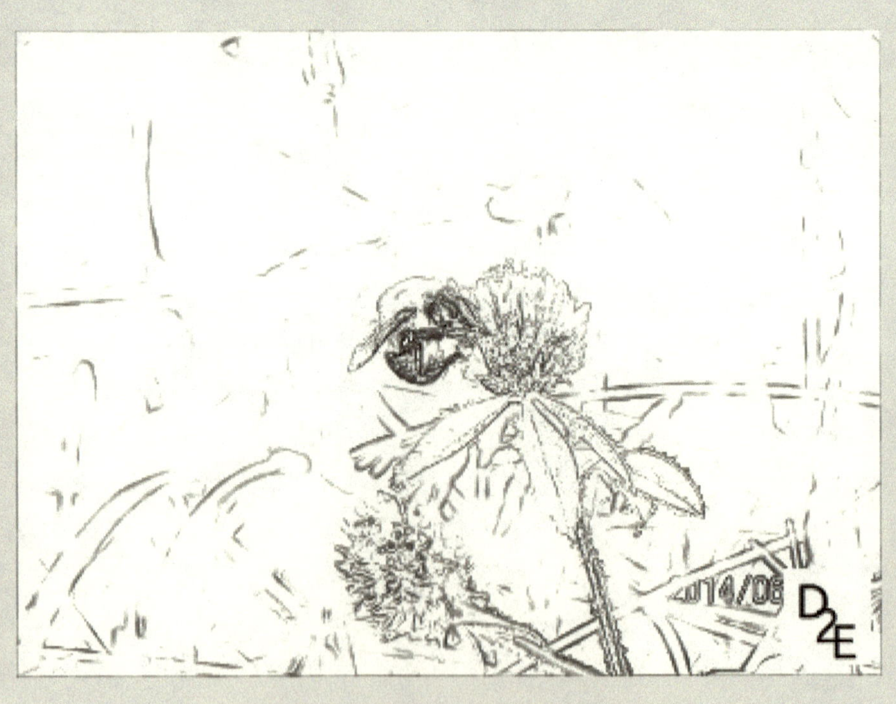
014/06
D2E

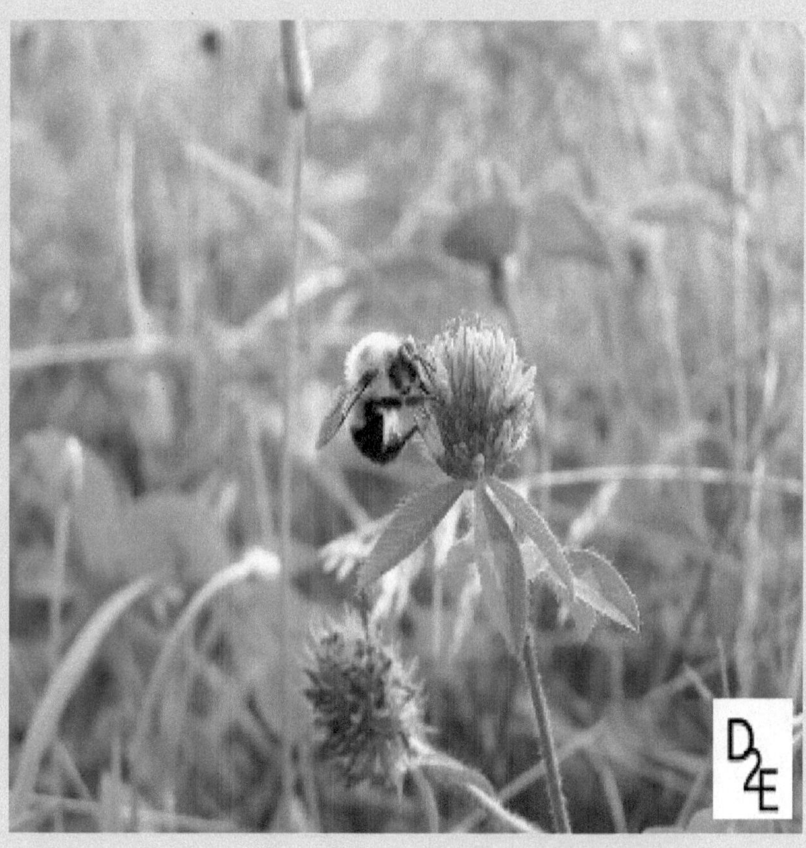

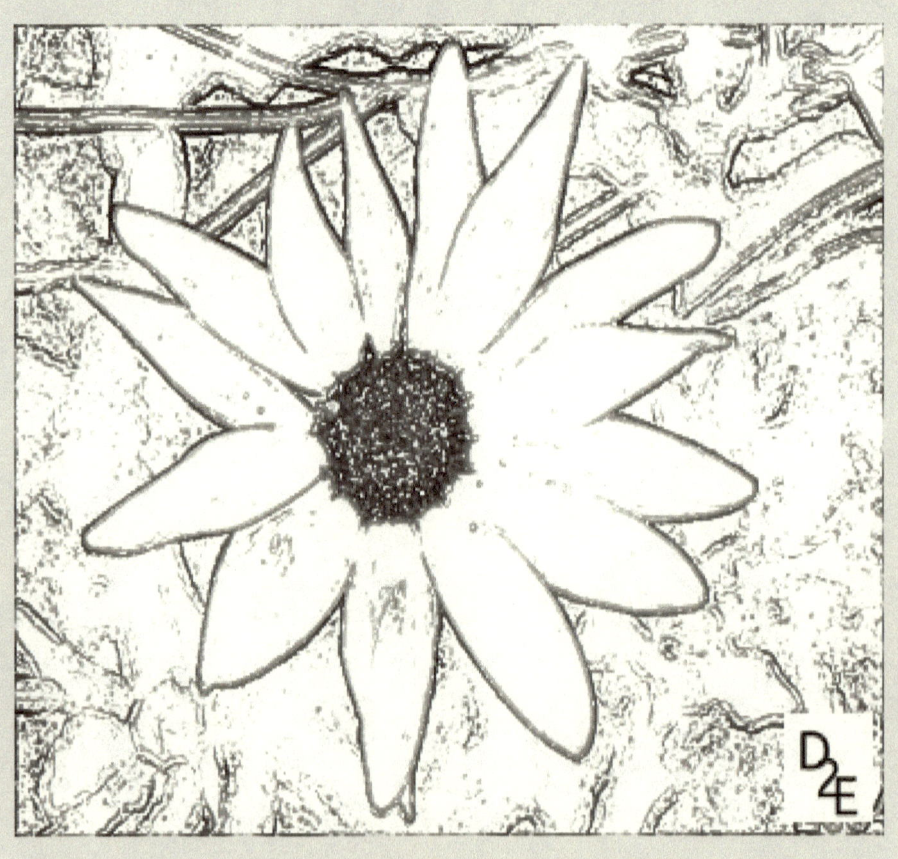
D2E

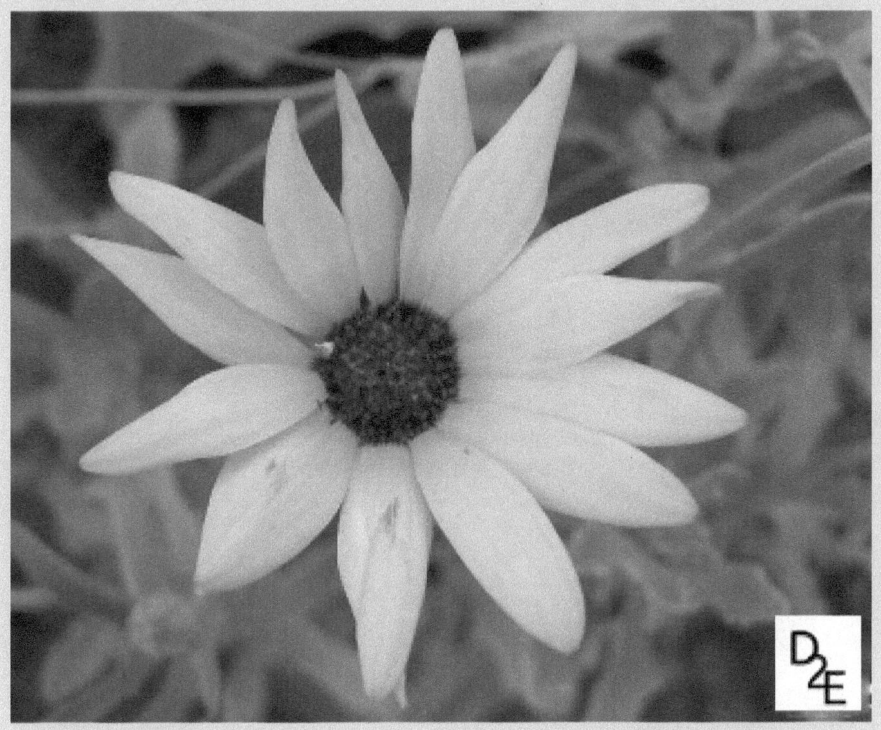

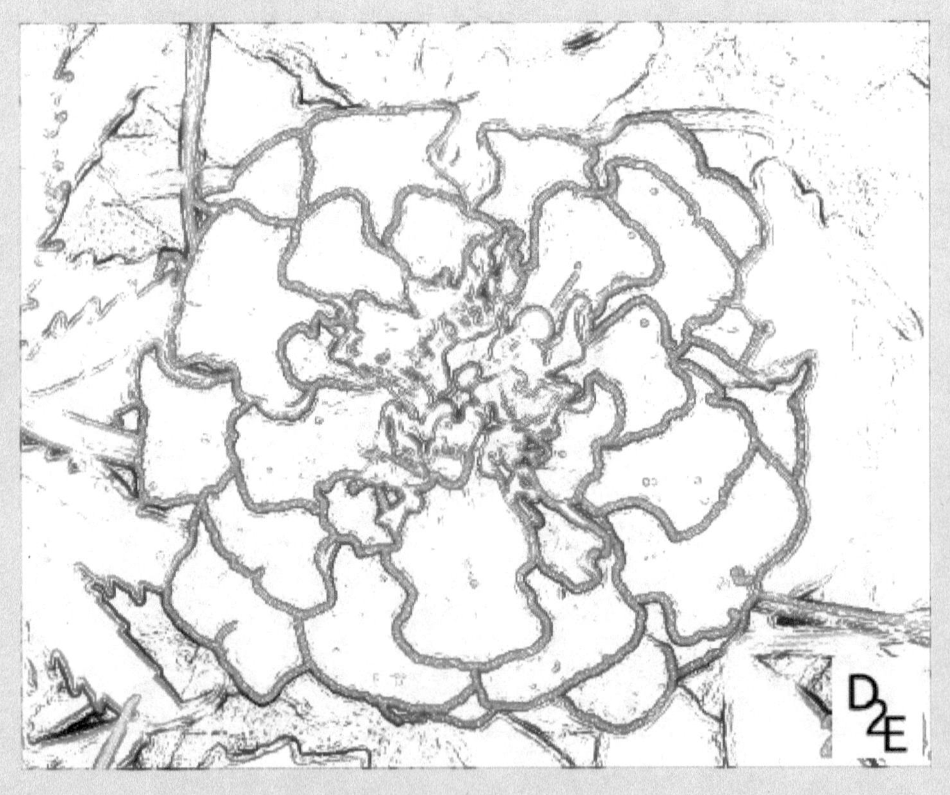
D2E

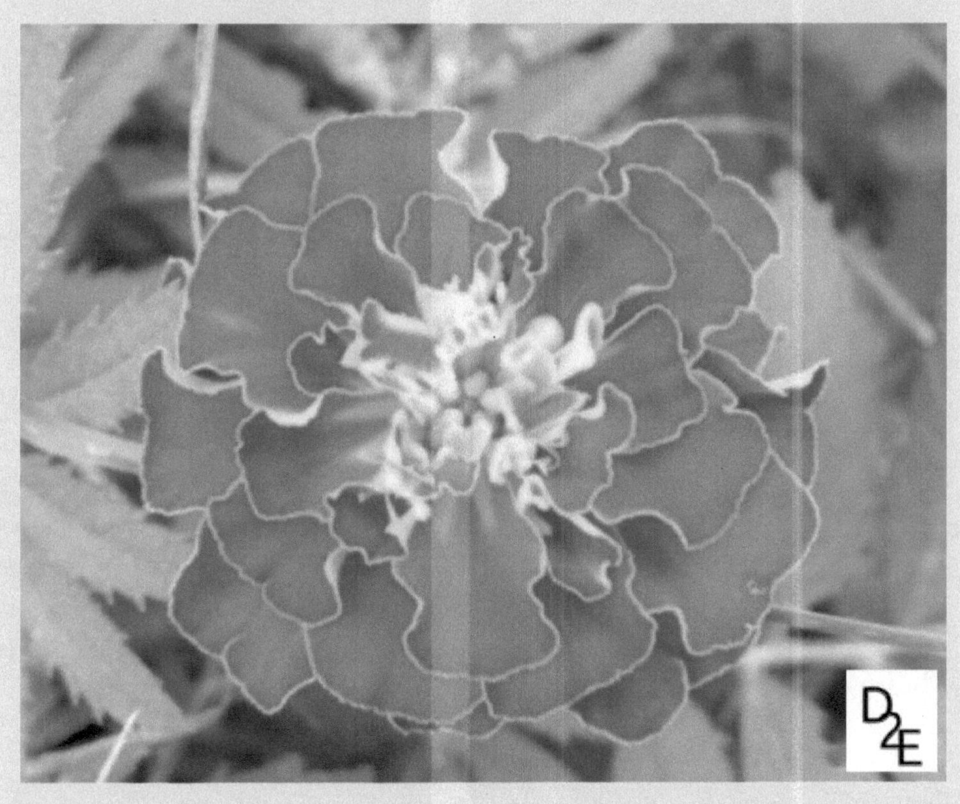

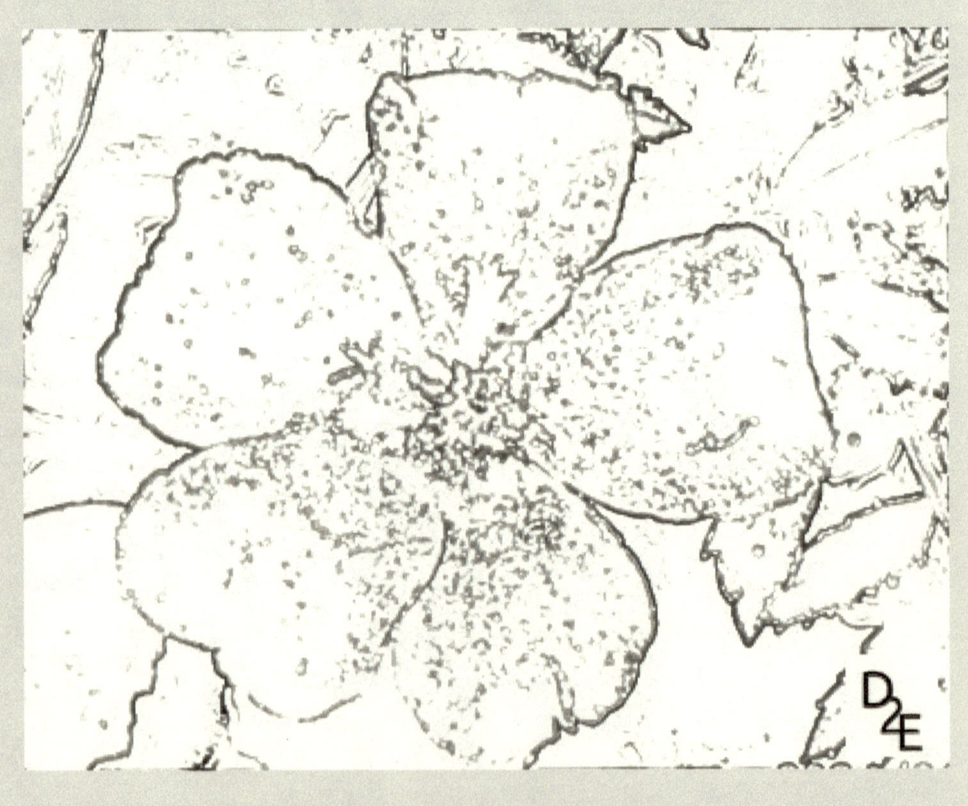
D2E

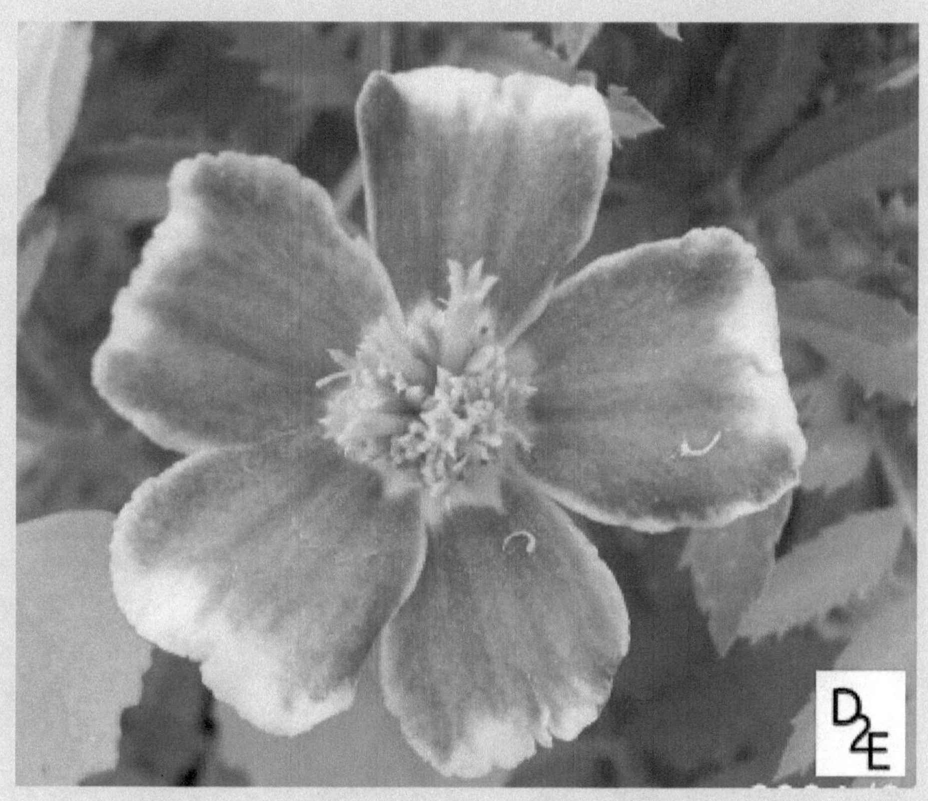
D2E

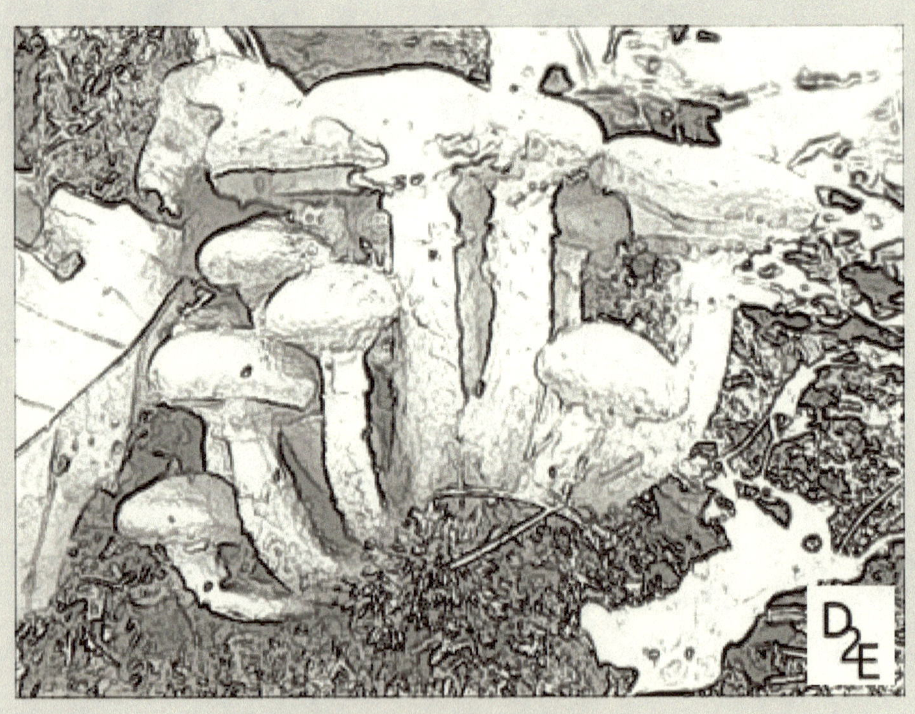
D2E

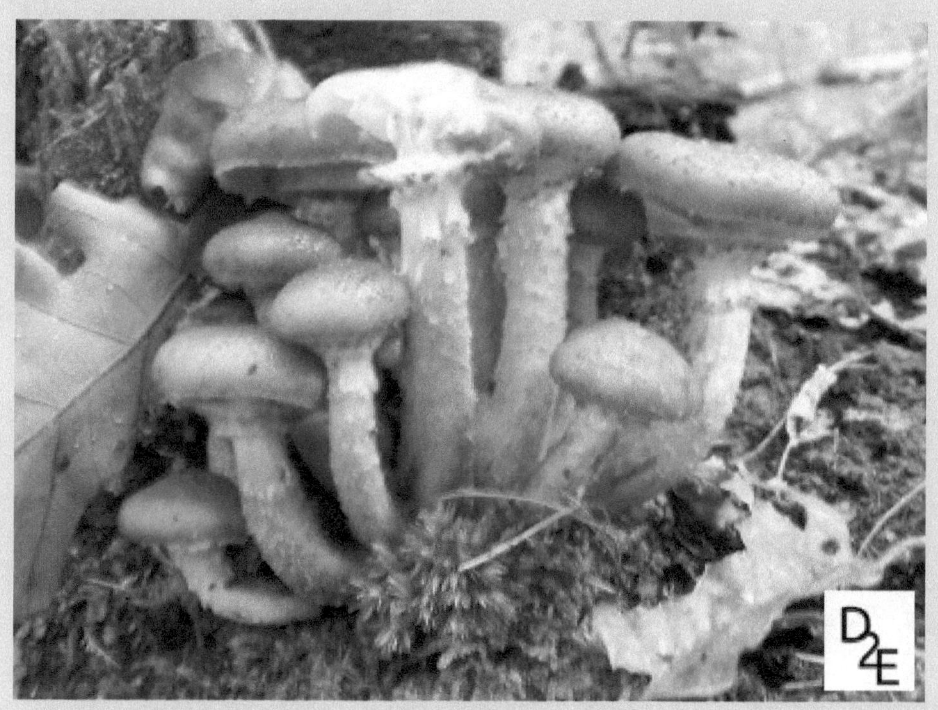
D2E

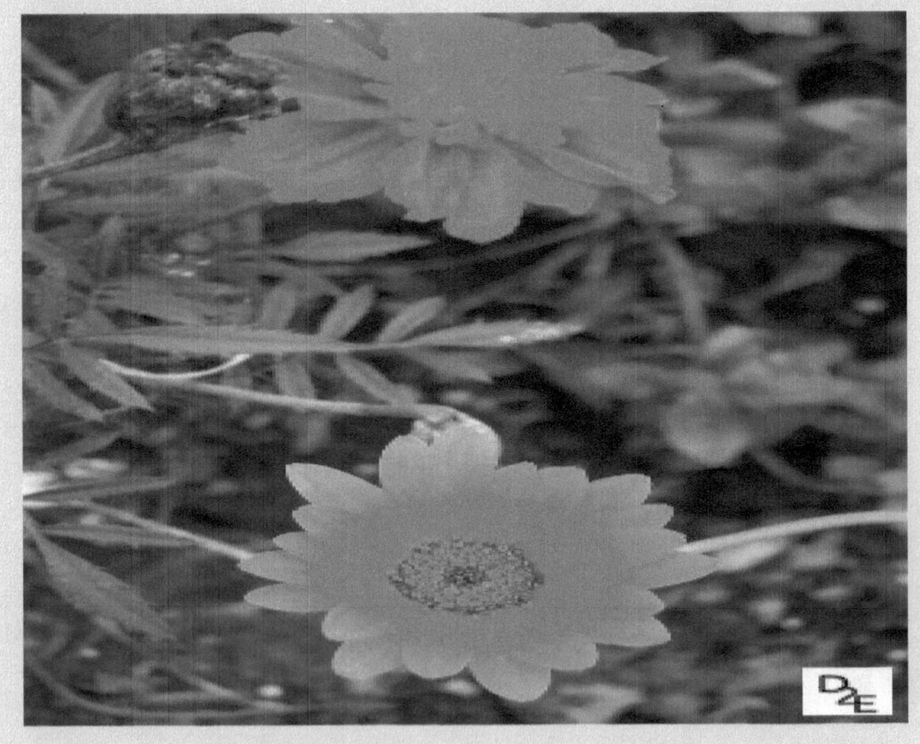
D2E

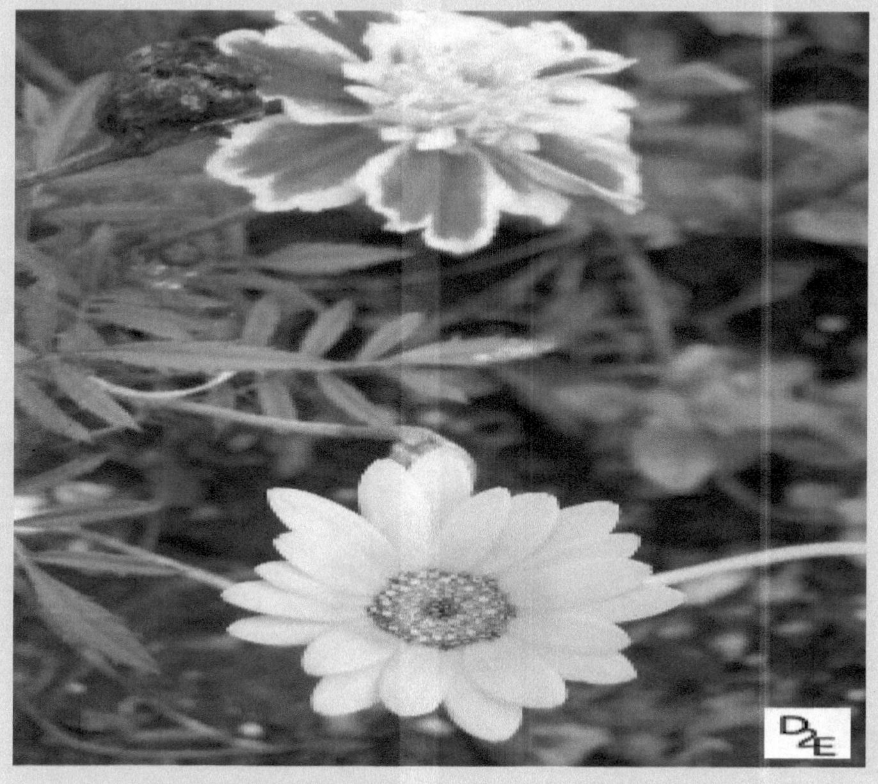
D2E

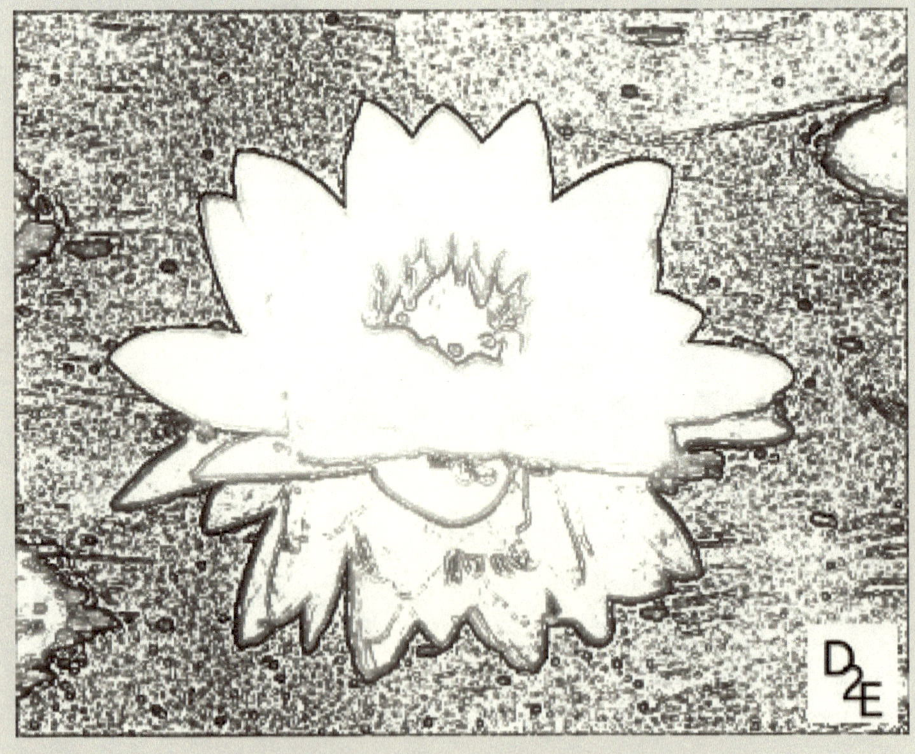
D2E

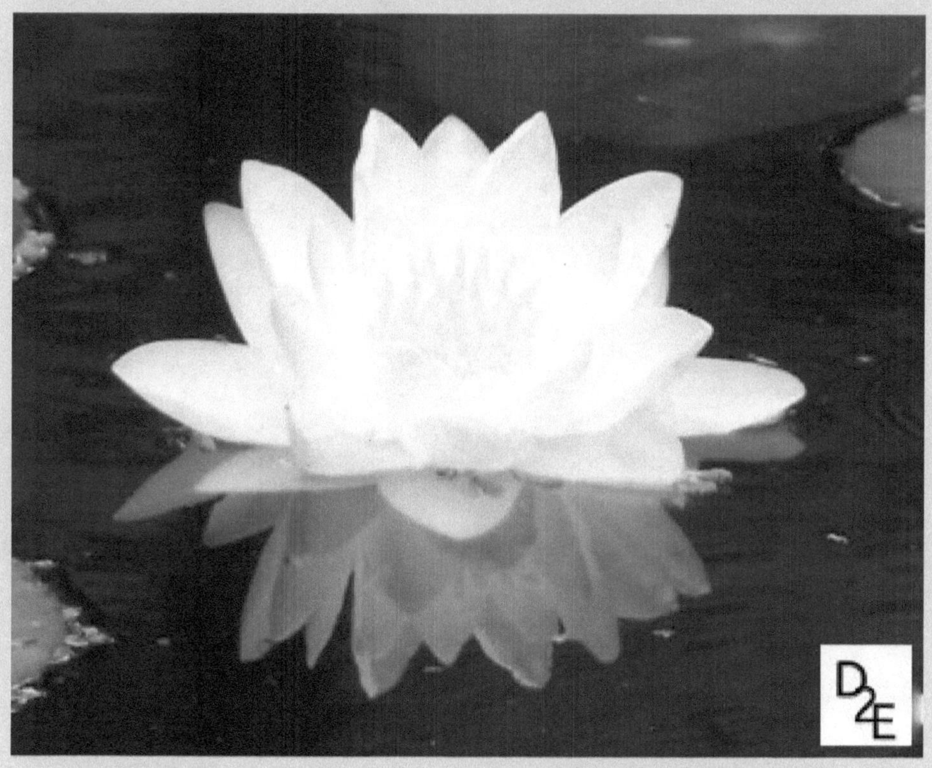
D2E

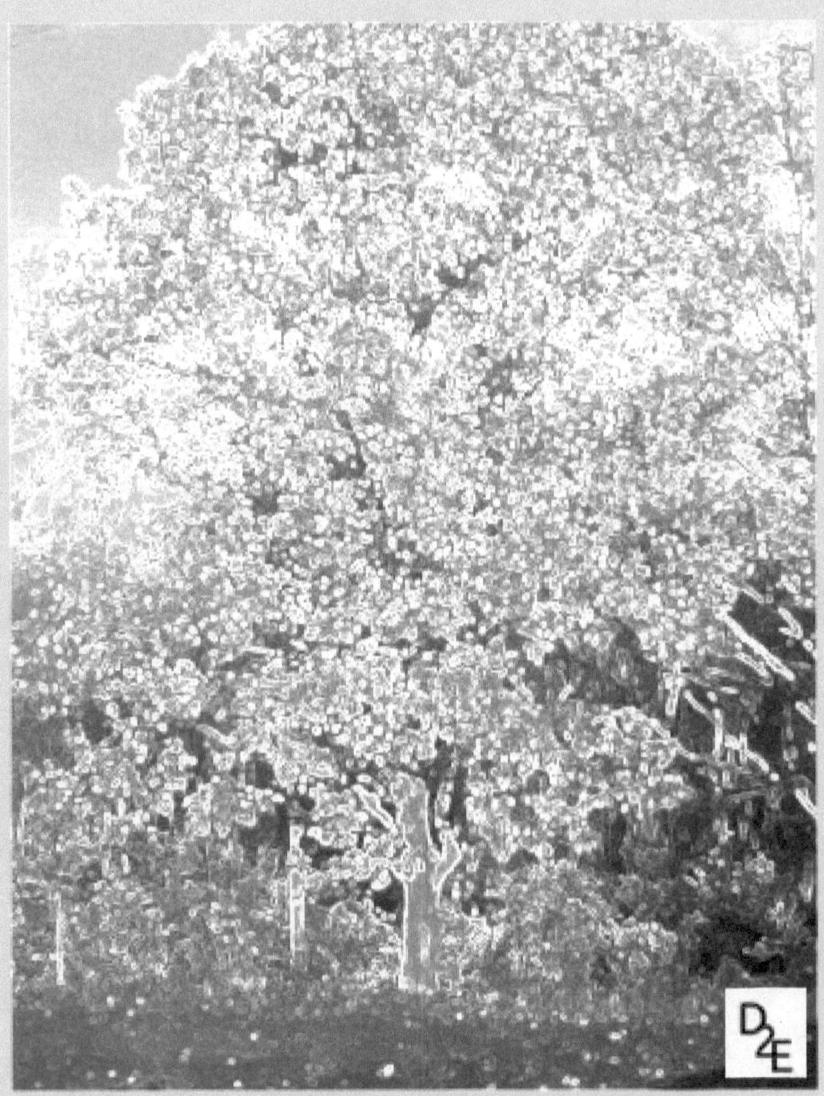
D2E

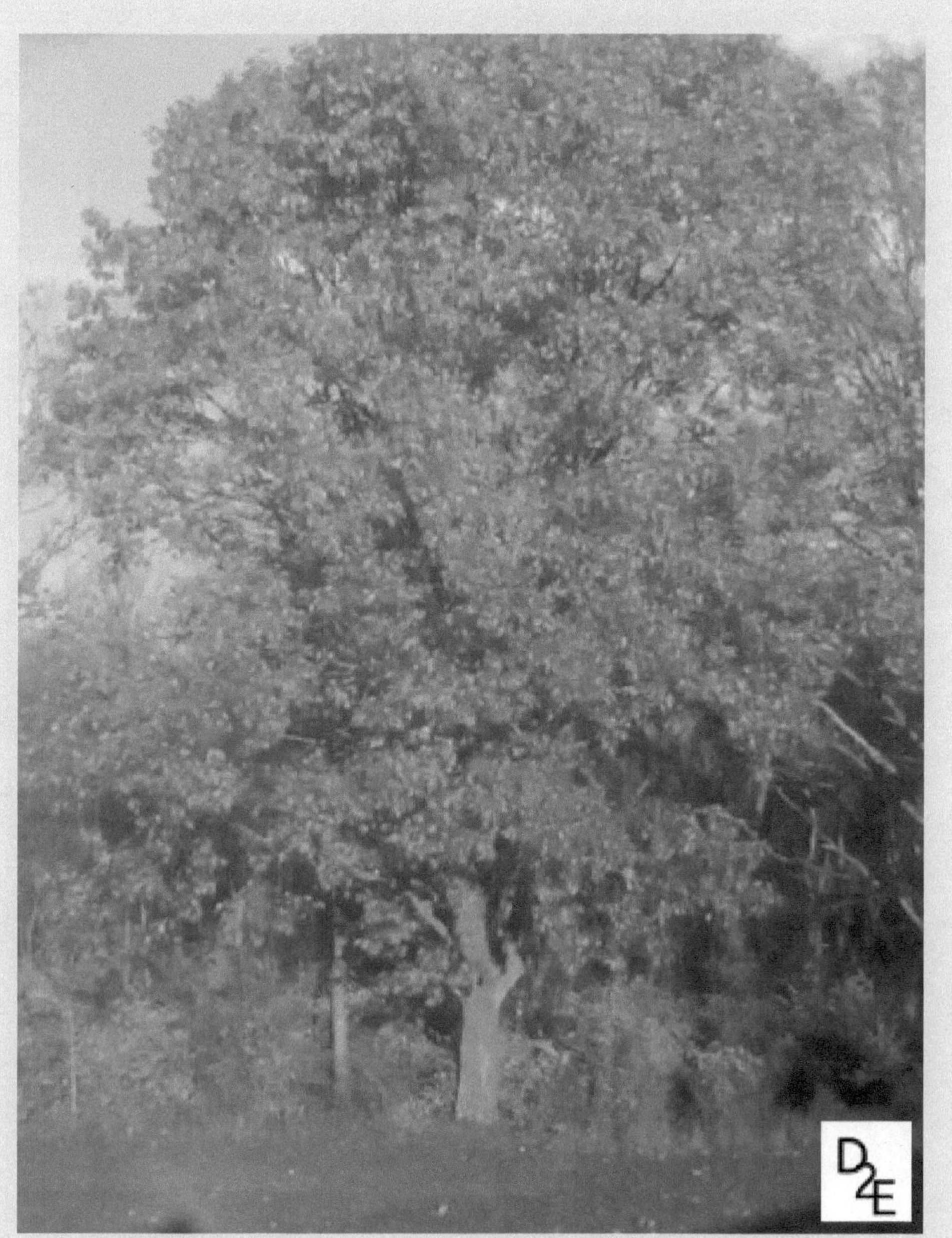
D2E

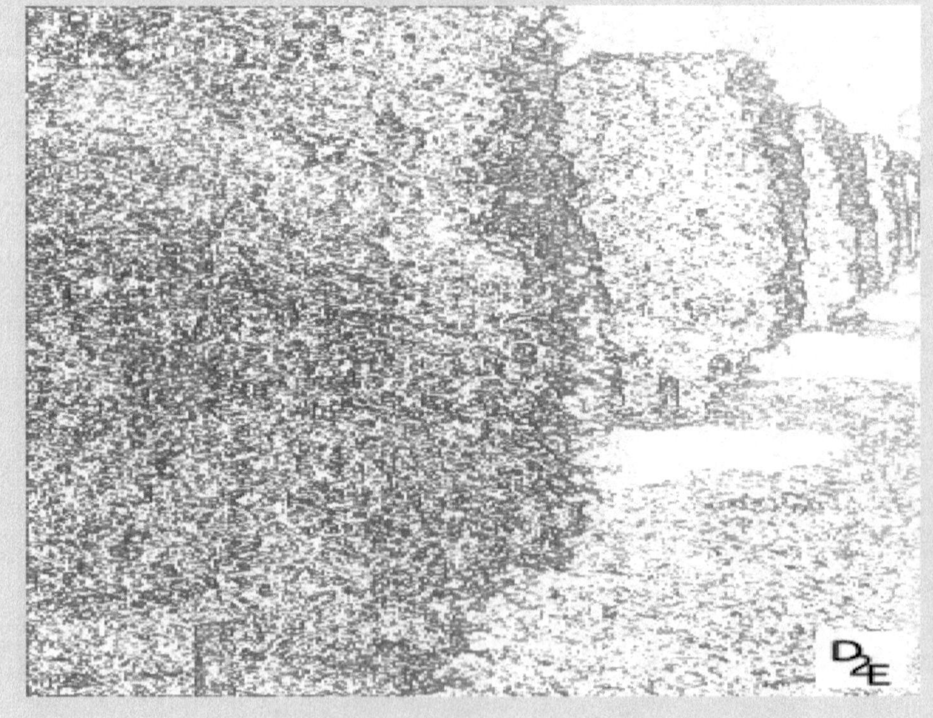

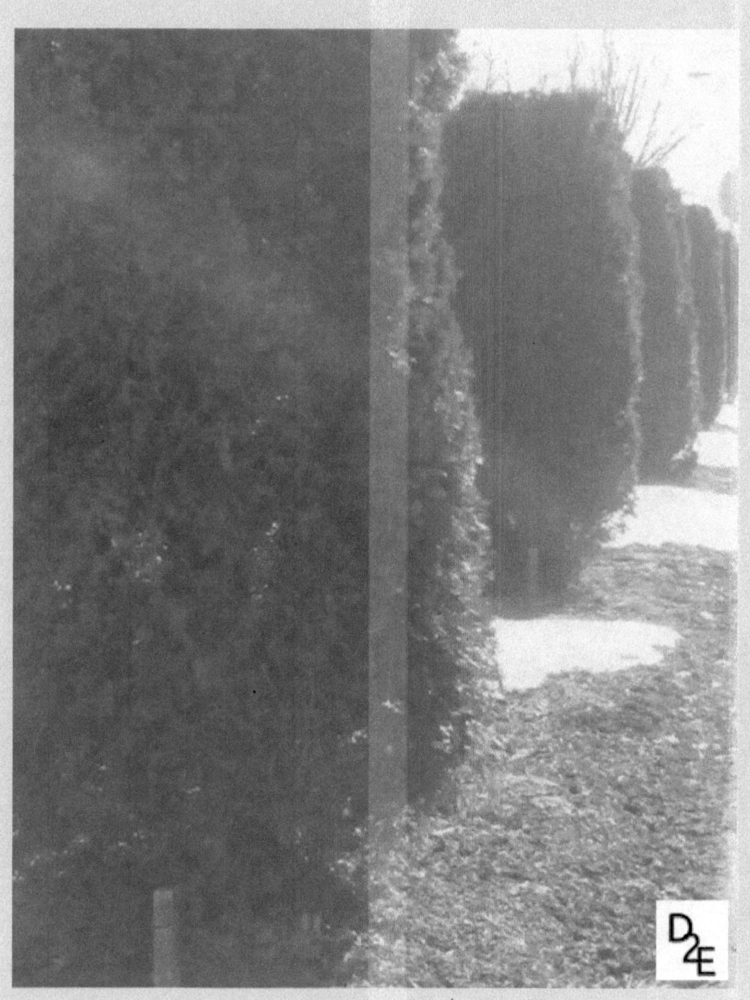
D2E

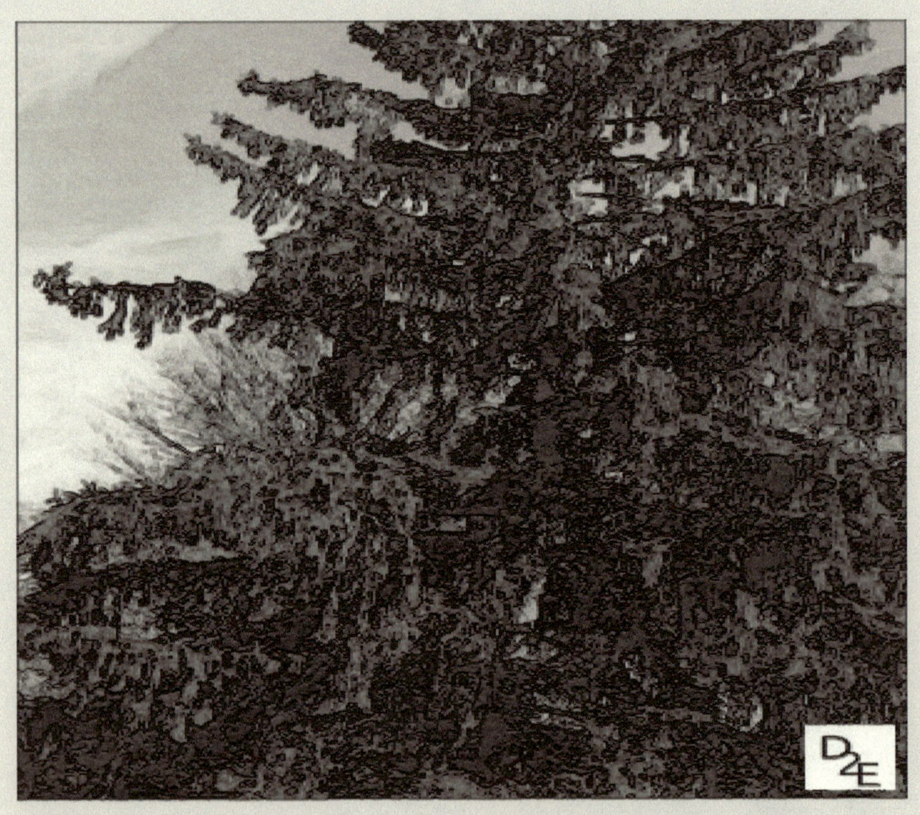
D2E

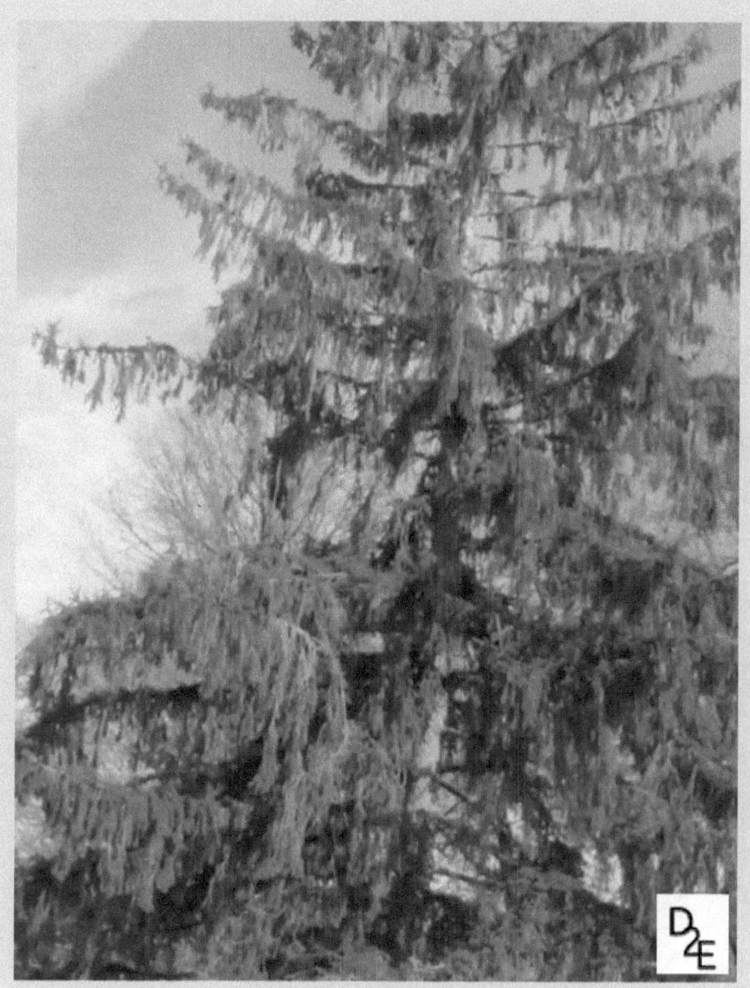
D2E

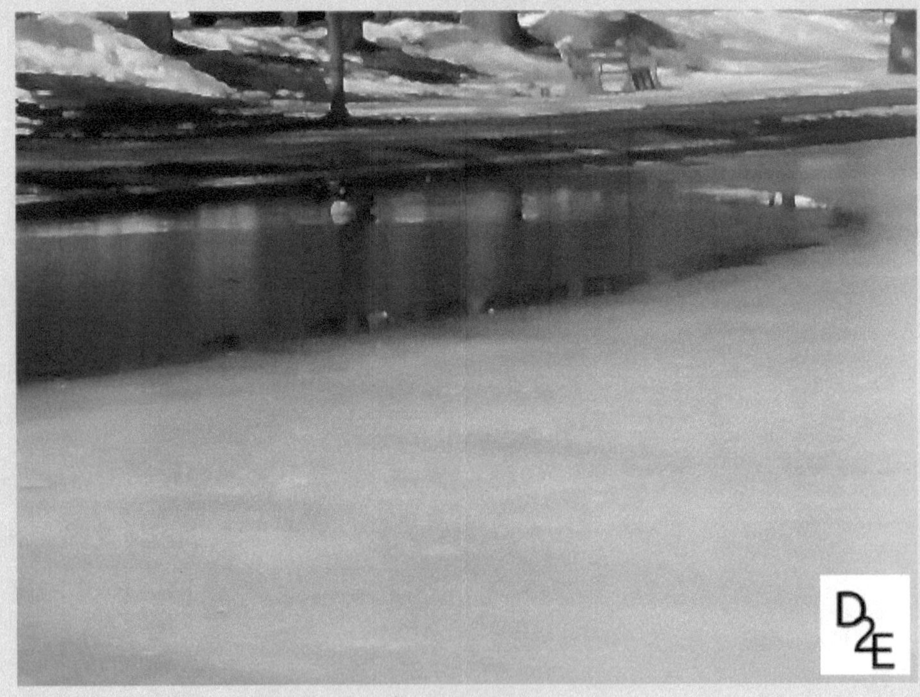

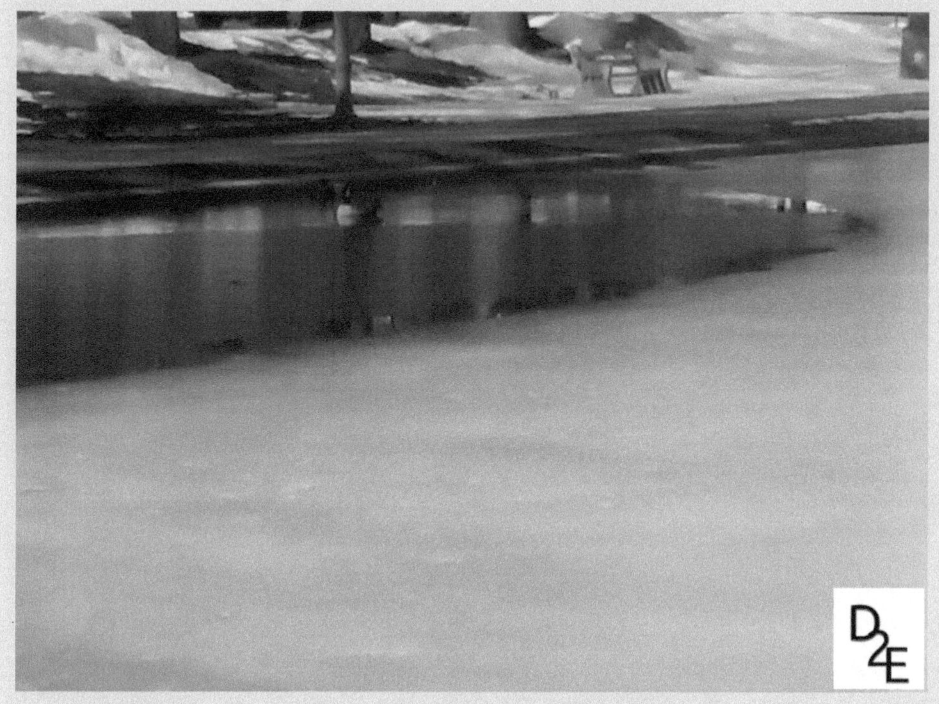
D2E

D2E

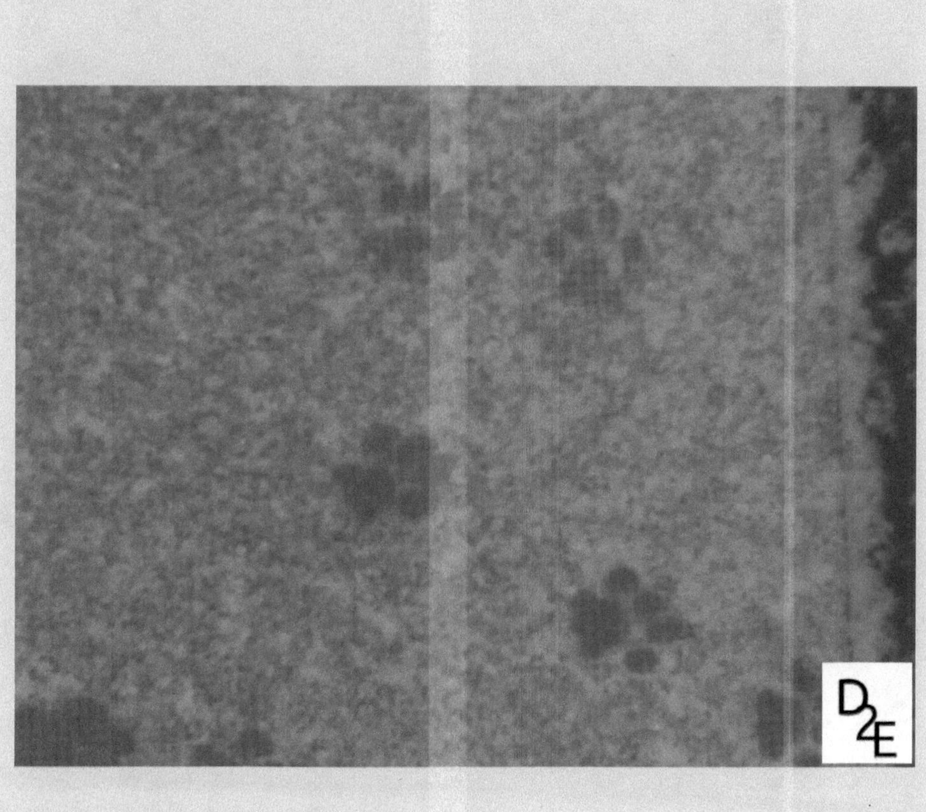
D2E

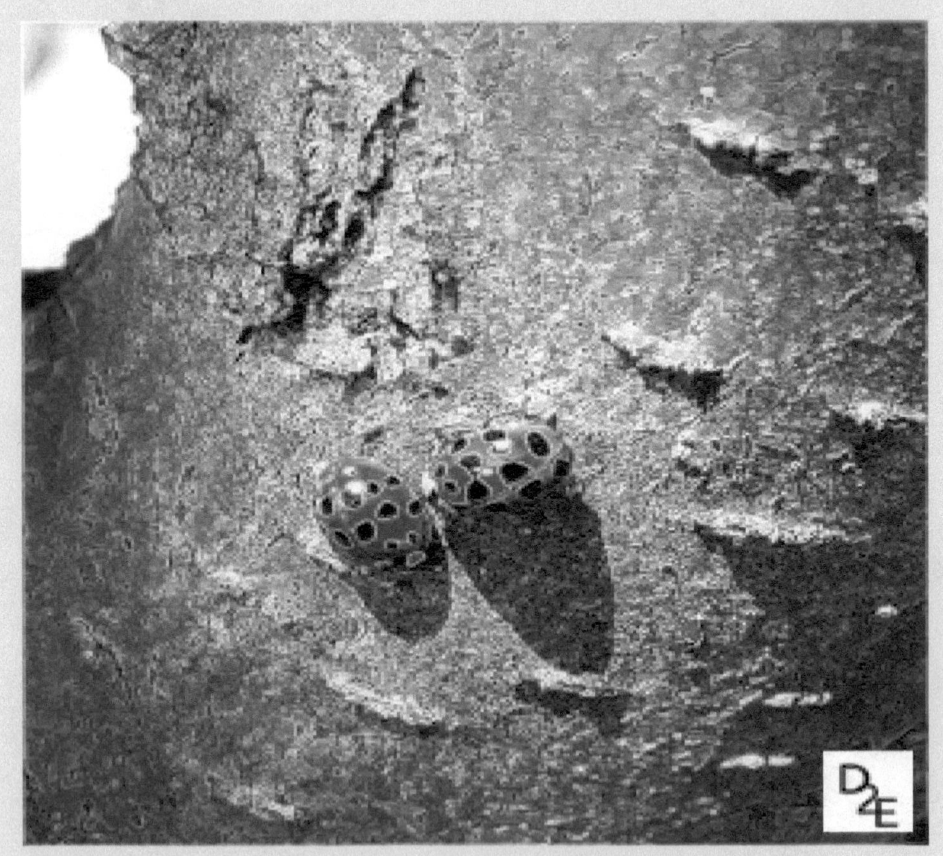
D2E

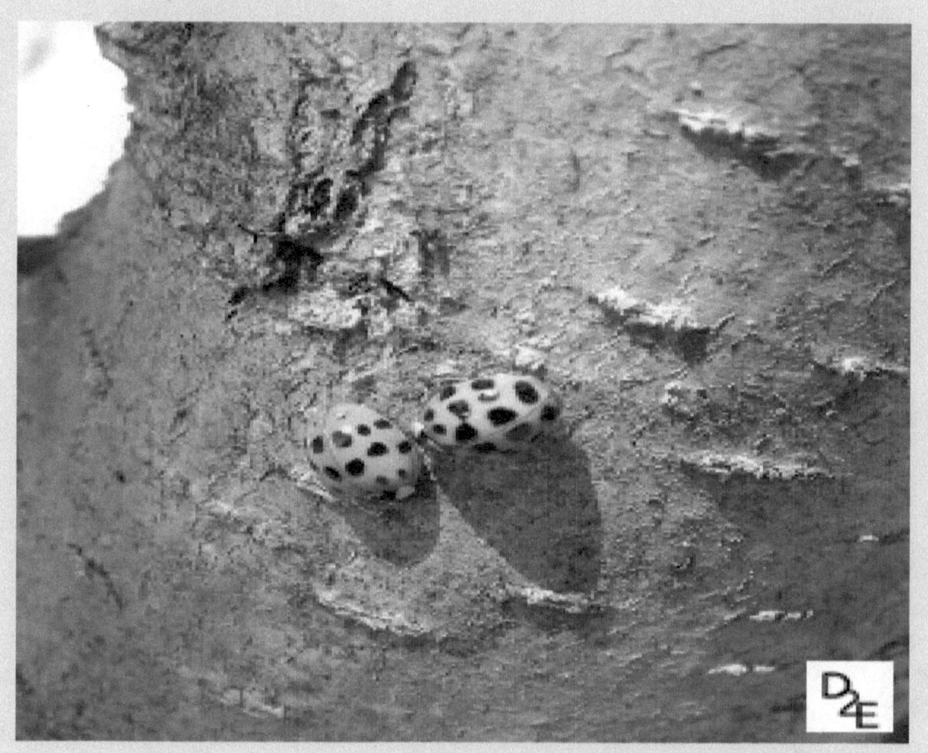
D2E

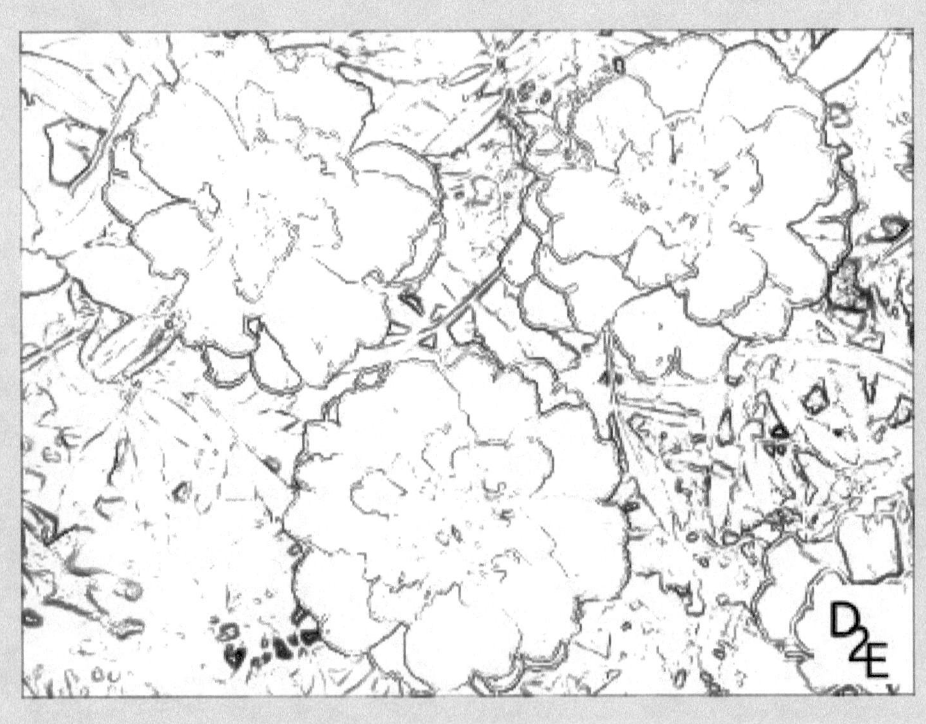
D2E

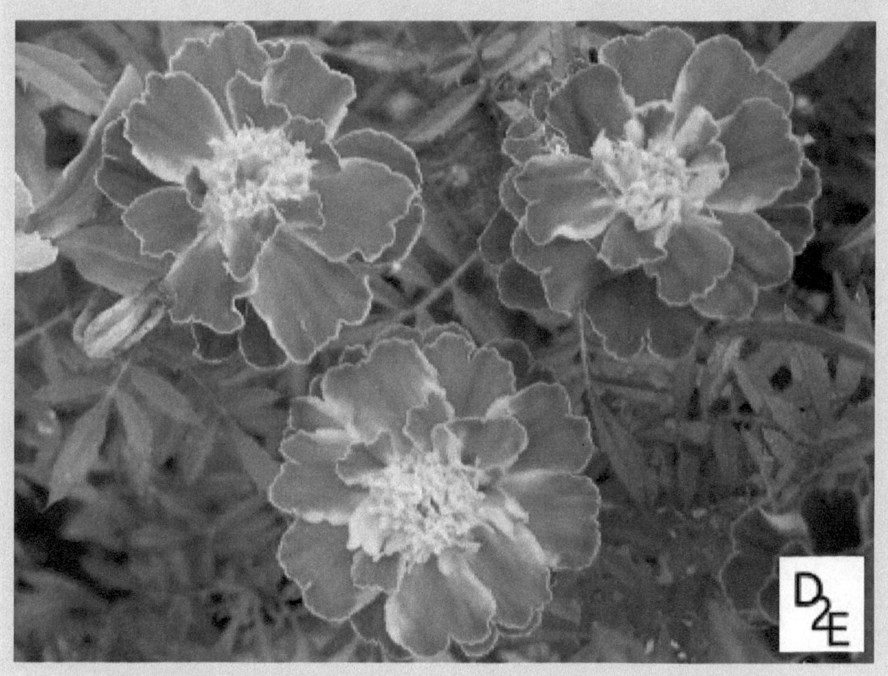
D2E

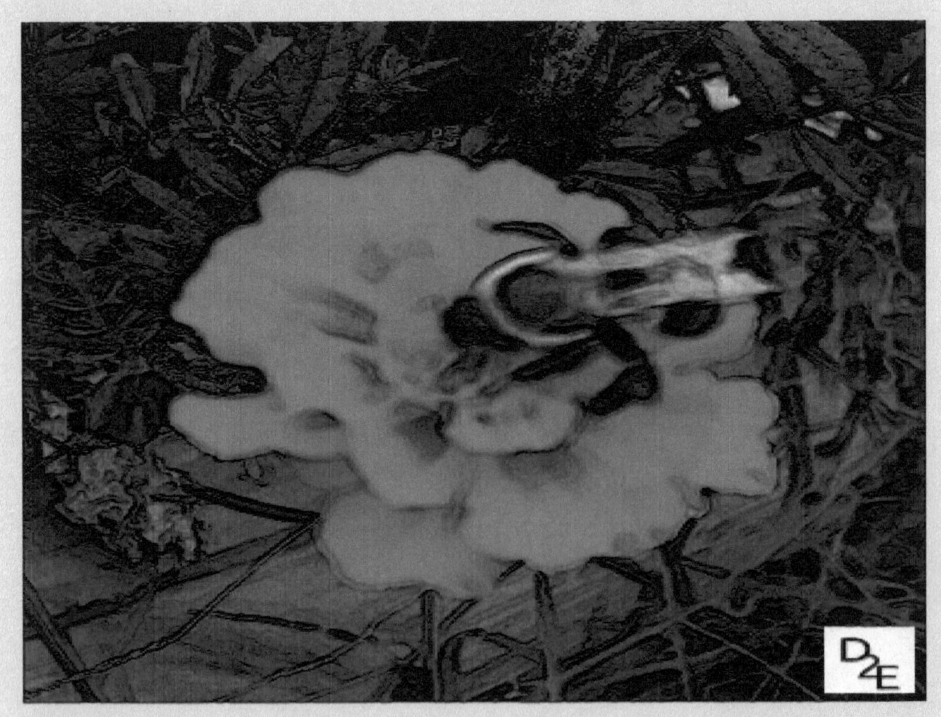

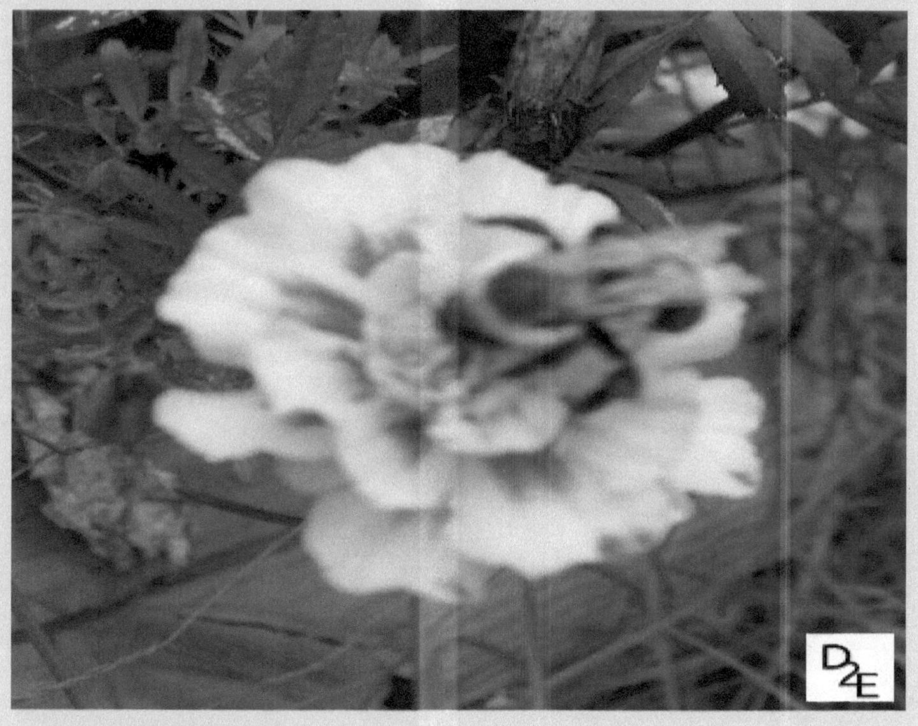
D2E

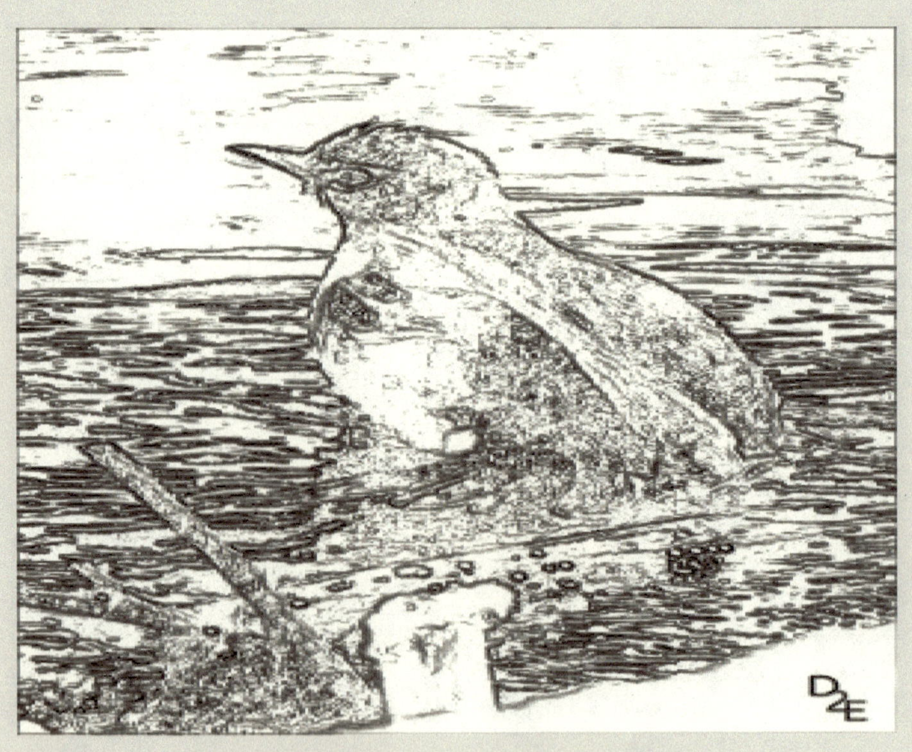

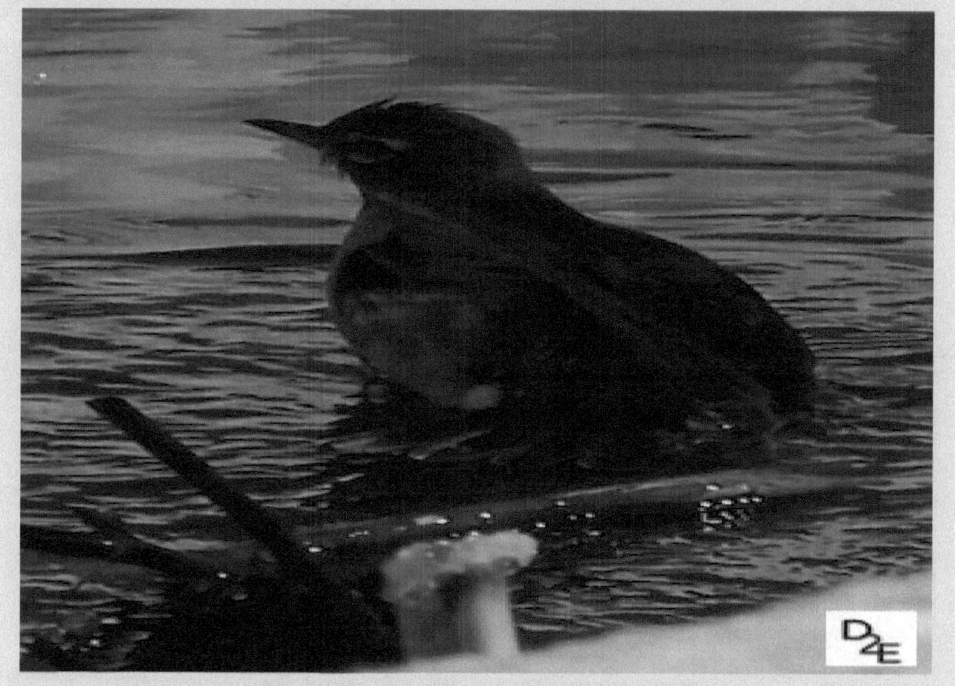
D2E

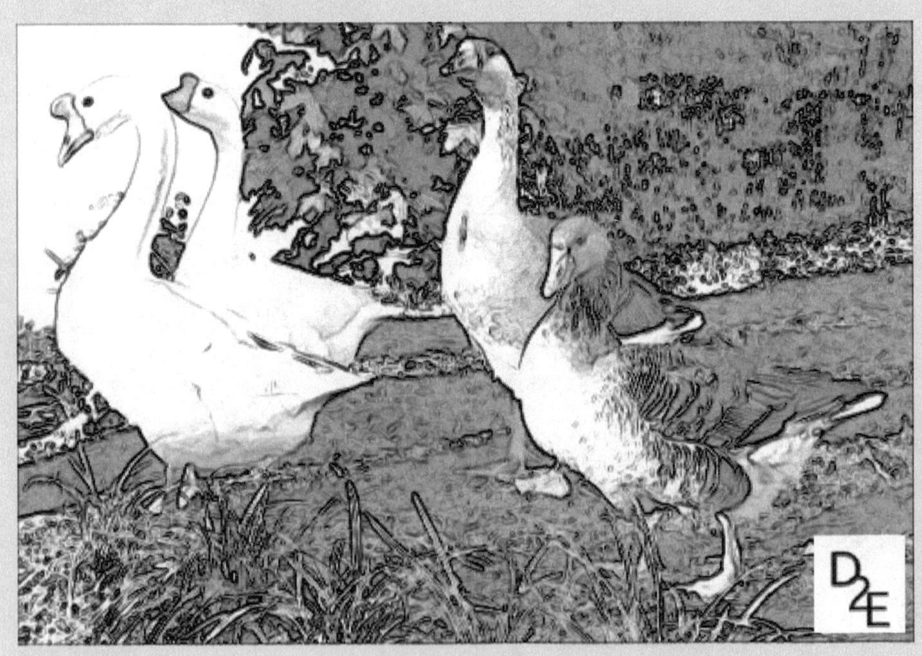
D2E

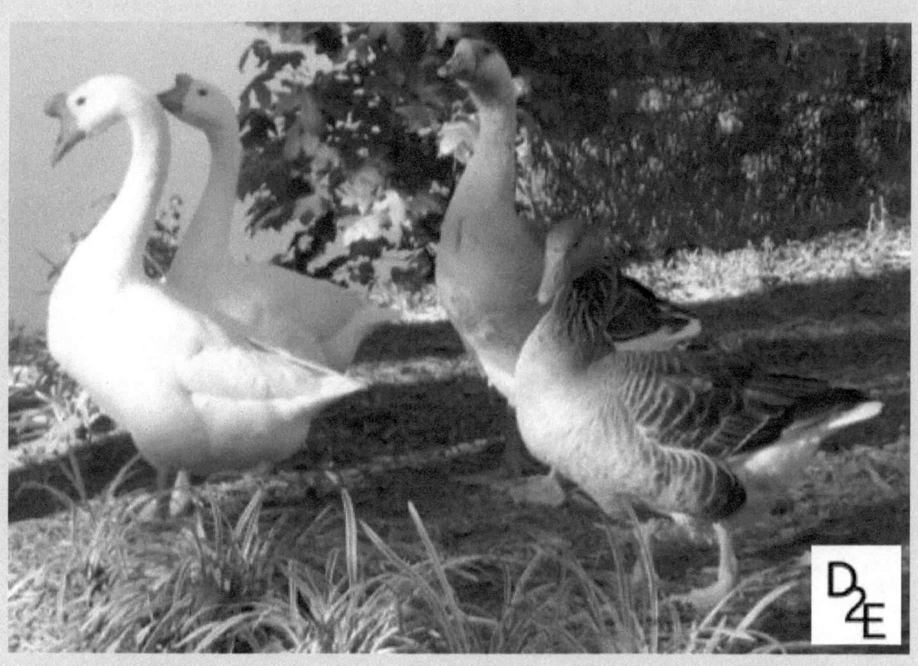
D2E

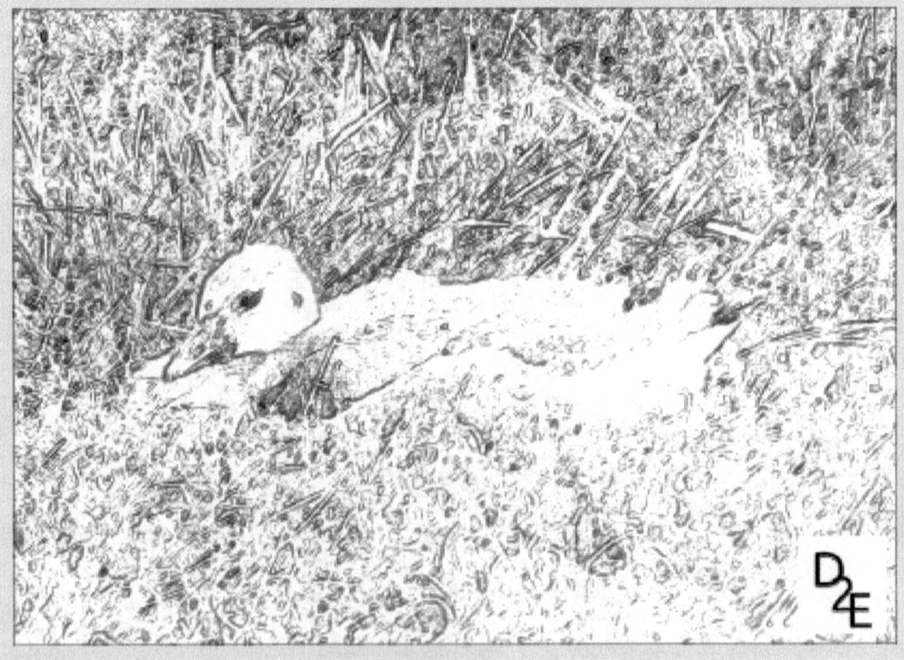
D2E

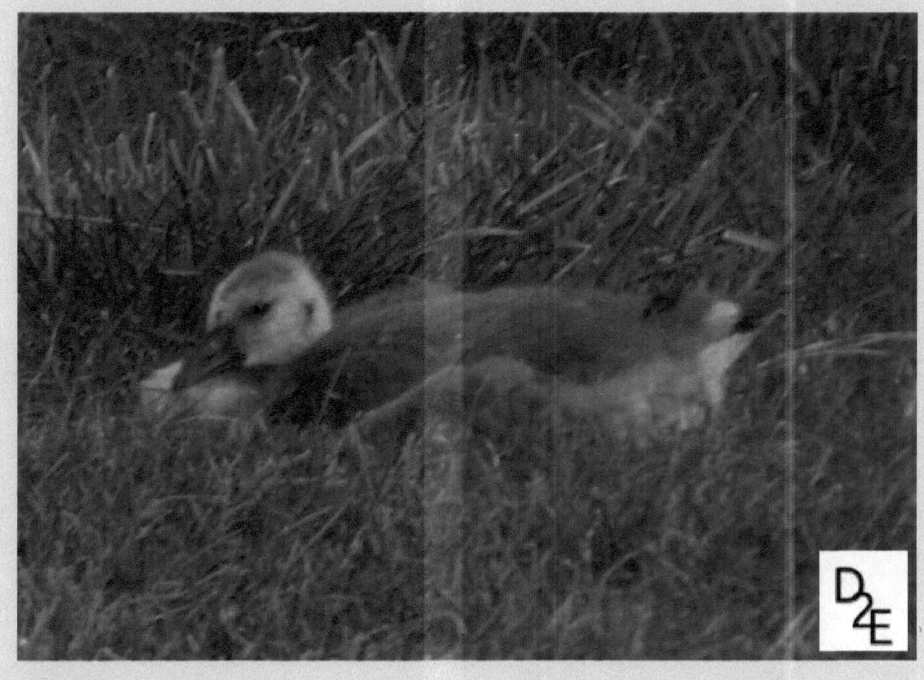
D2E

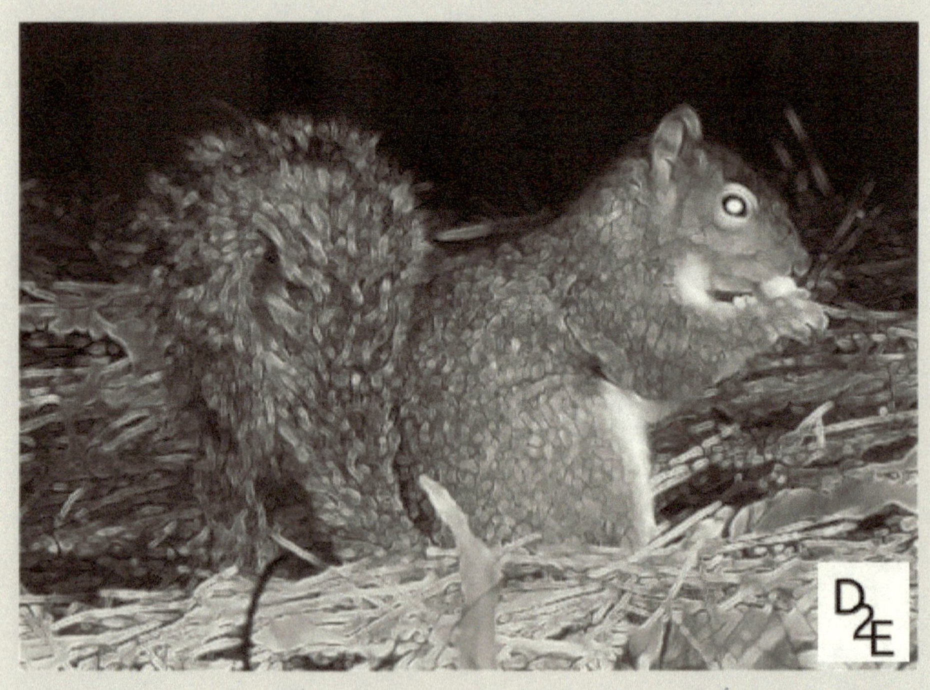

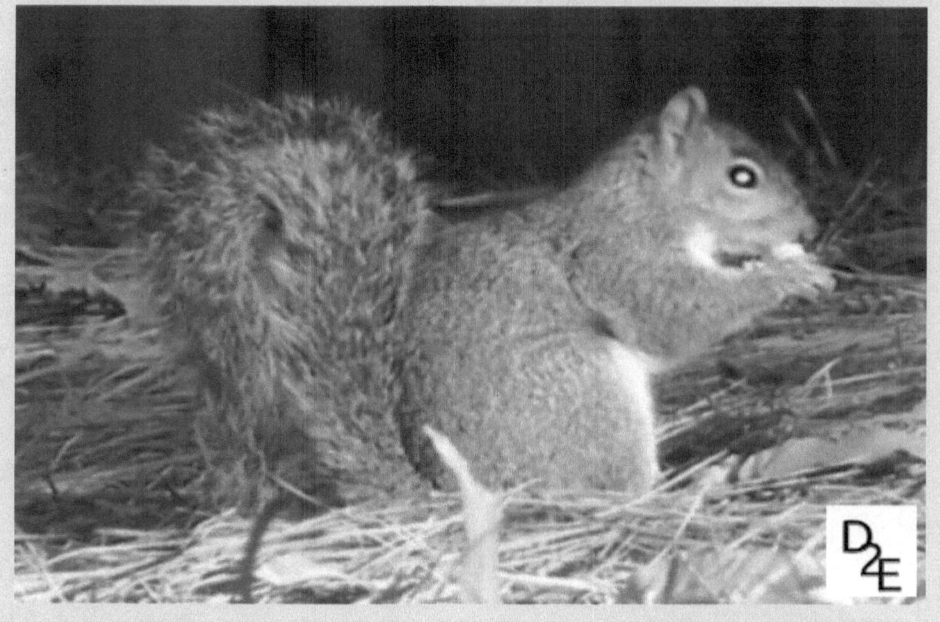
D2E

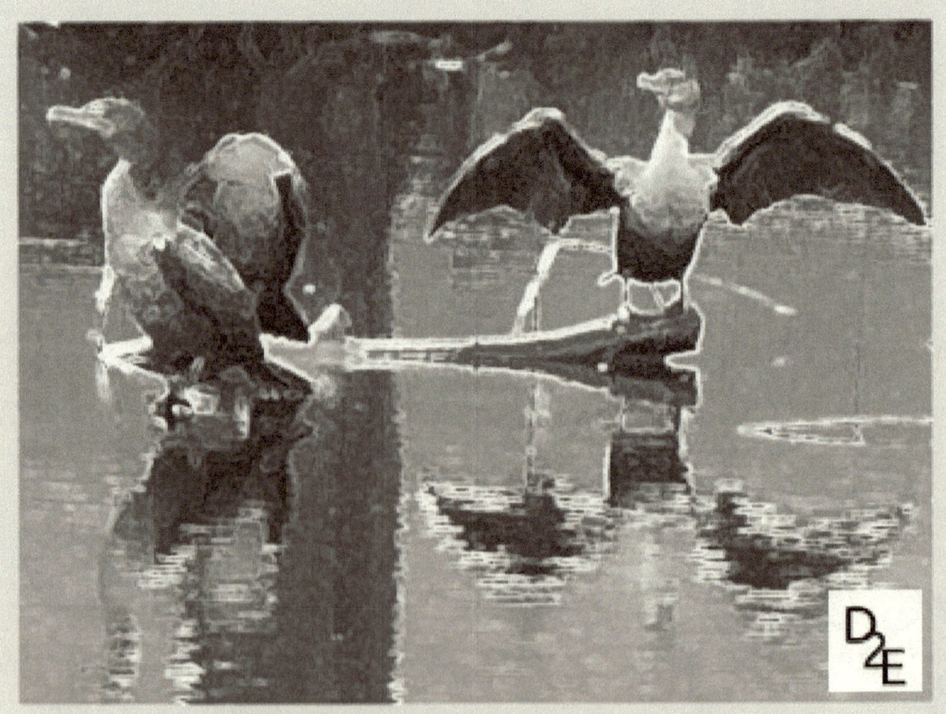

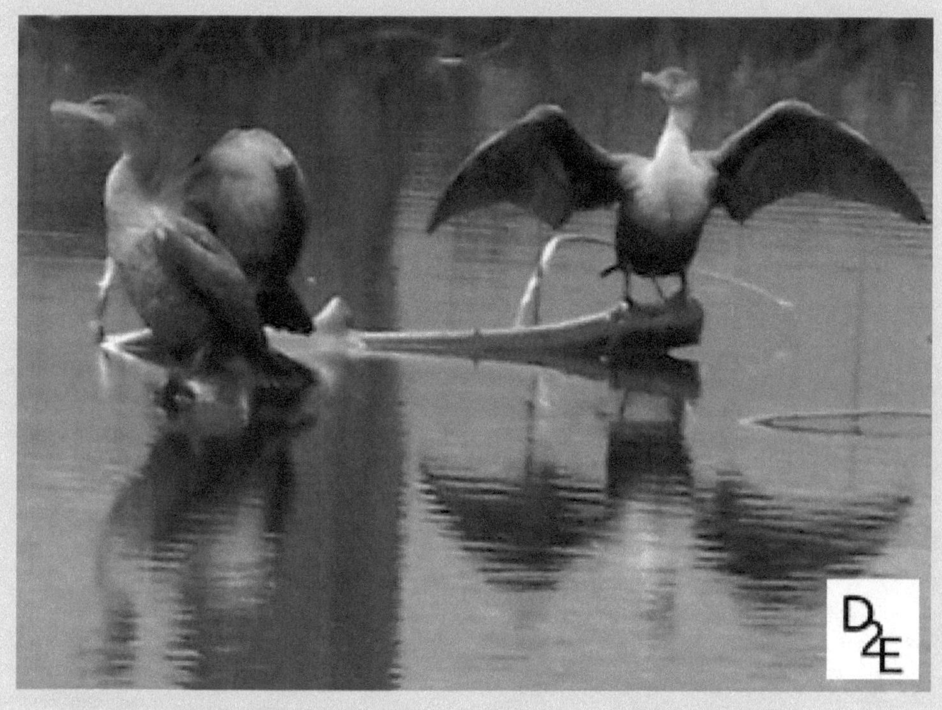

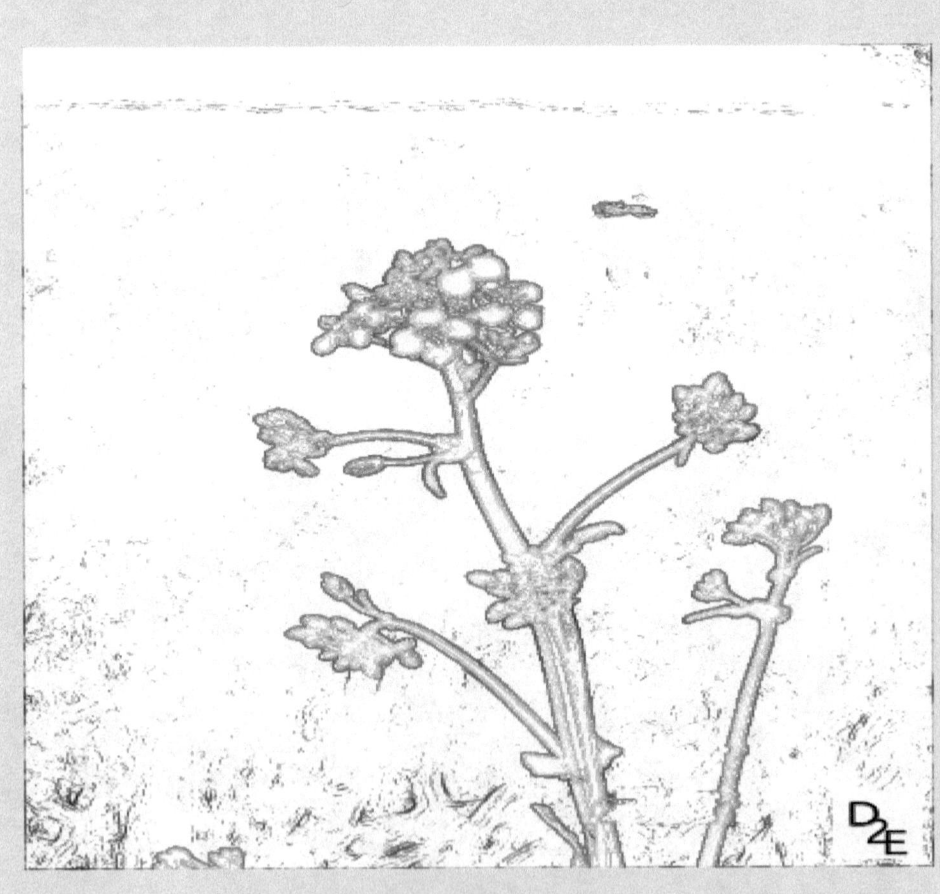
D2E

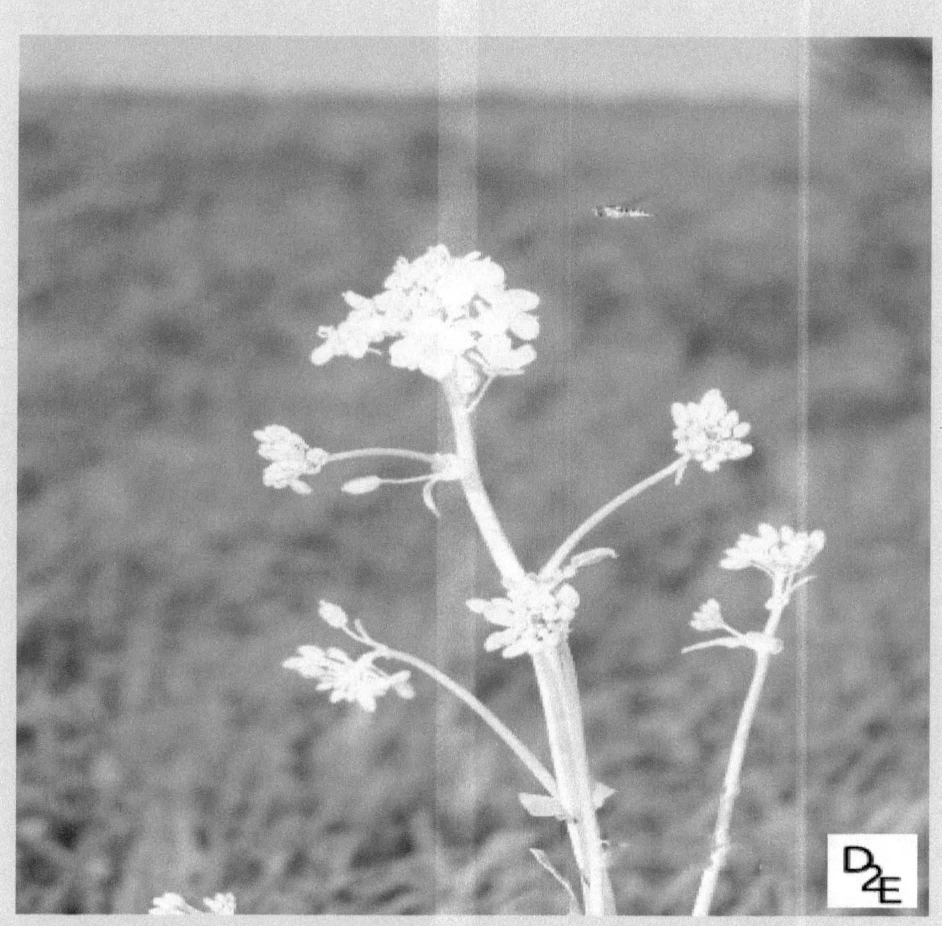
D2E

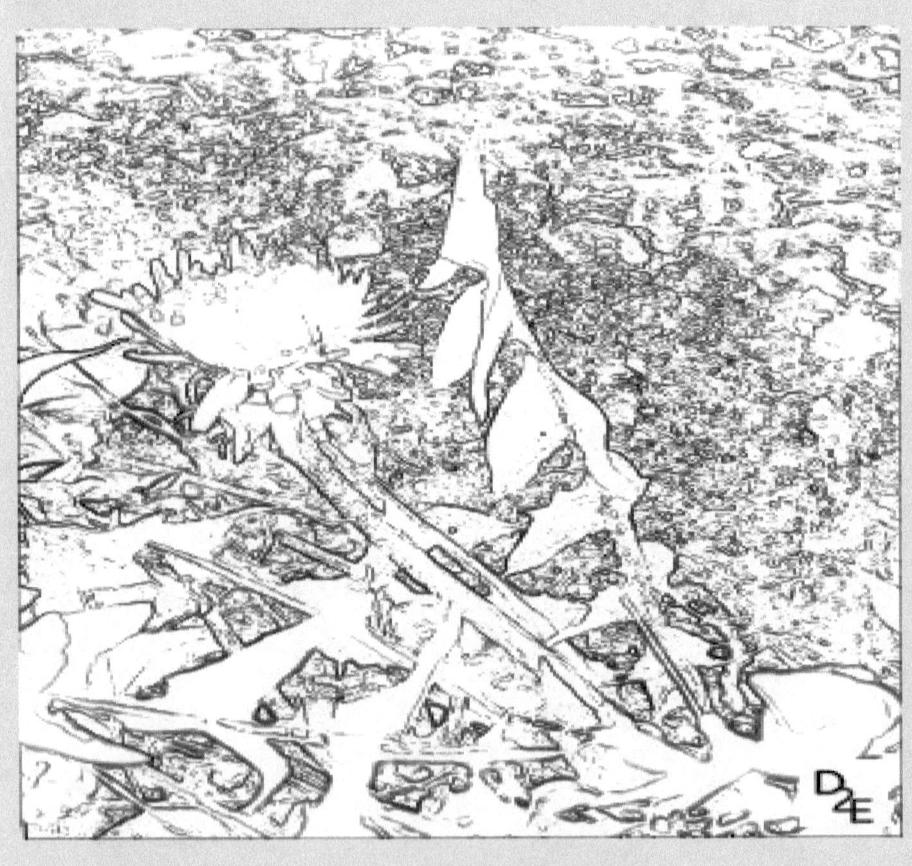

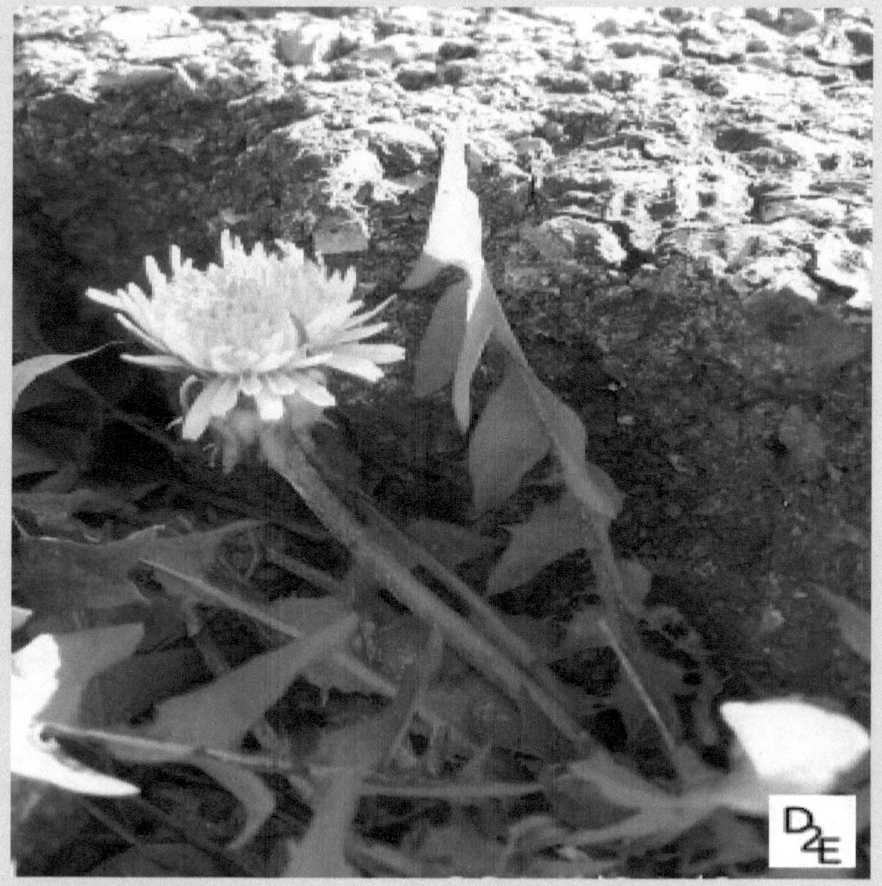
D2E

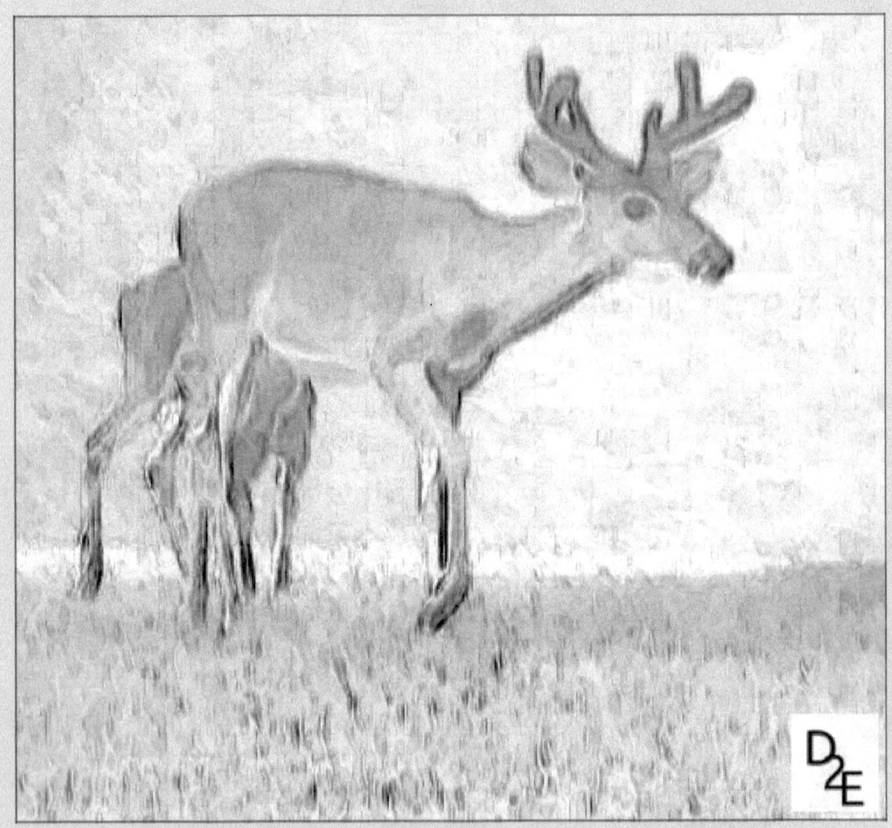
D2E

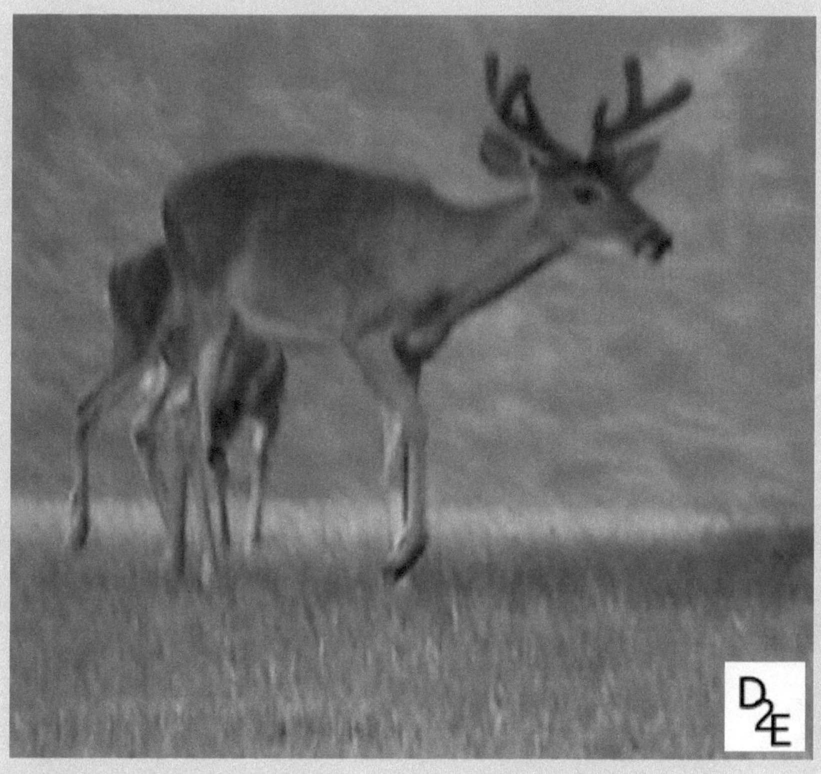

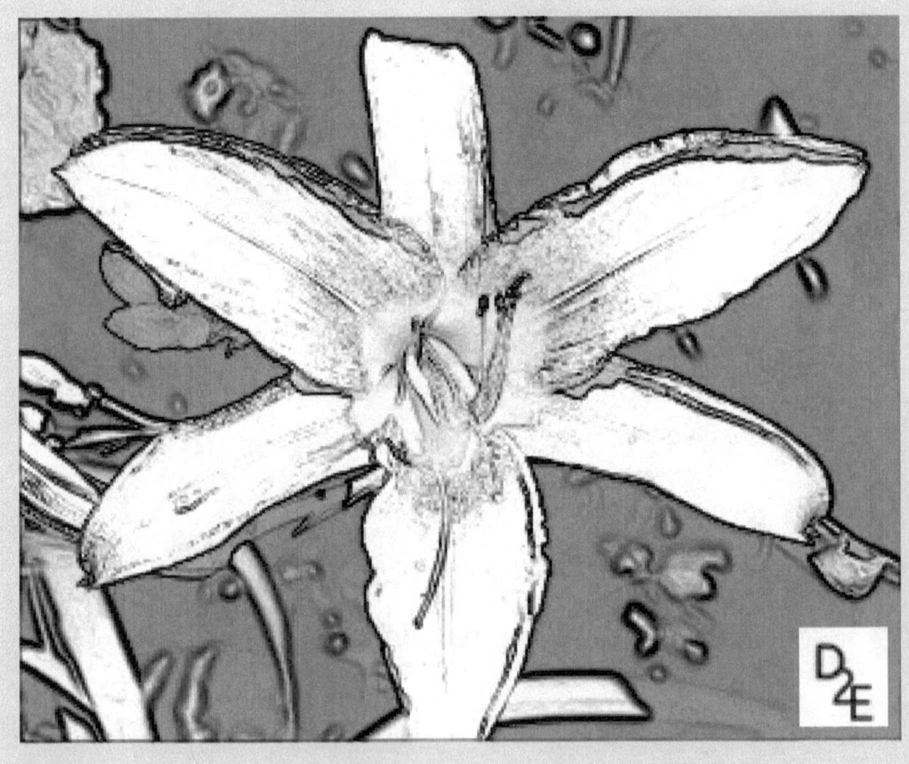
D2E

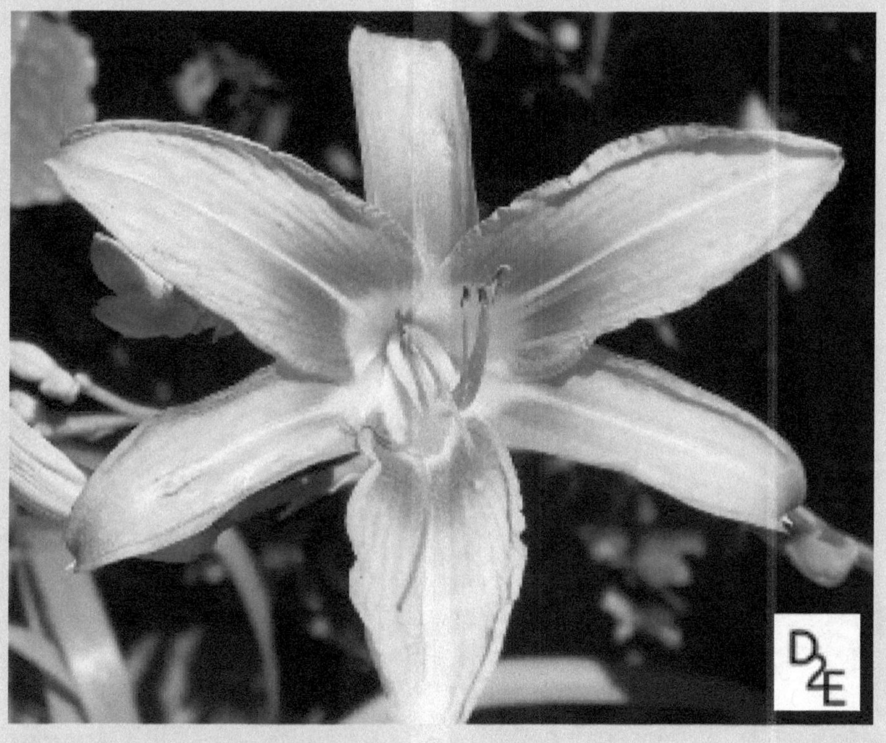

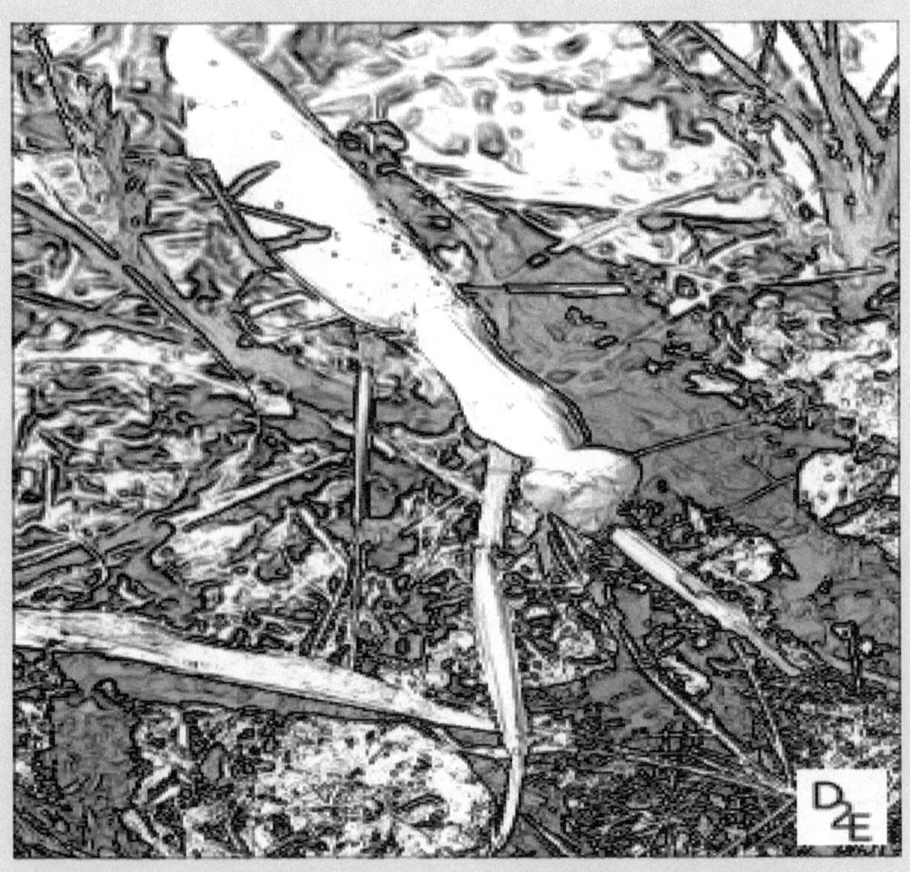
D2E

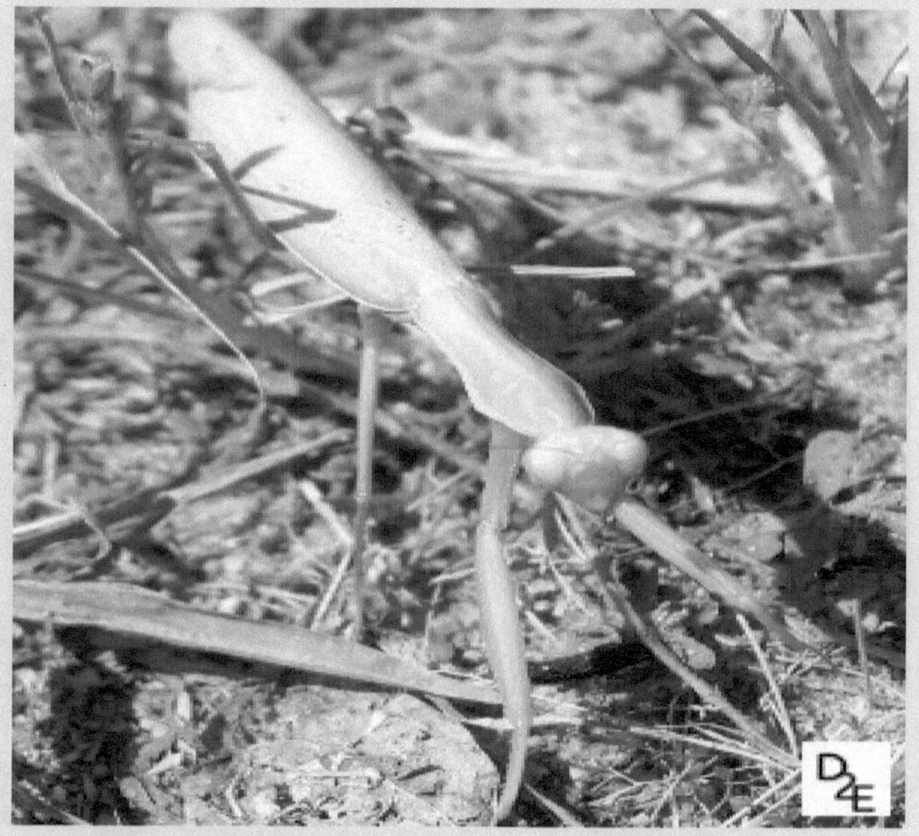
D2E

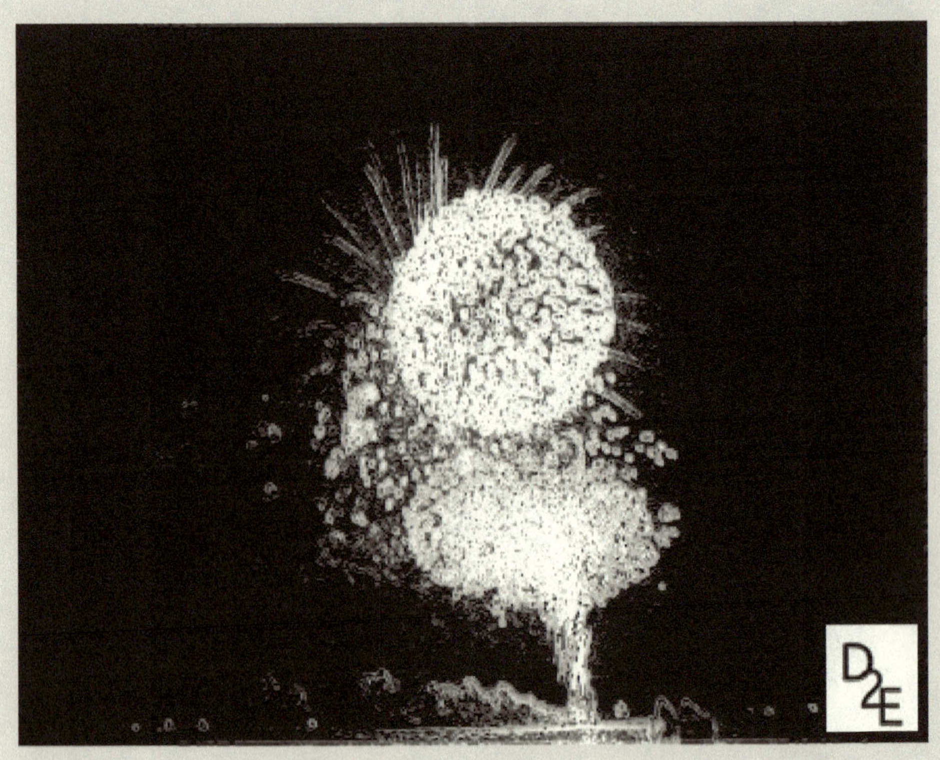
D2E

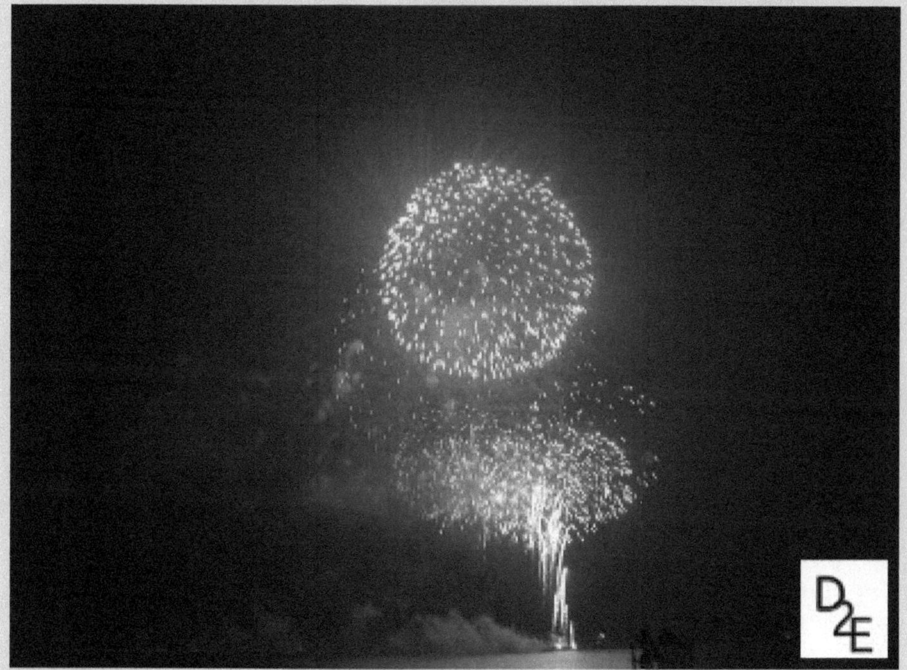
D2E

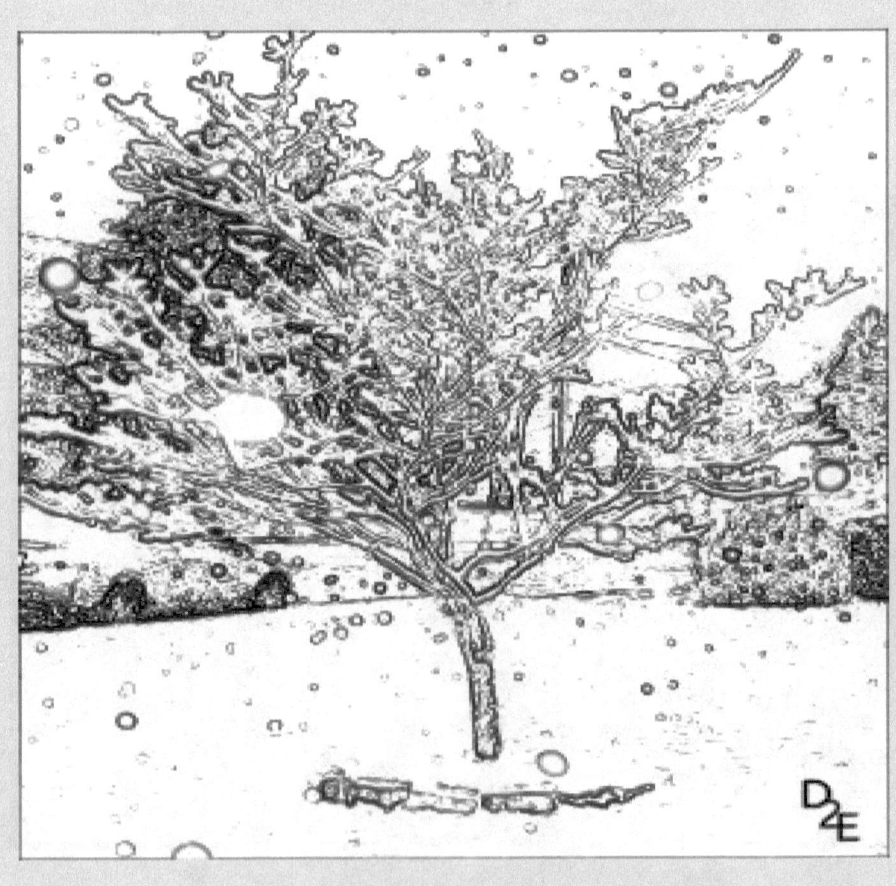
D2E

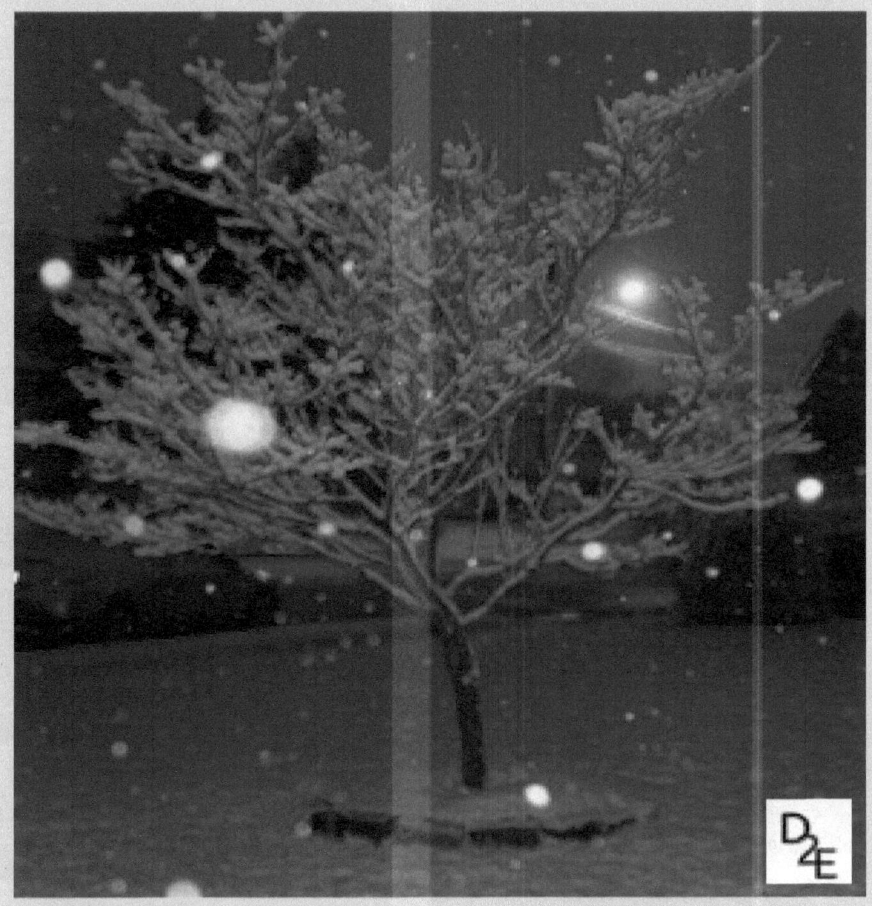

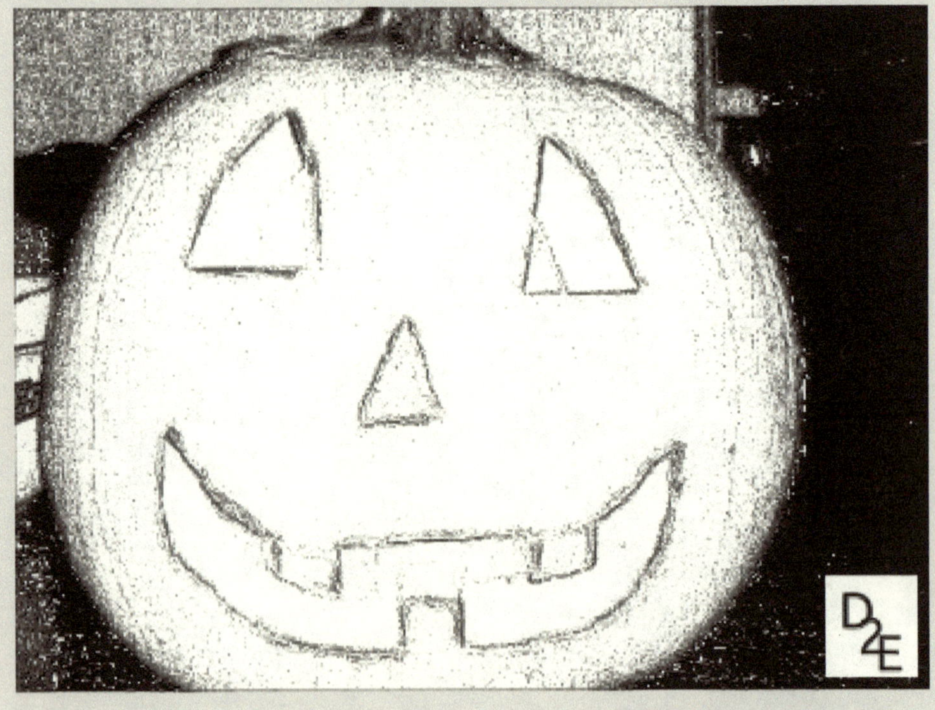
D2E

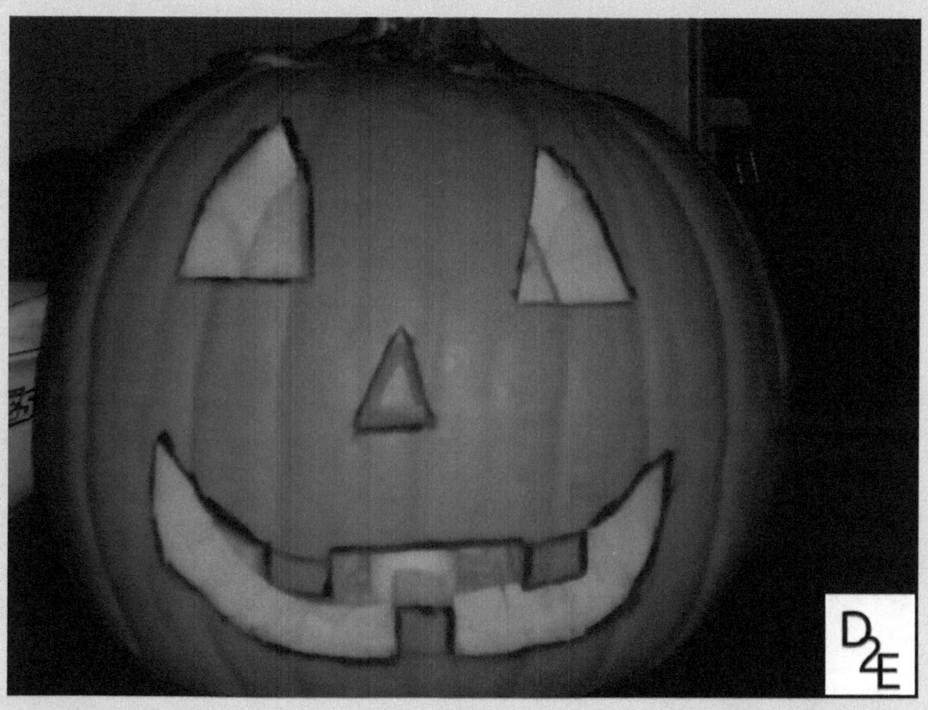
D2E

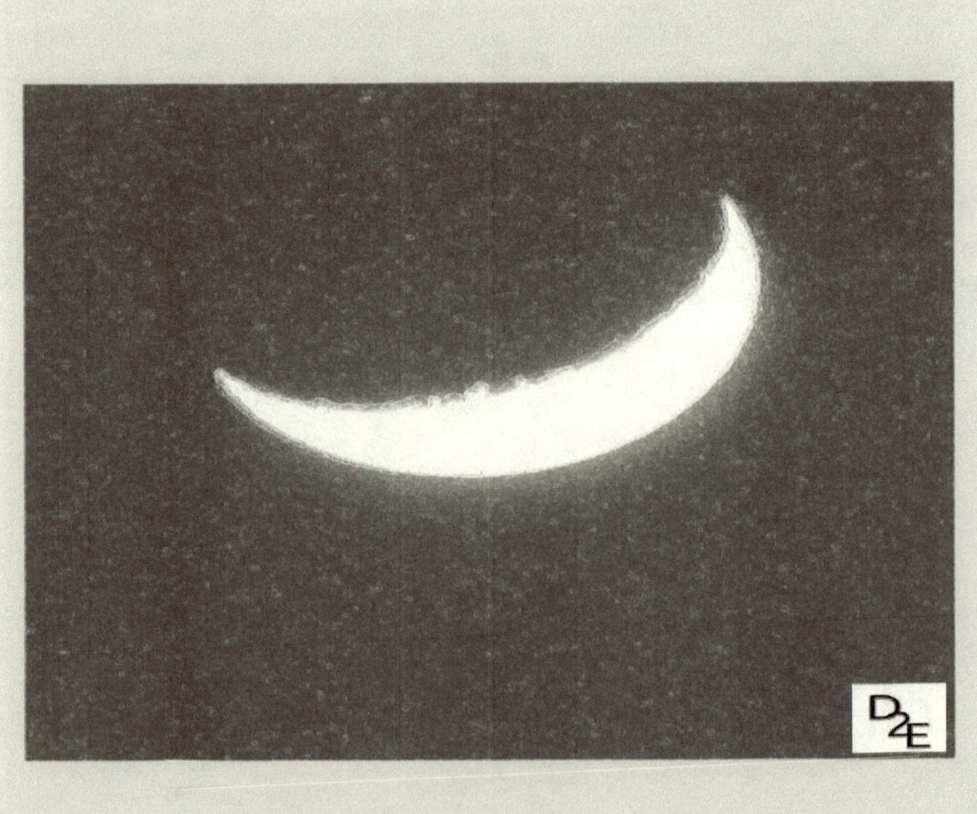
D2E

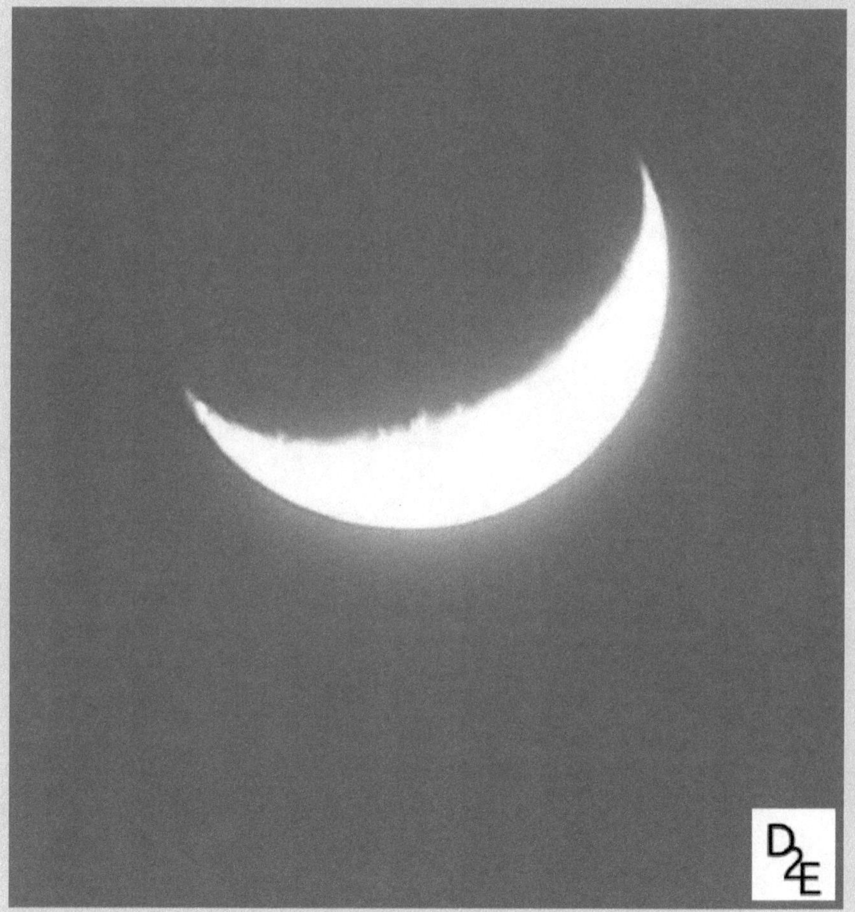
D2E

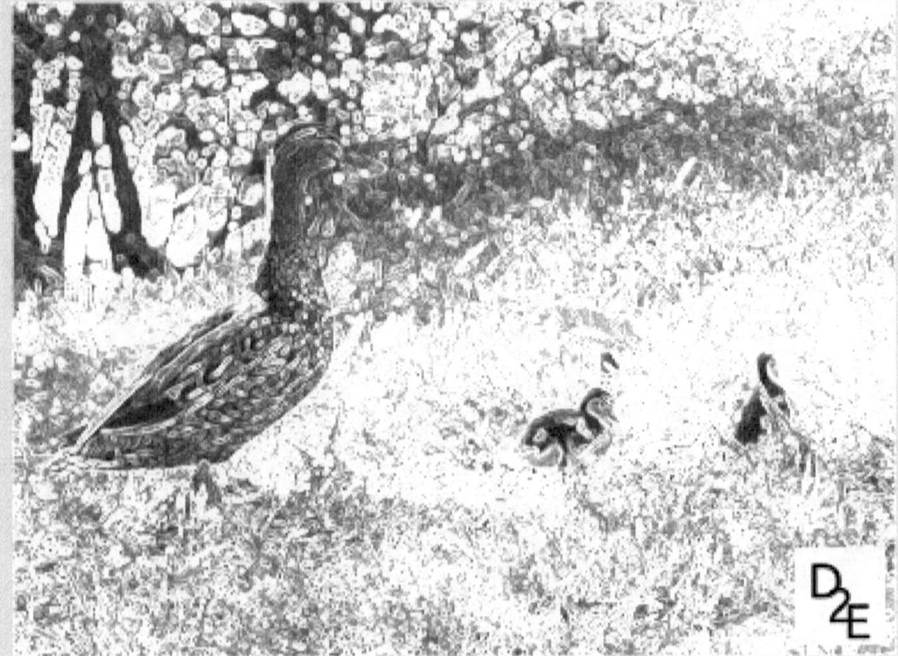
D2E

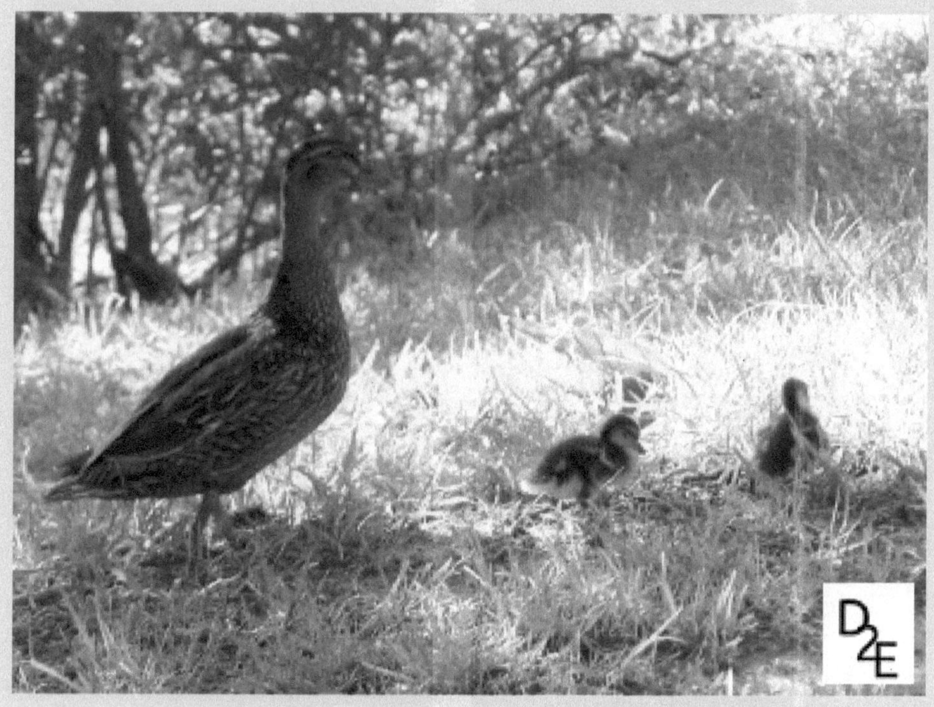
D2E

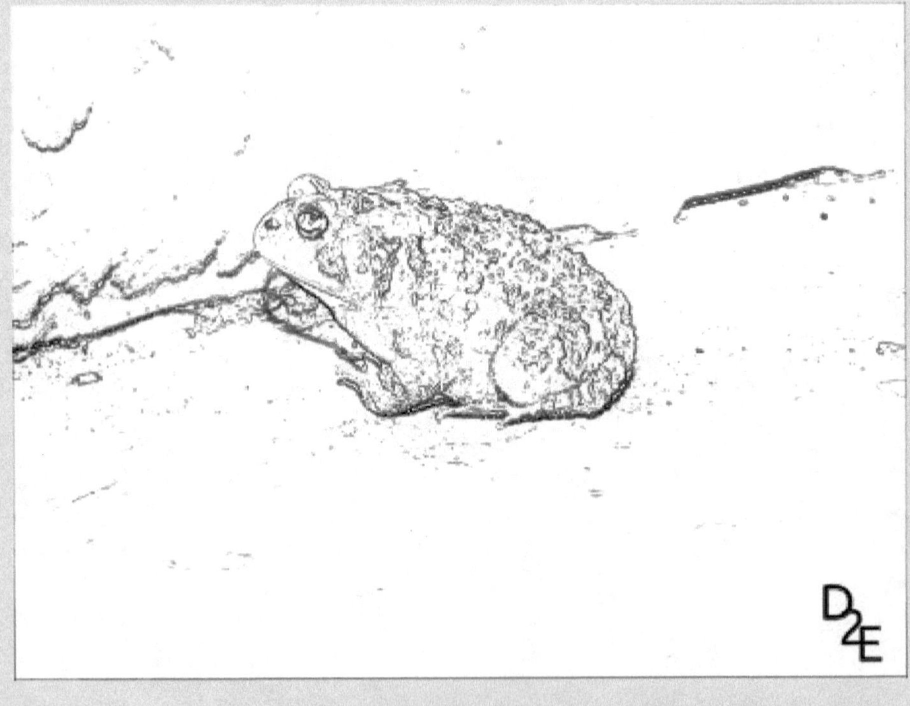
D2E

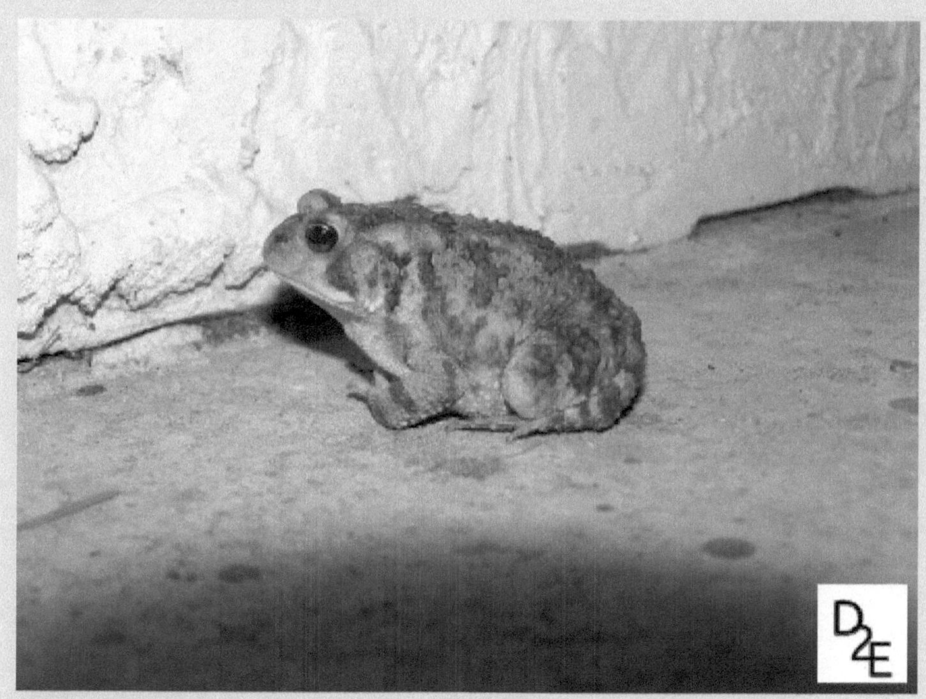
D2E

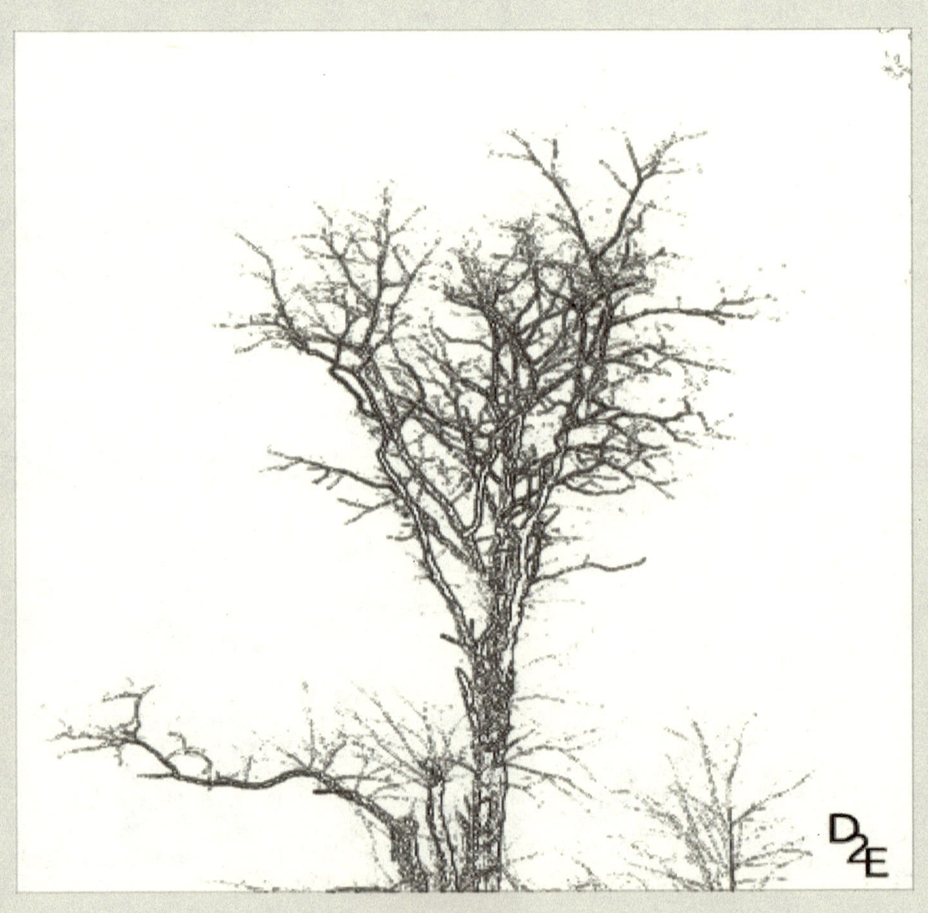
D2E

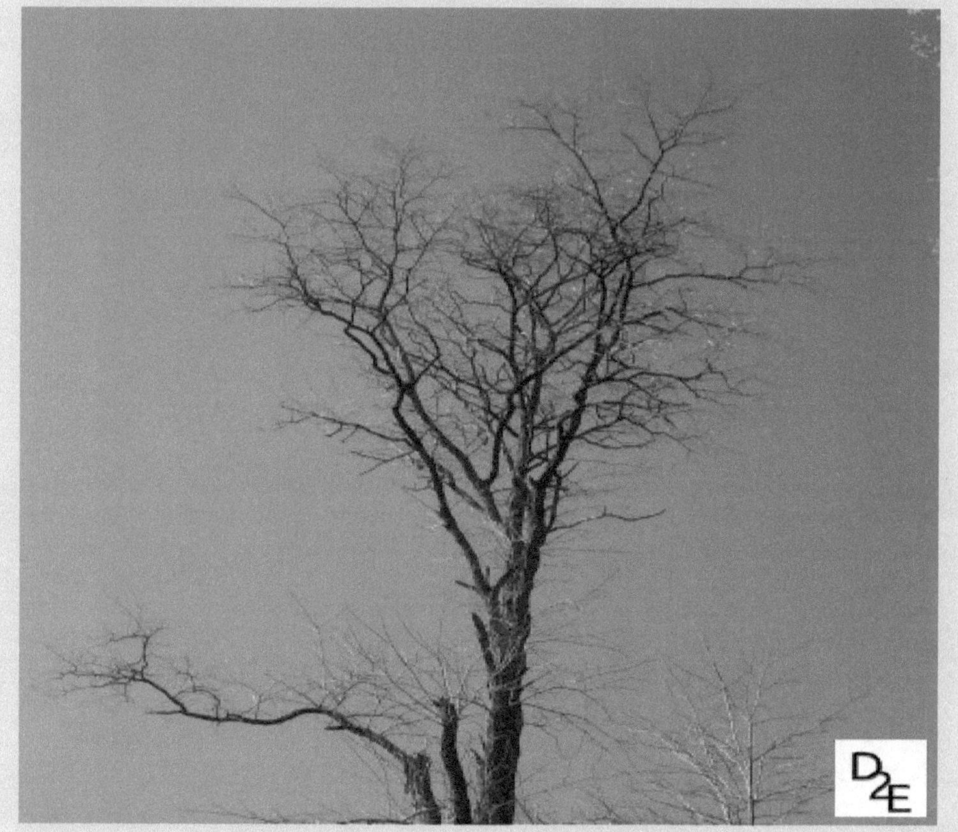
D2E

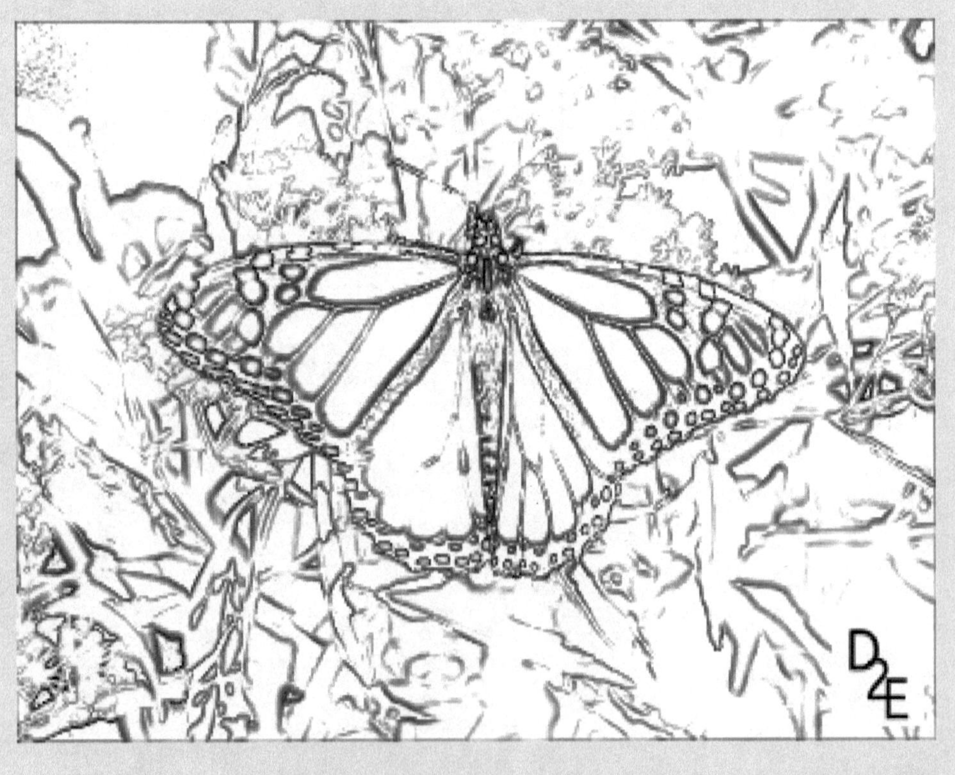
D2E

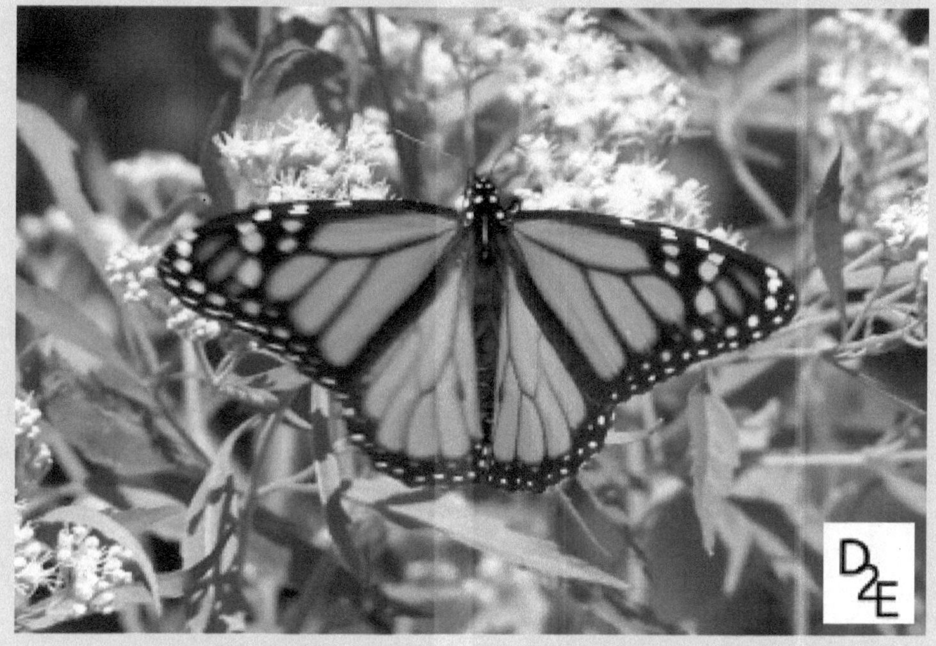

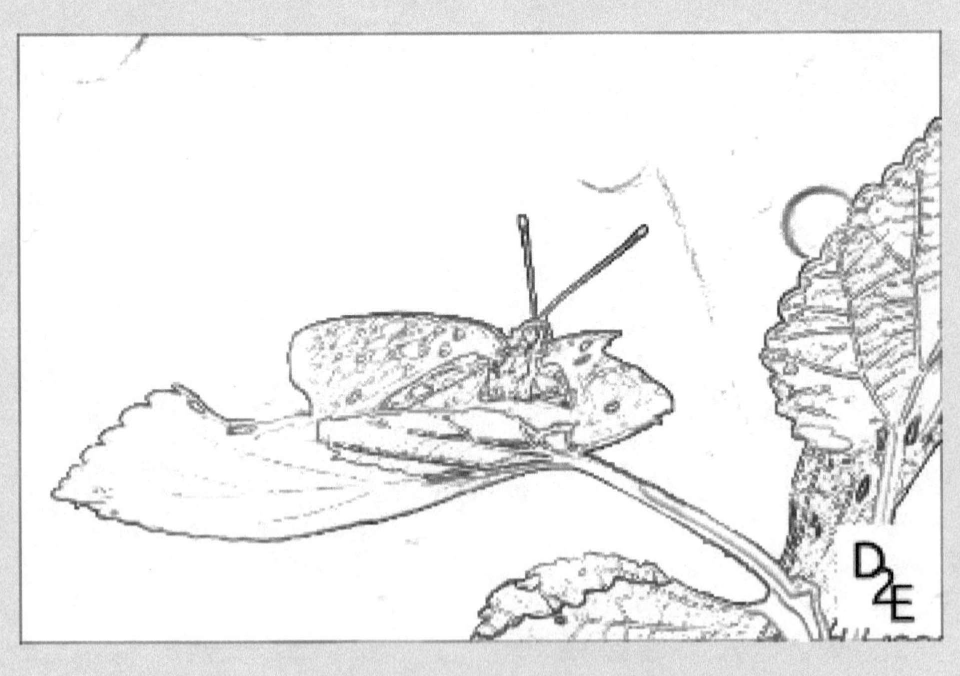
D2E

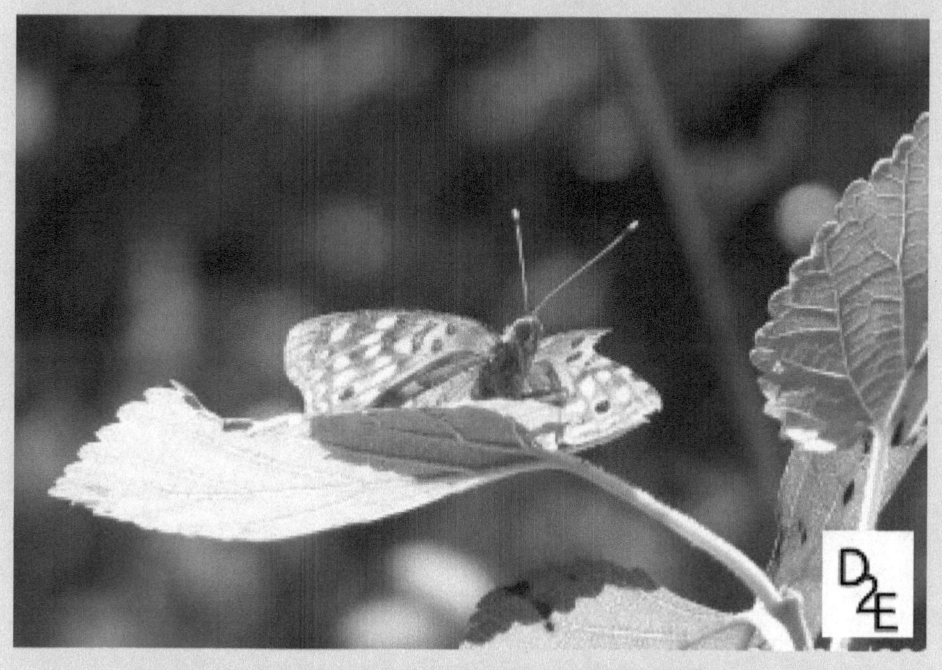
D2E

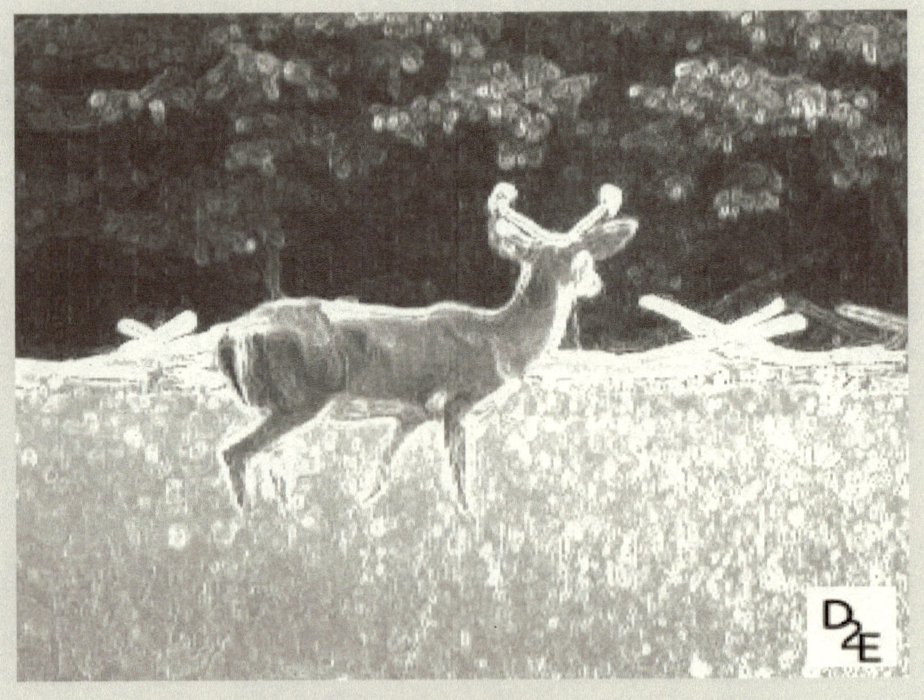
D2E

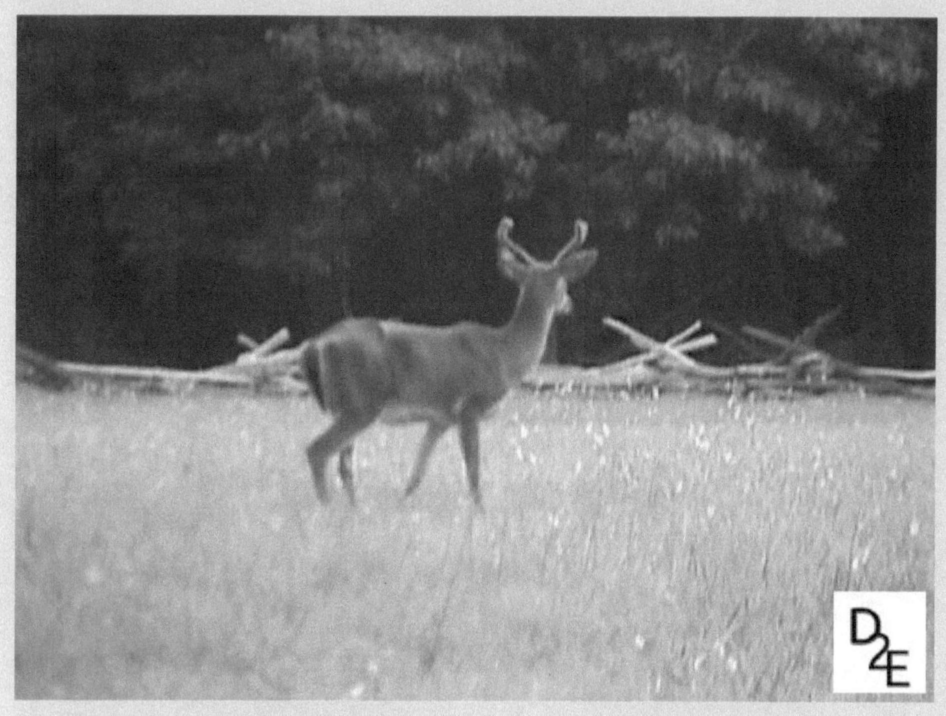

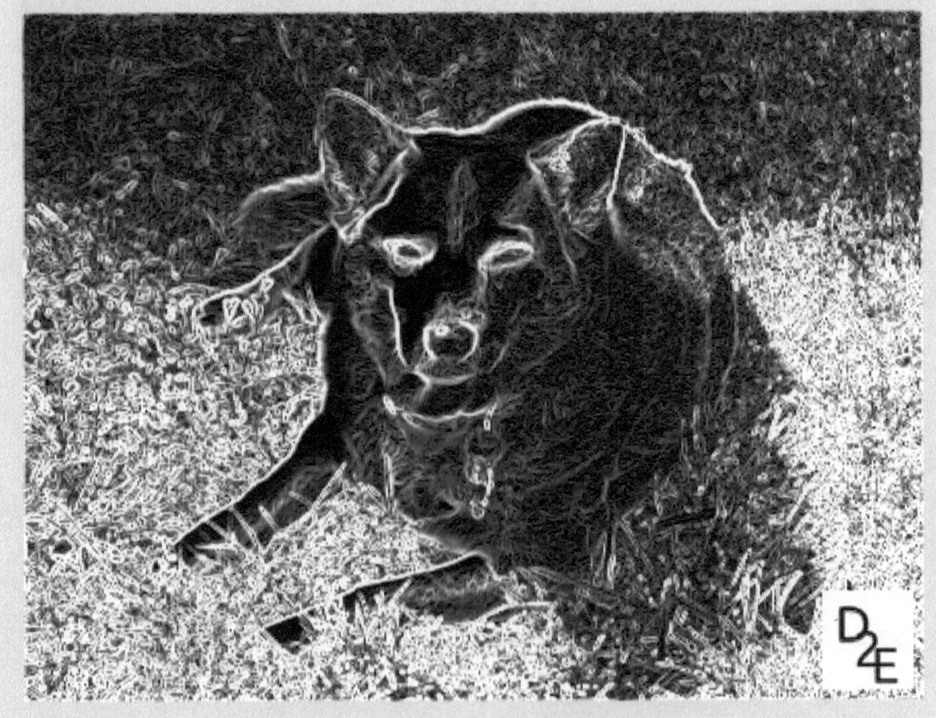
D2E

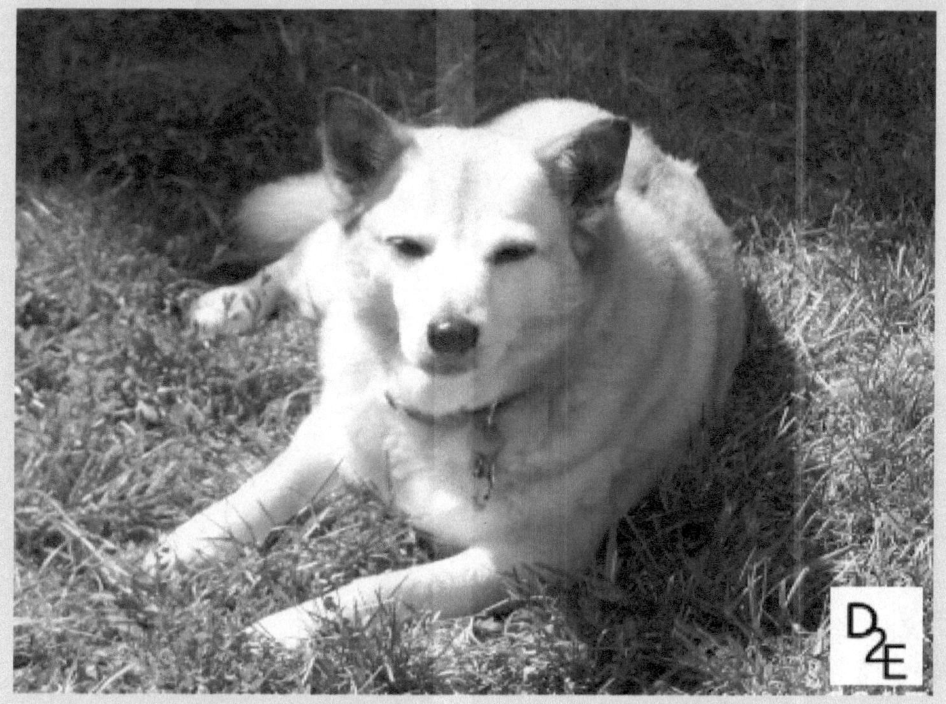
D2E

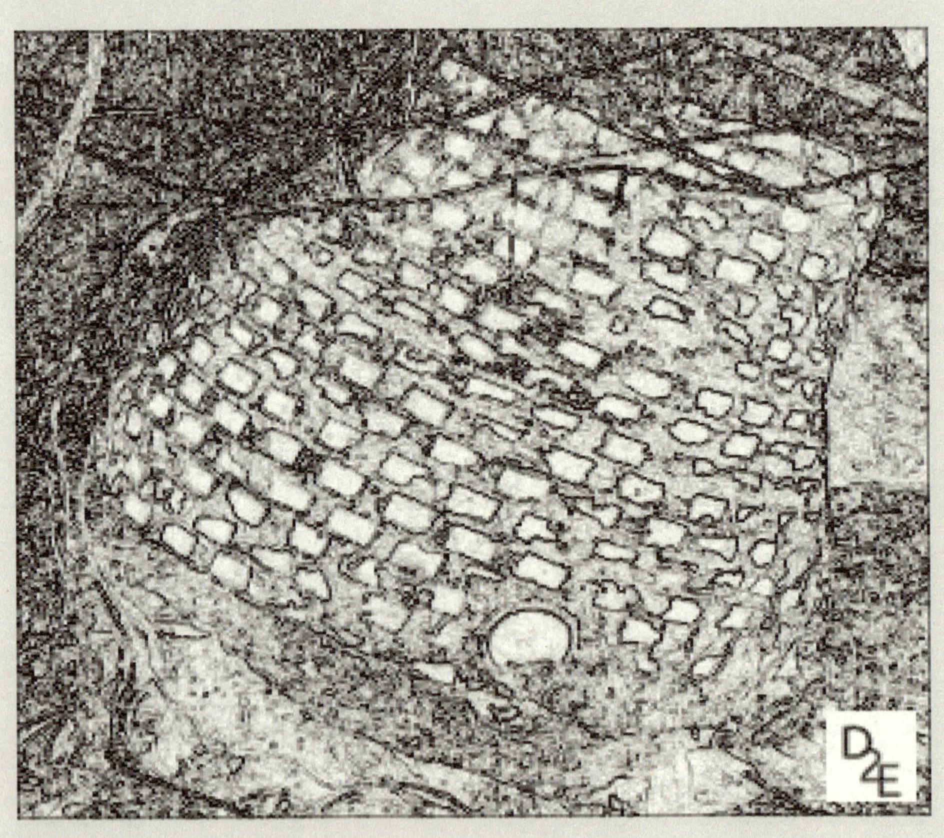
D4E

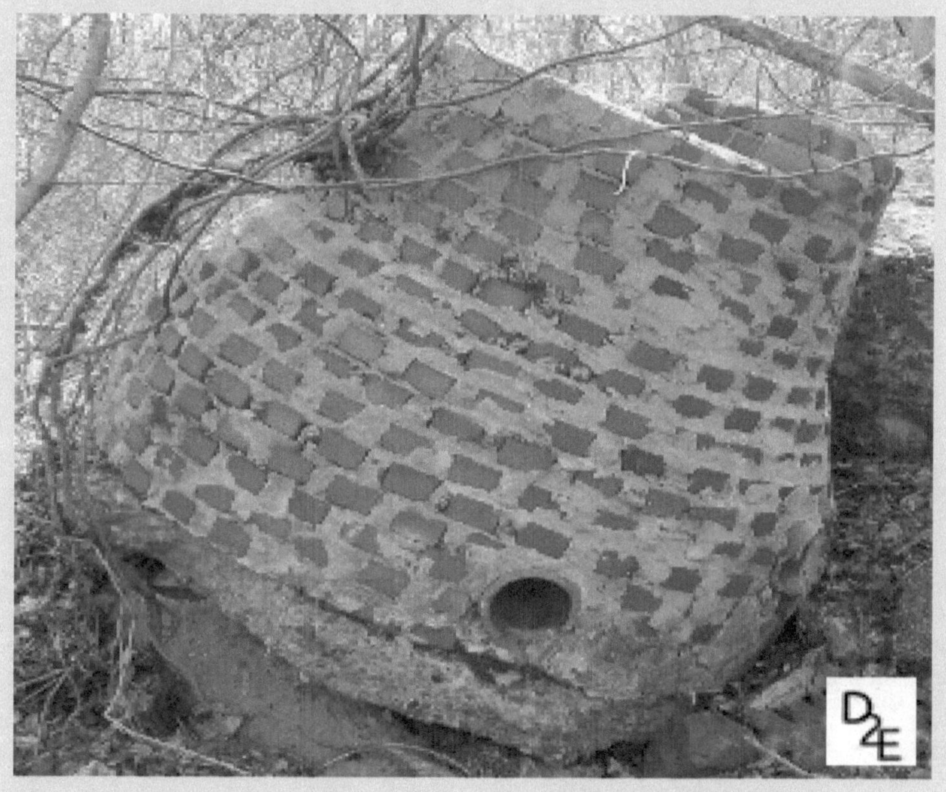
D4E

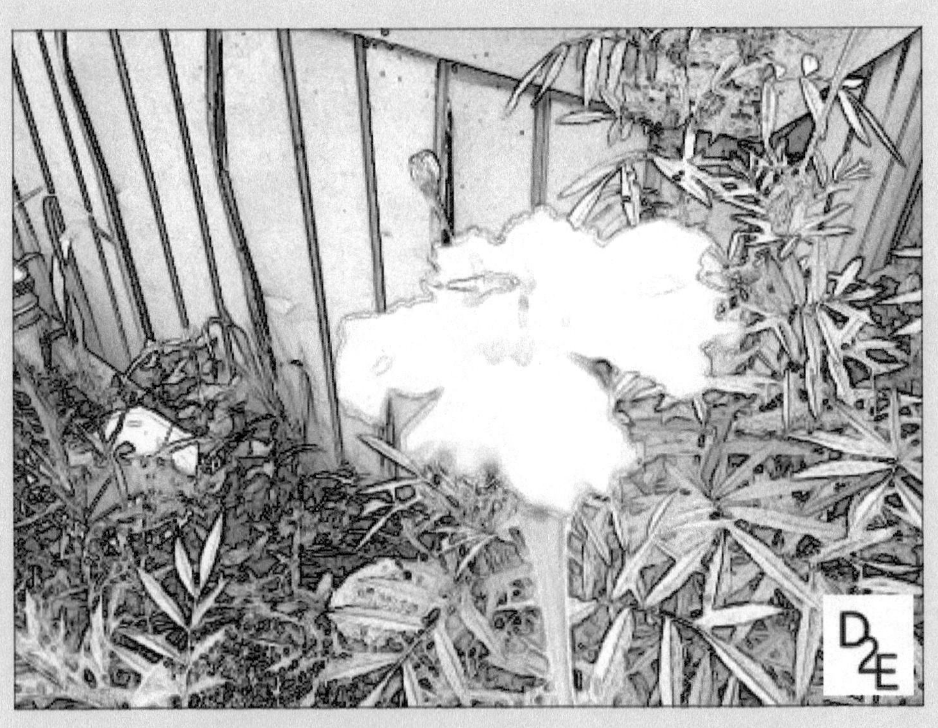

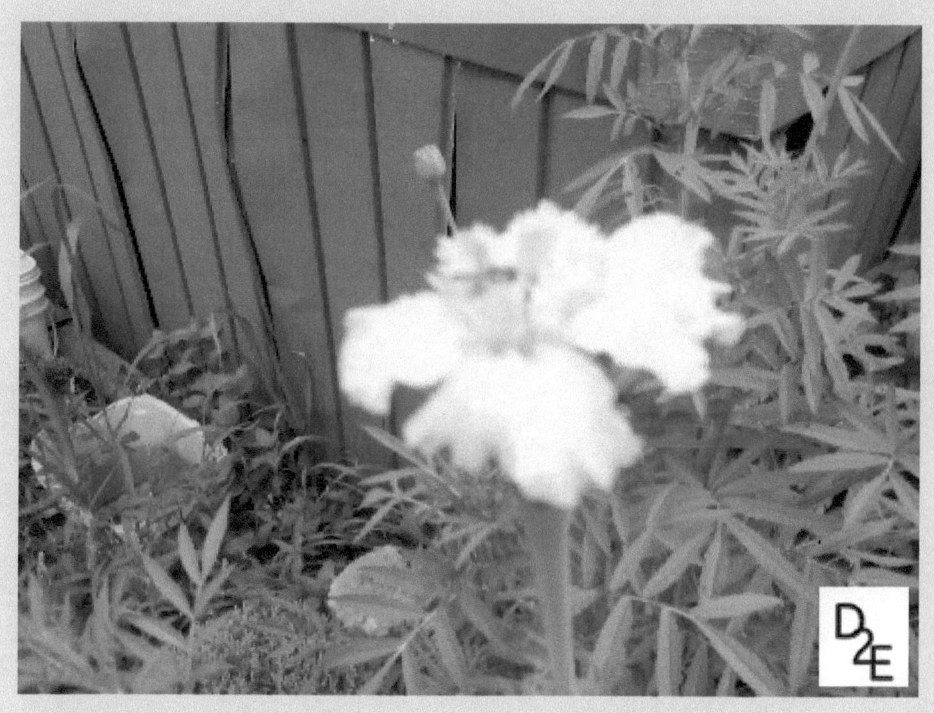
D2E

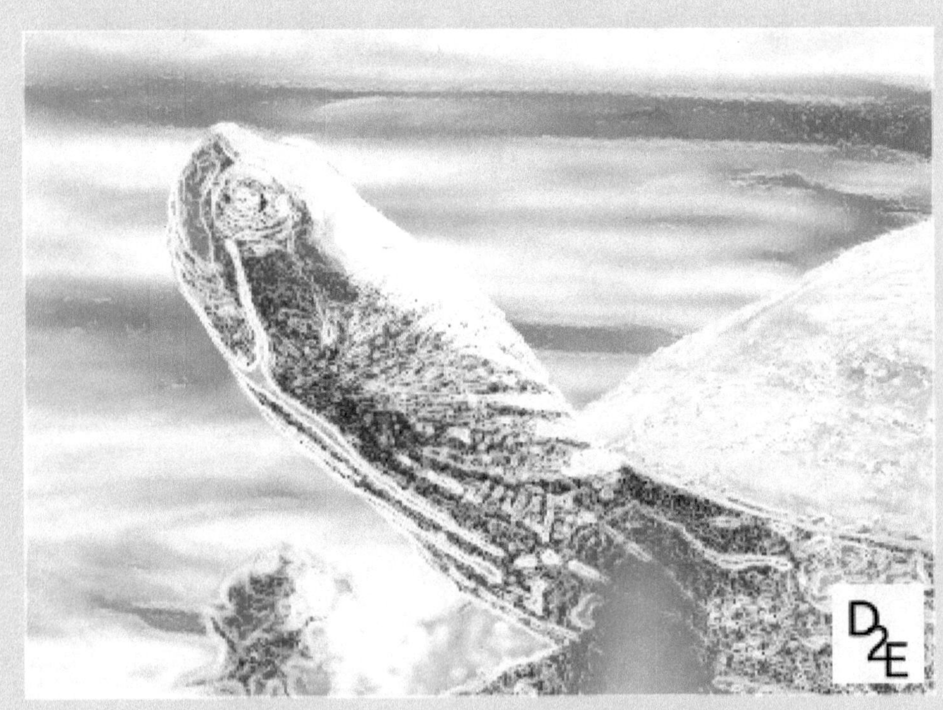
D2E

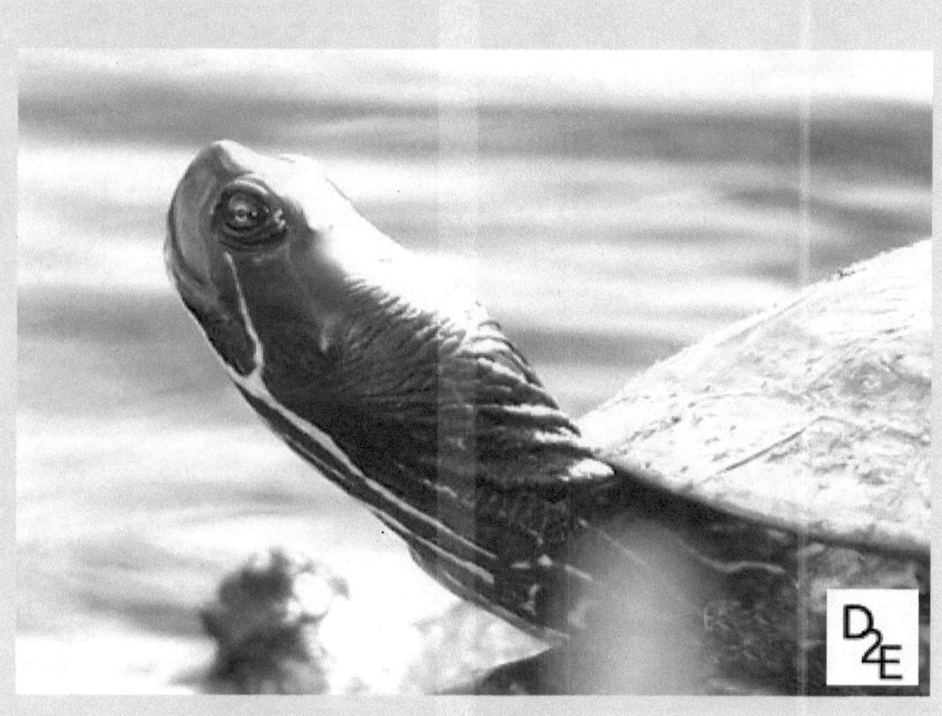
D2E

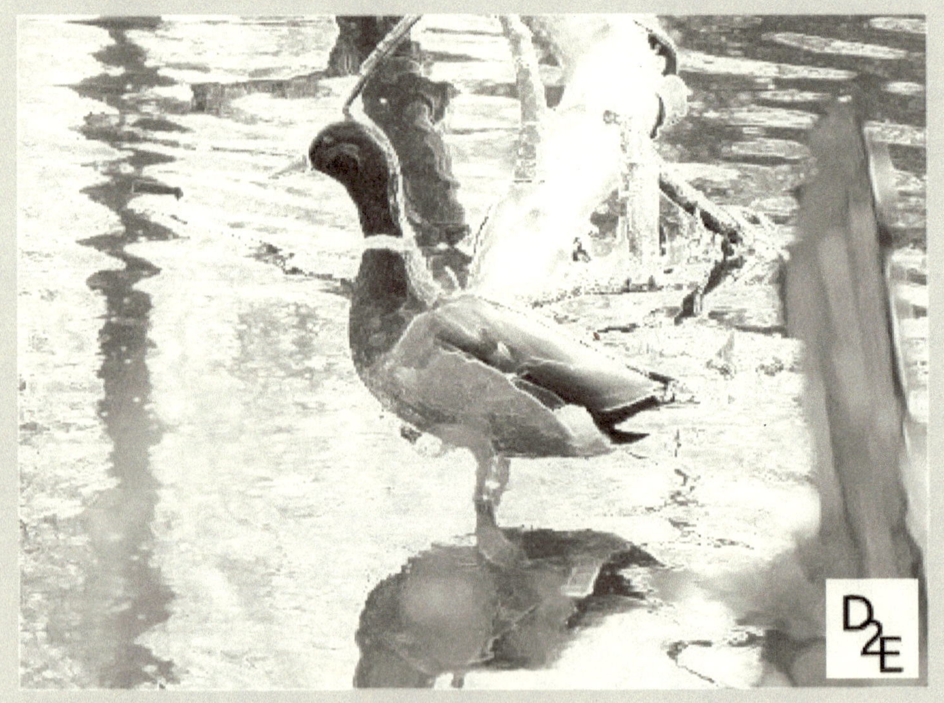

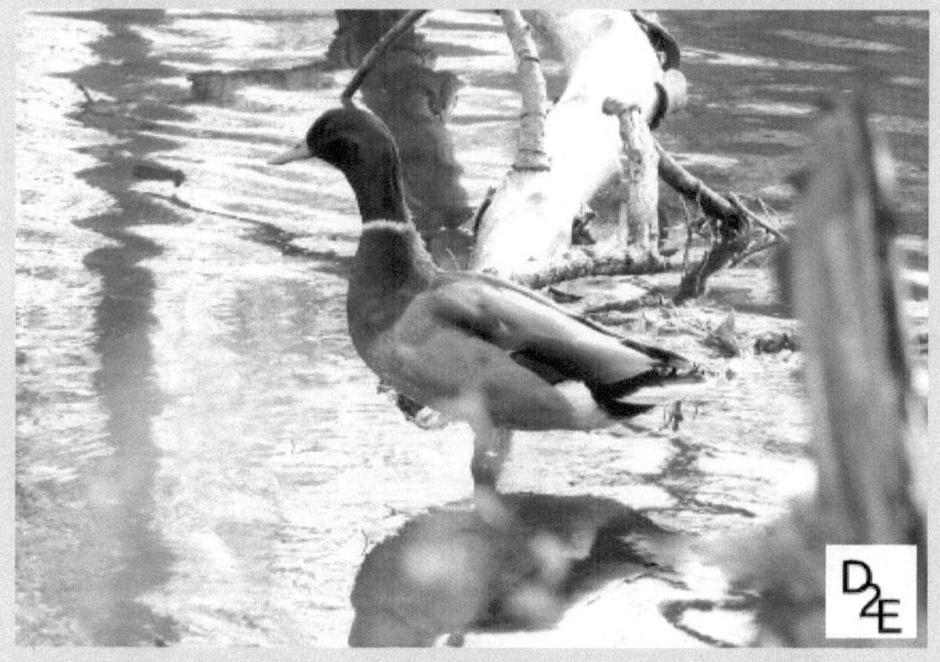
D2E

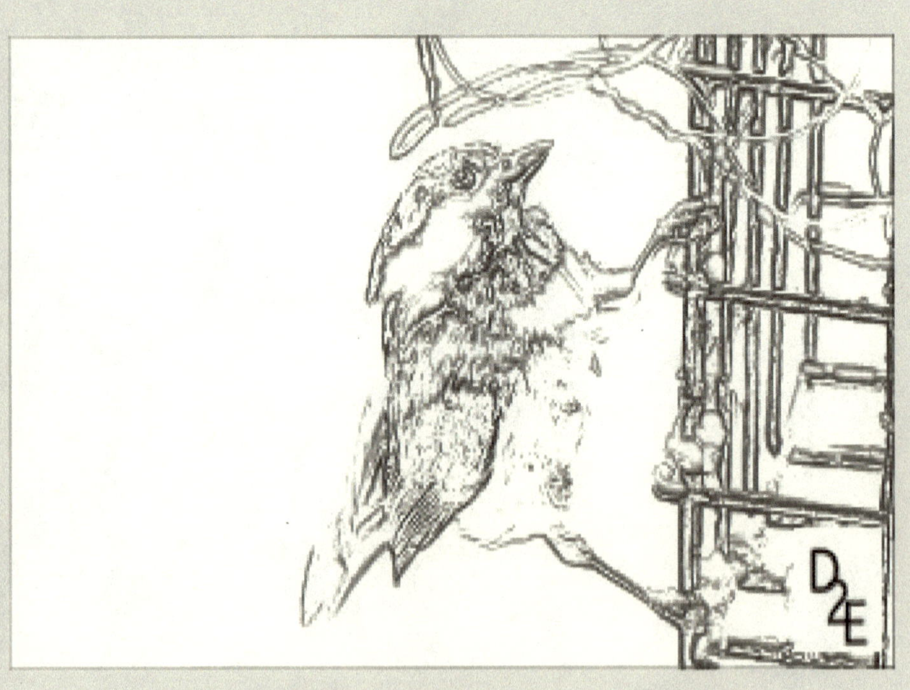

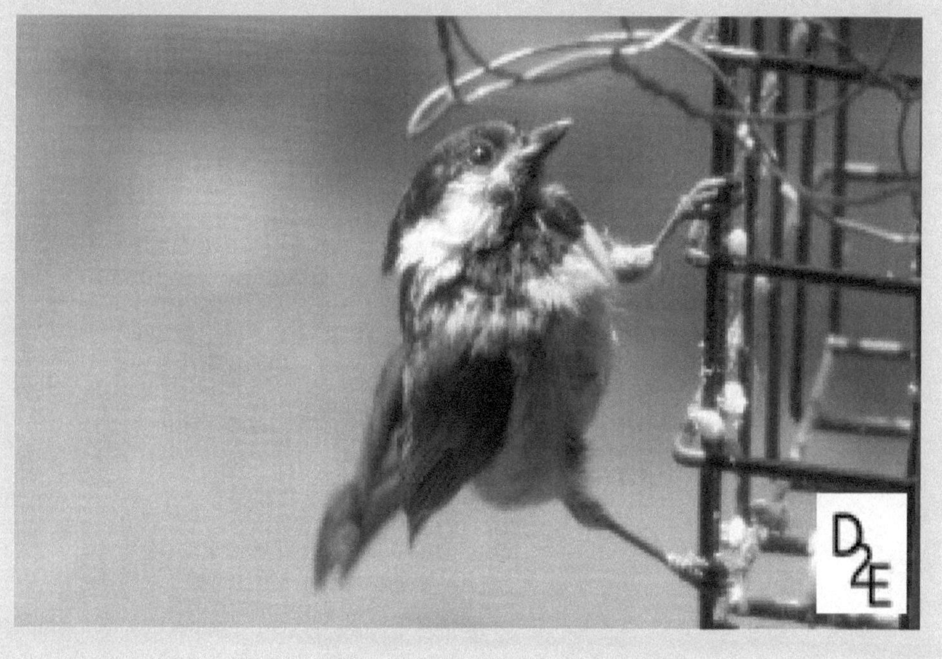
D2E

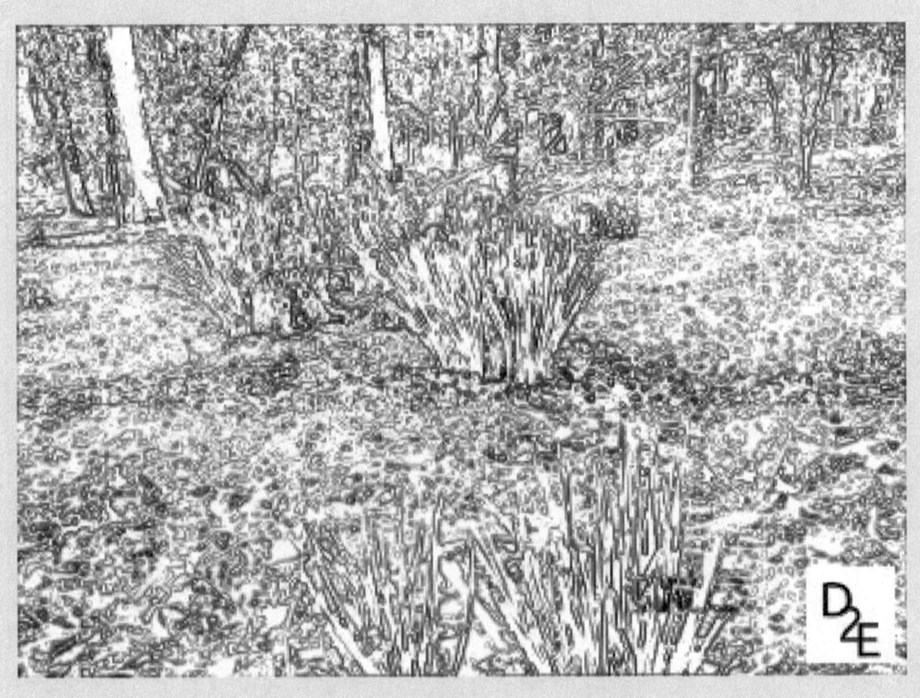
D2E

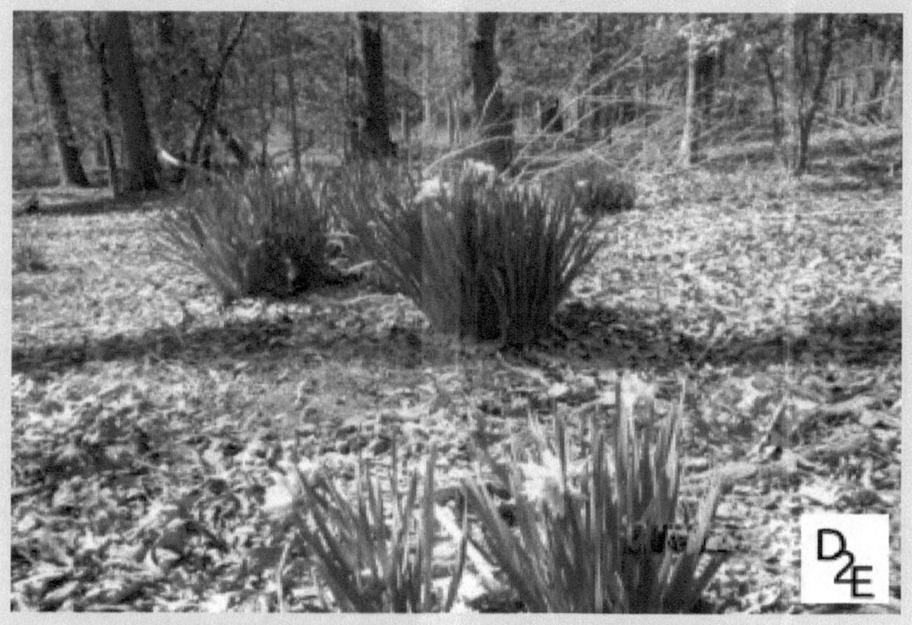
D2E

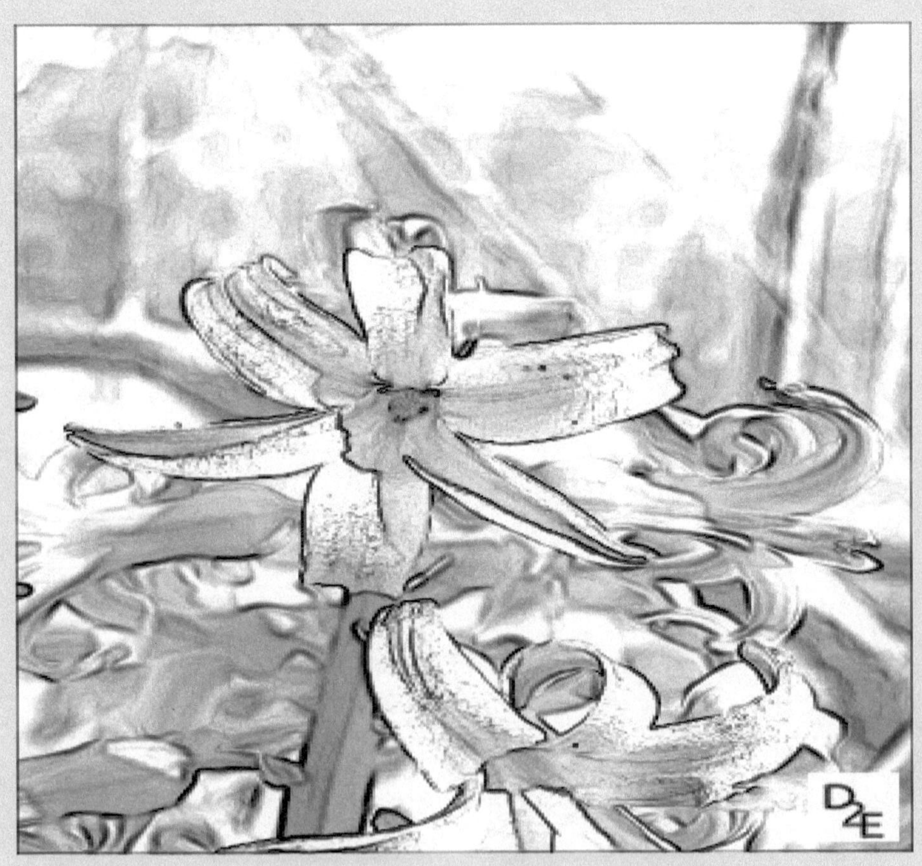
D2E

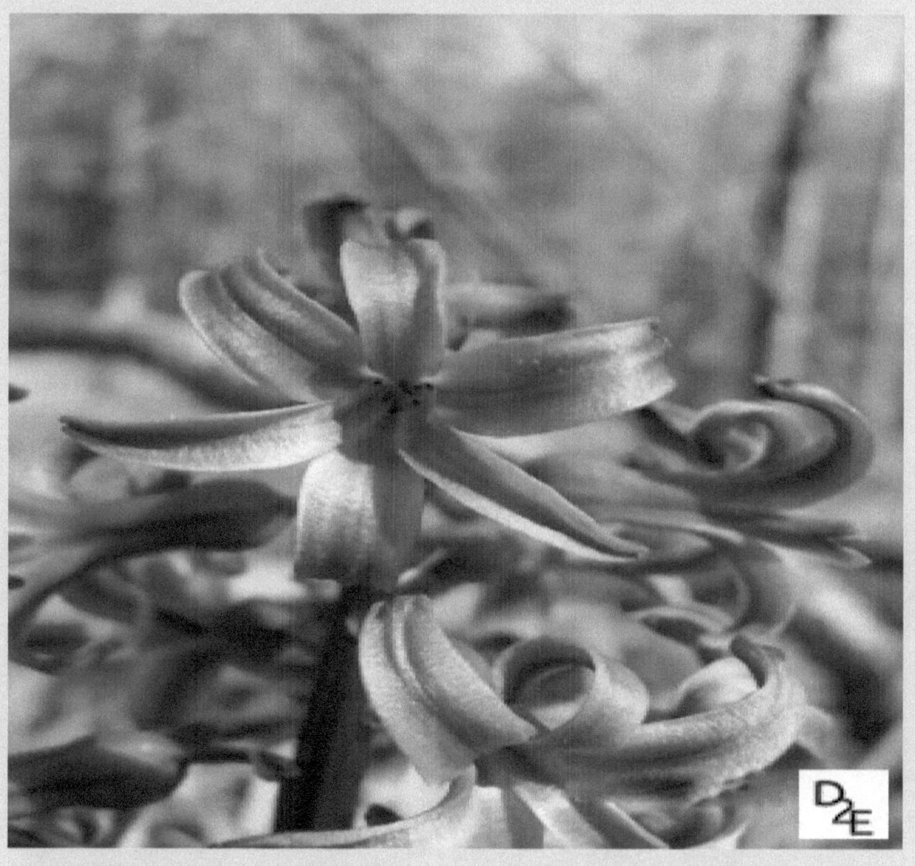
D2E

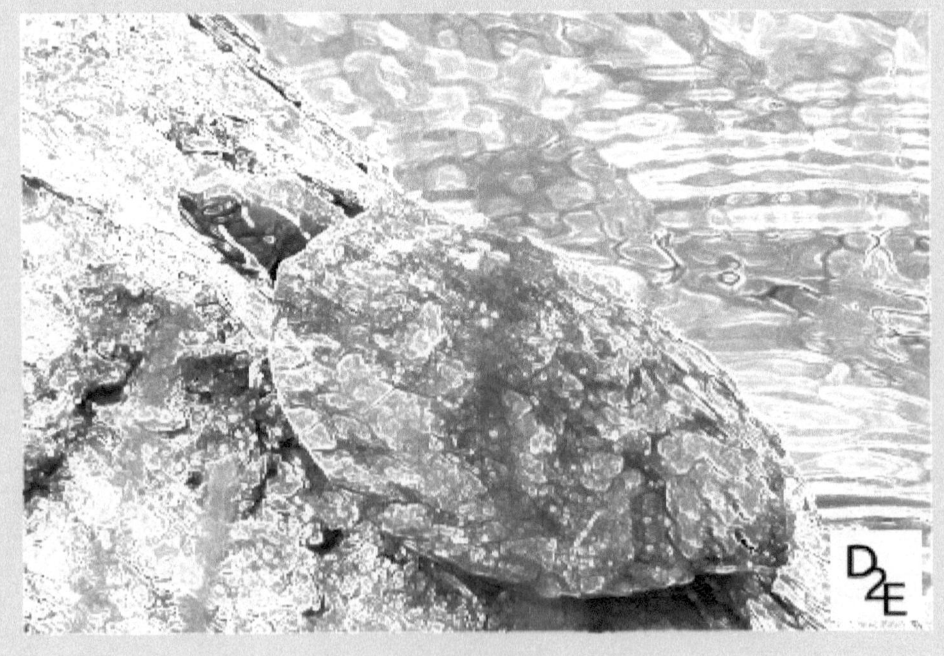
D2E

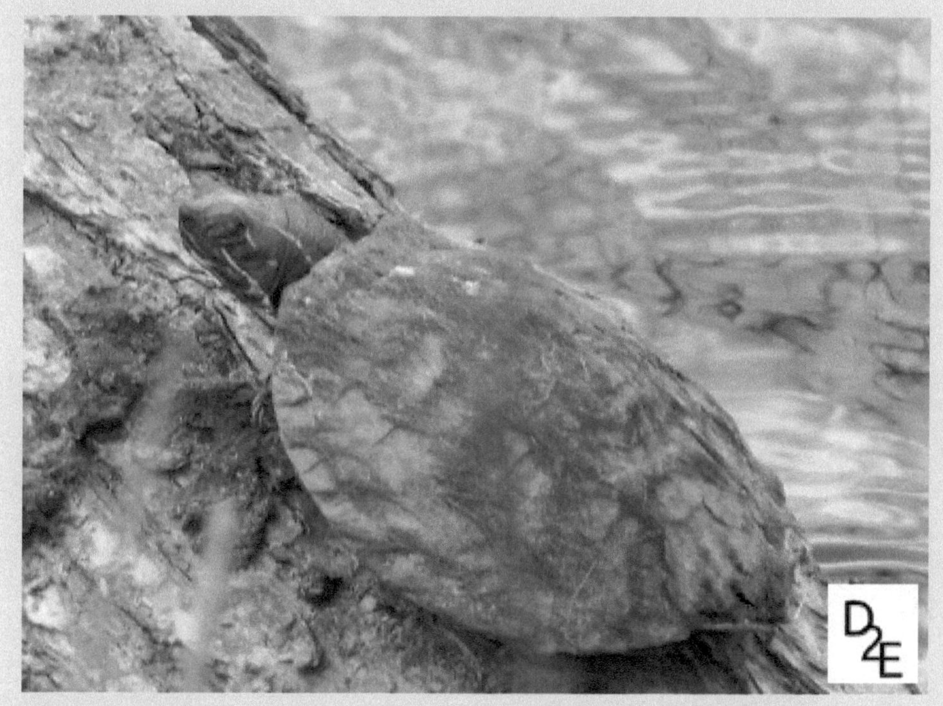
D2E

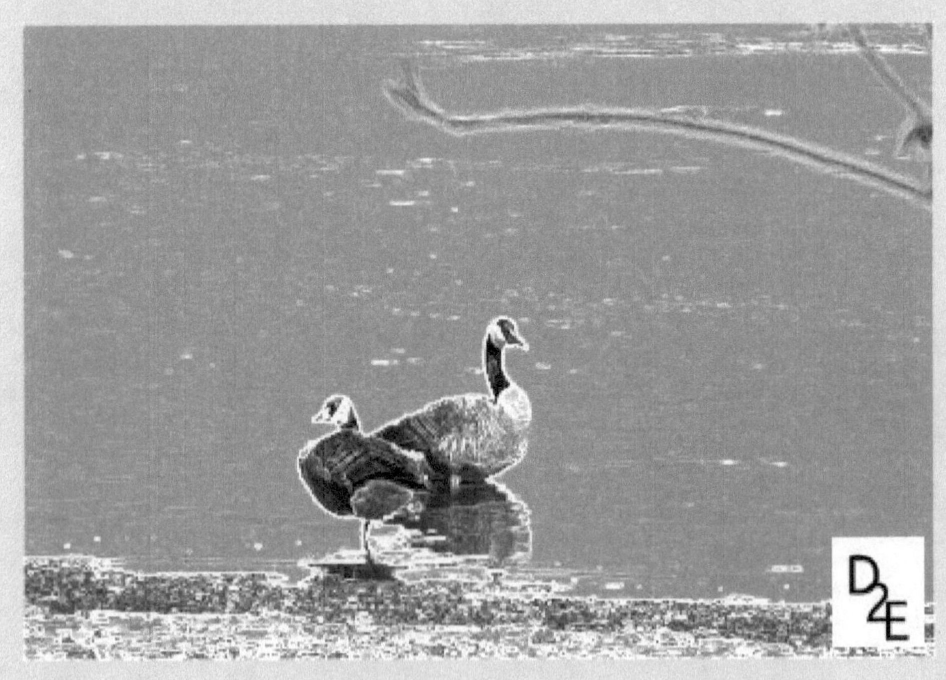
D2E

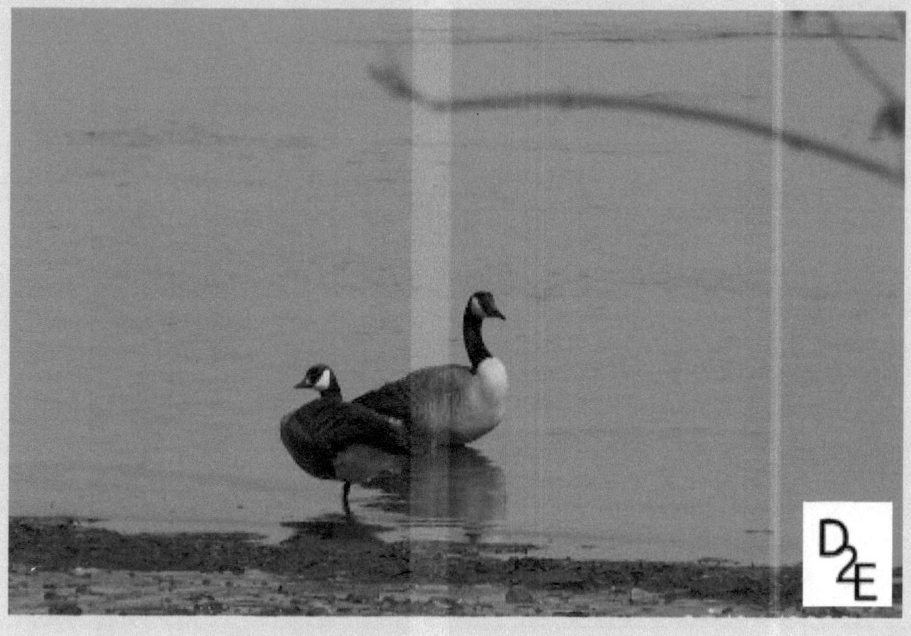
D2E

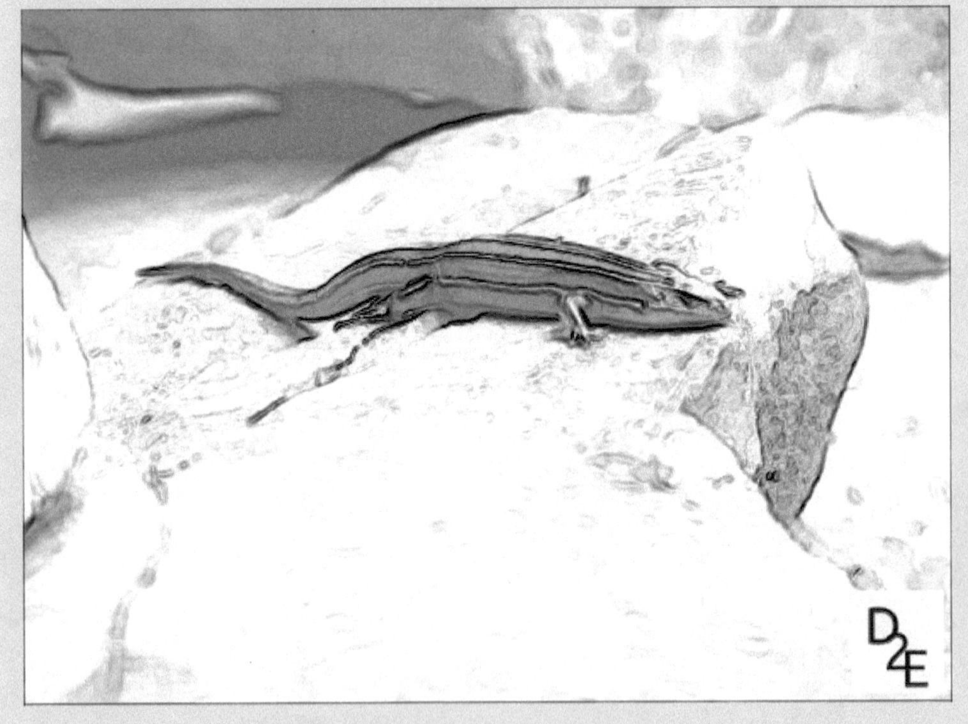

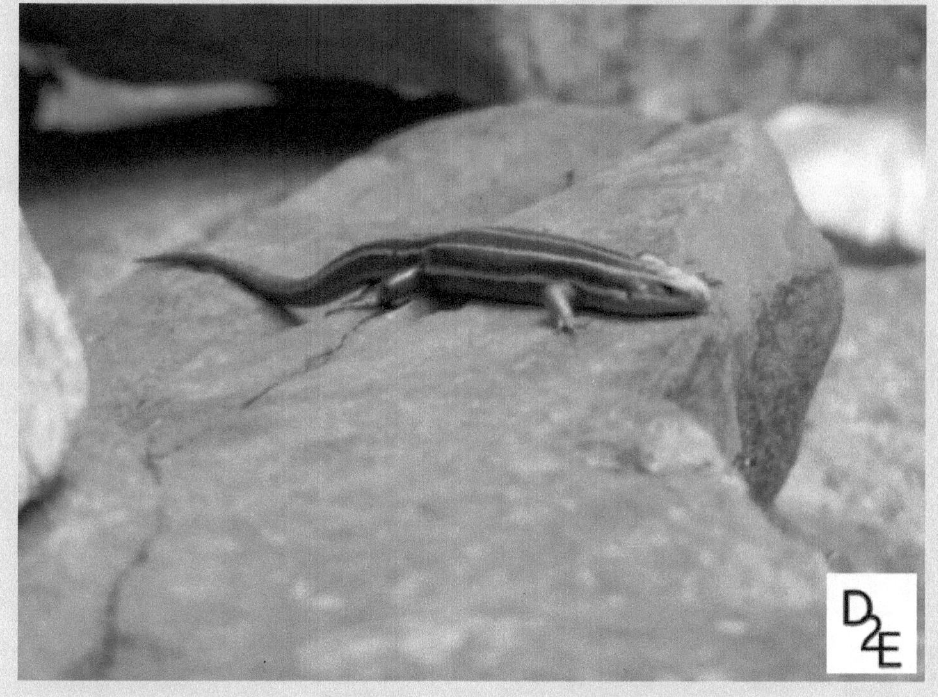
D2E

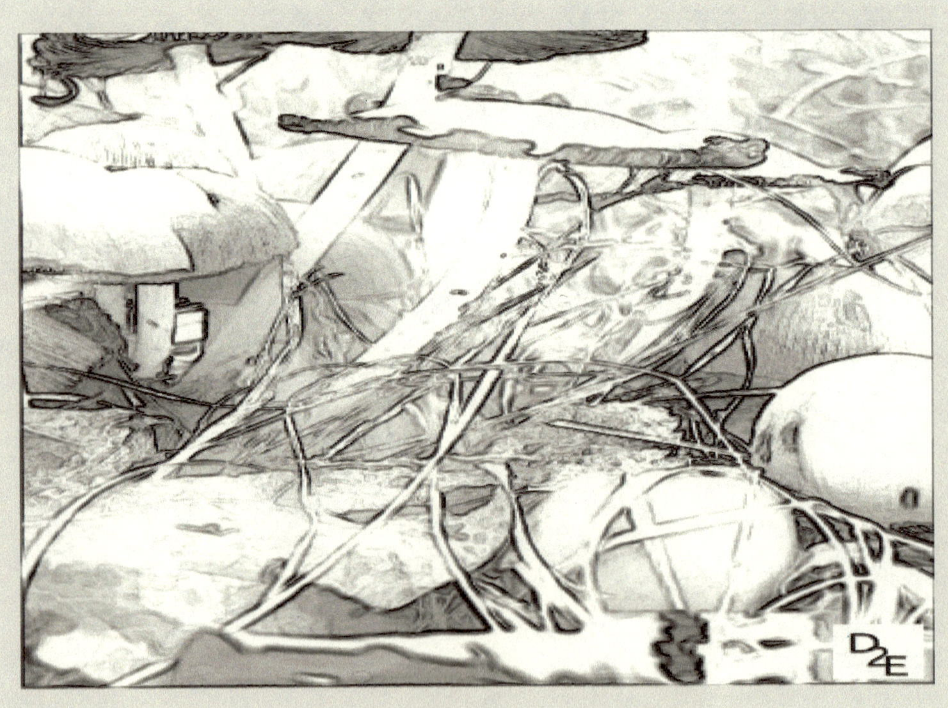

D2E

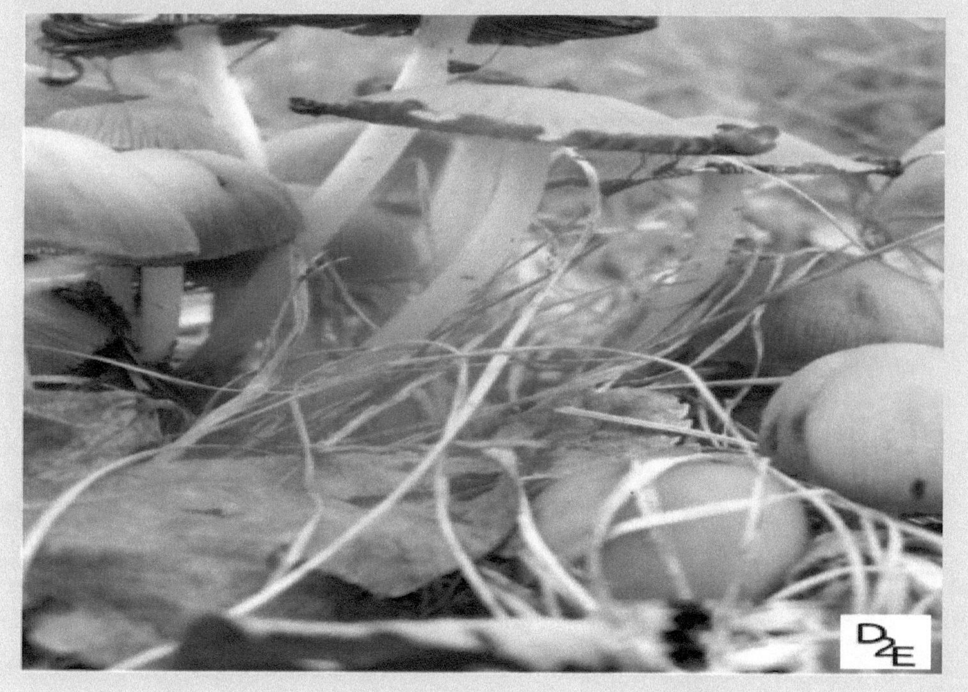
D2E

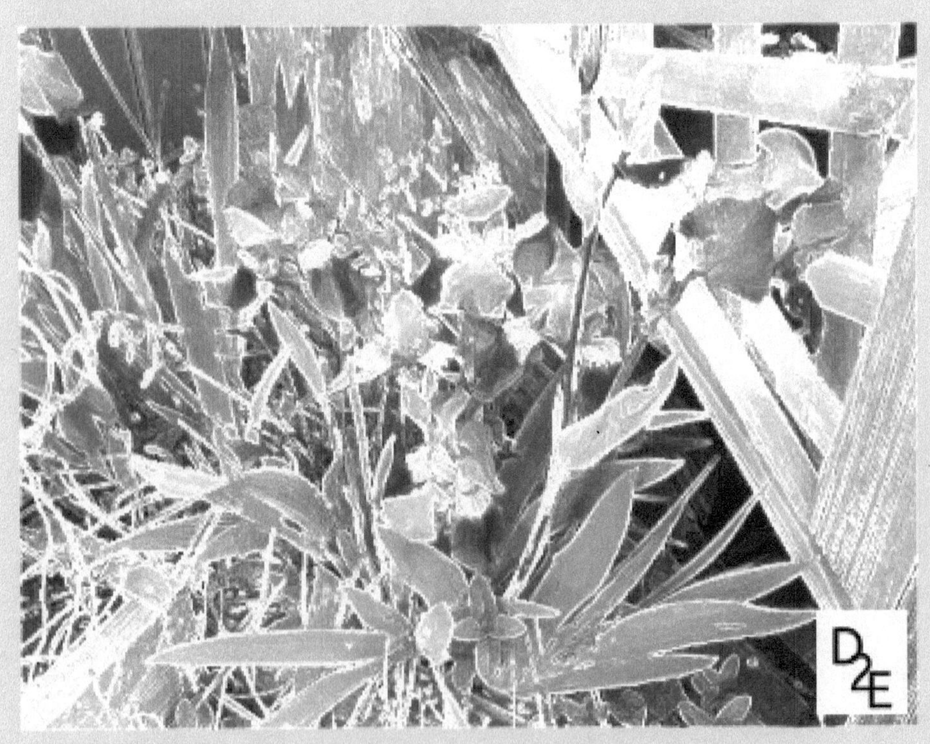
D2E

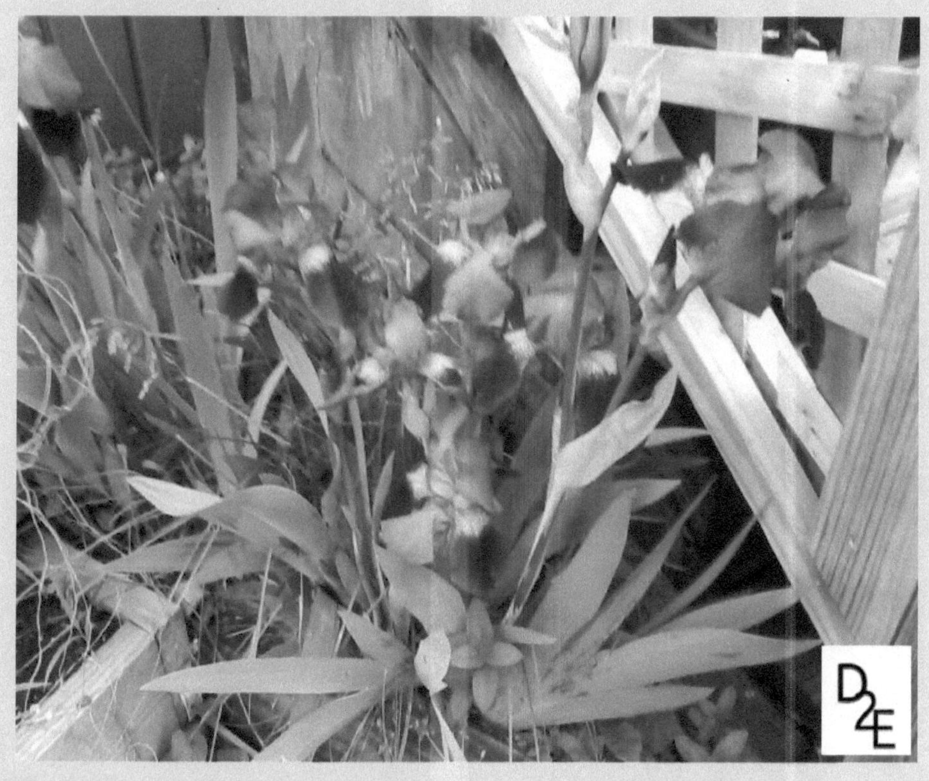
D2E

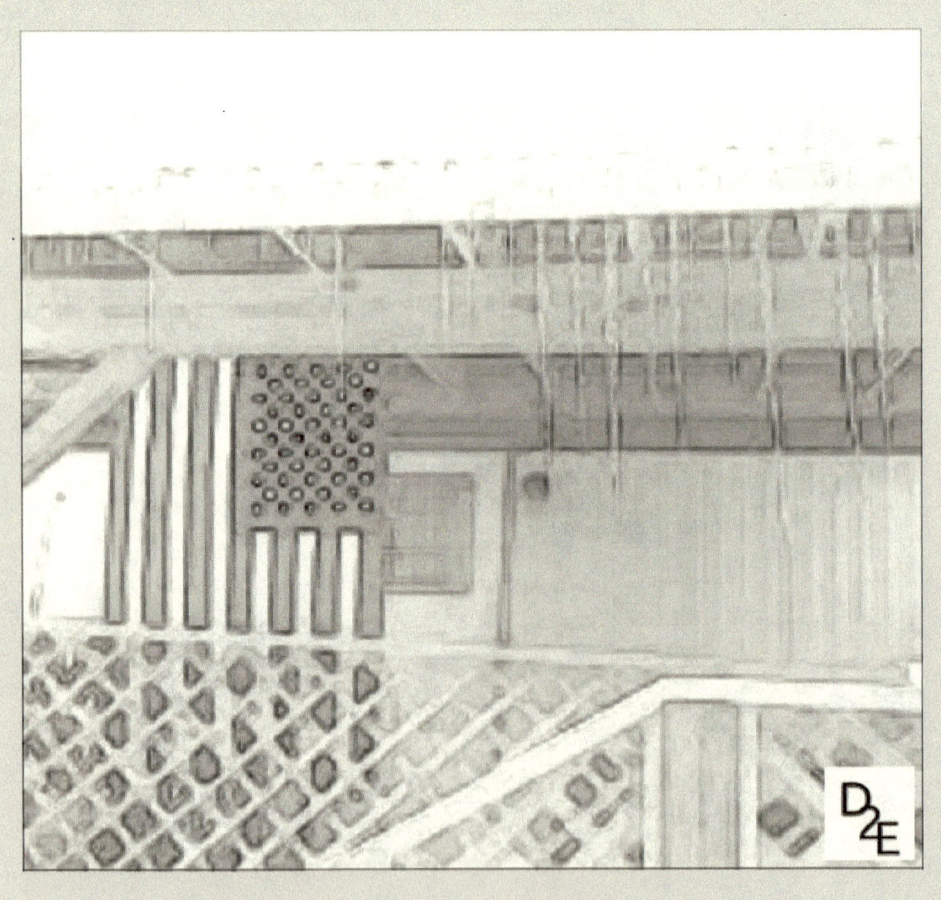

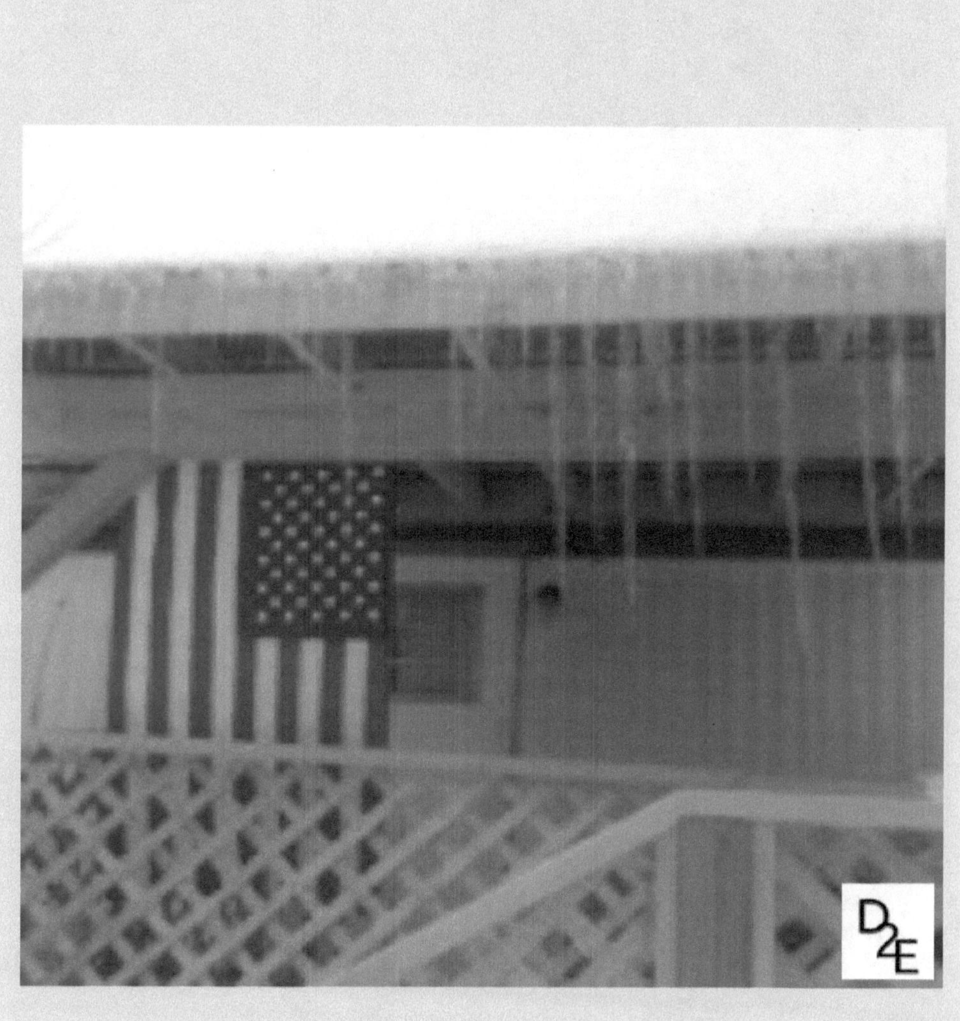

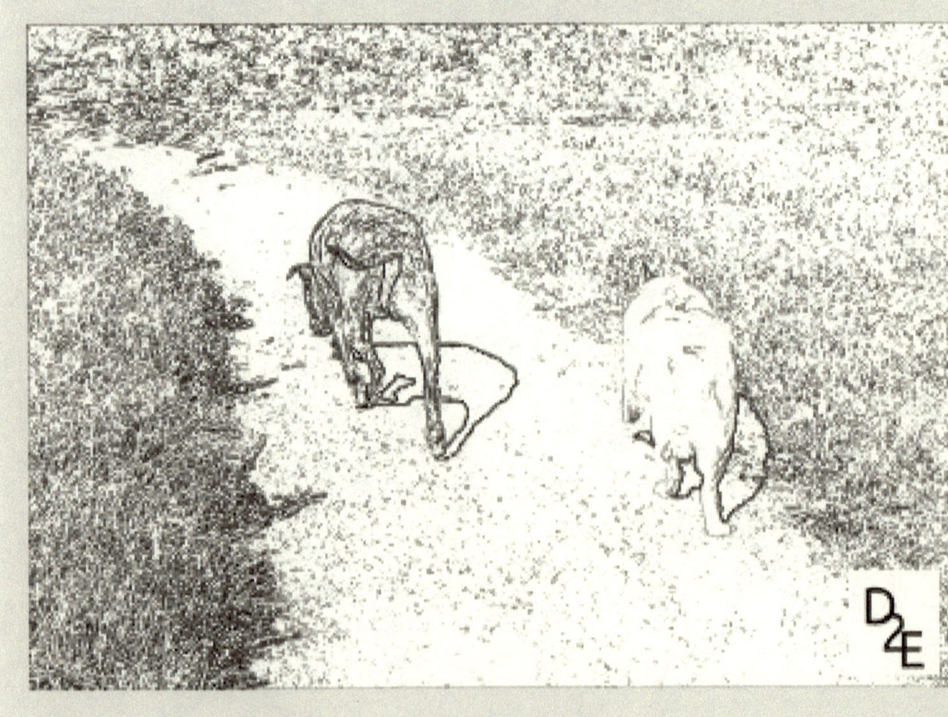
D2E

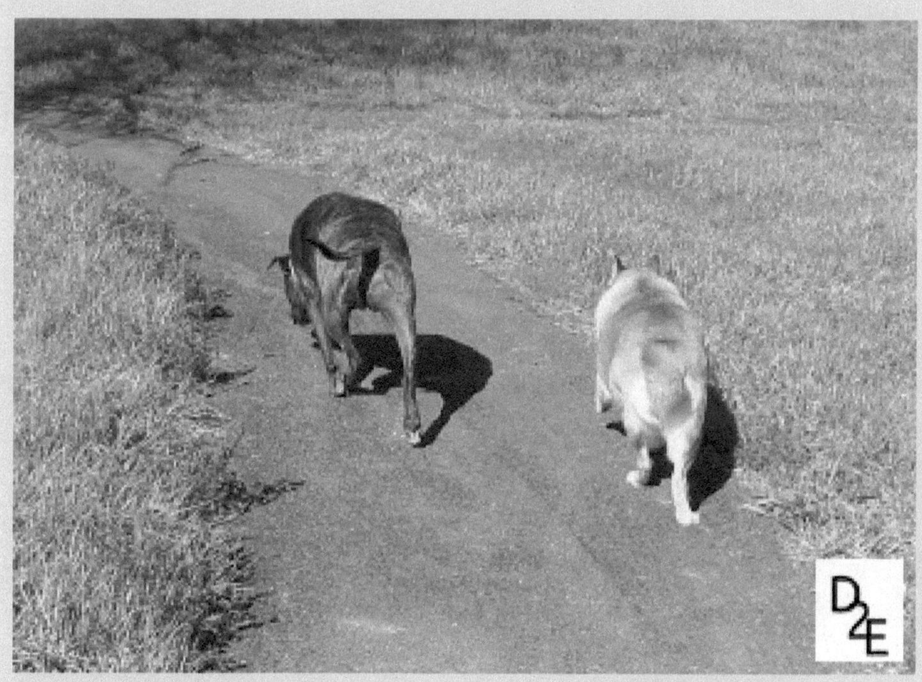
D2E

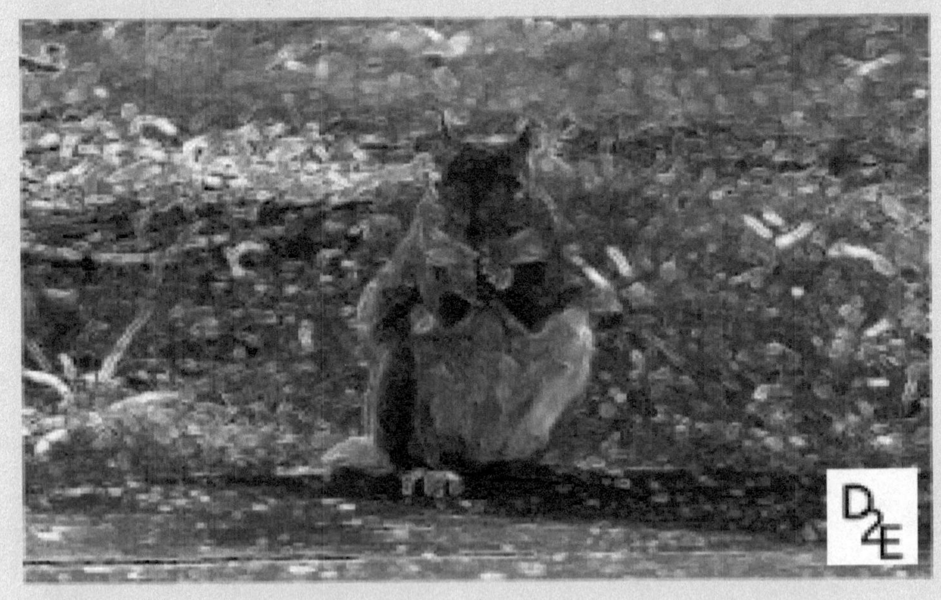

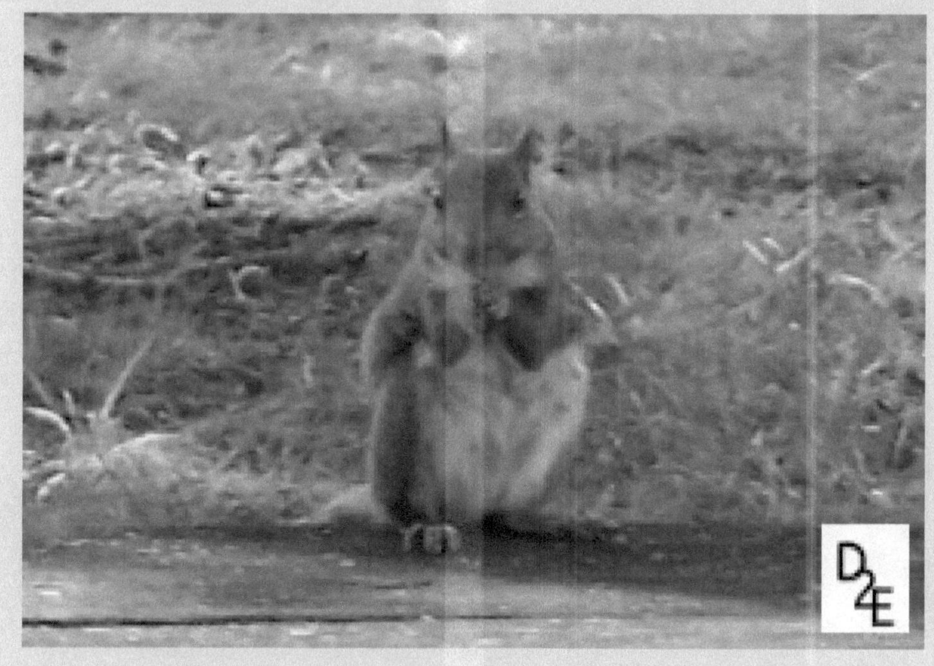
D2E

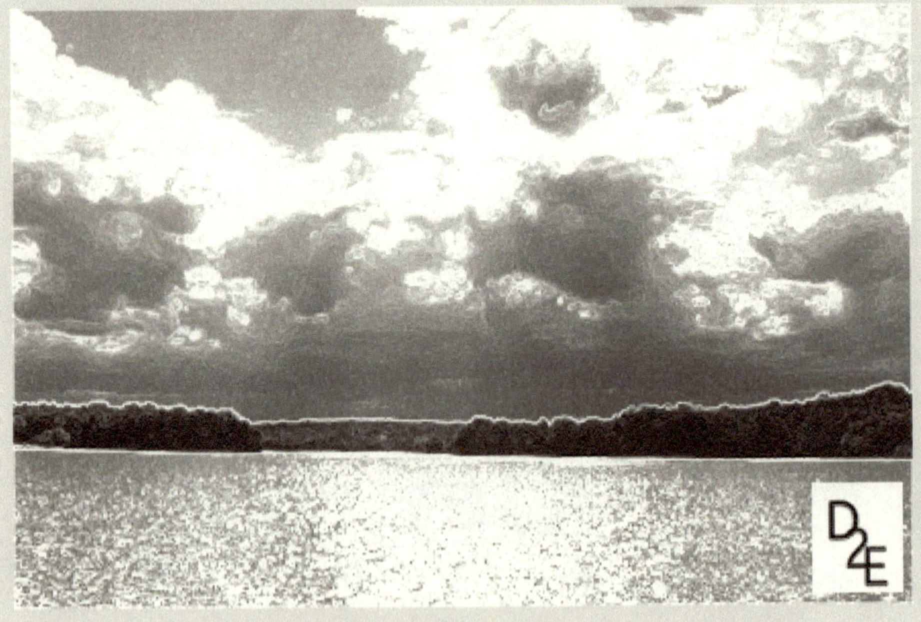
D2E

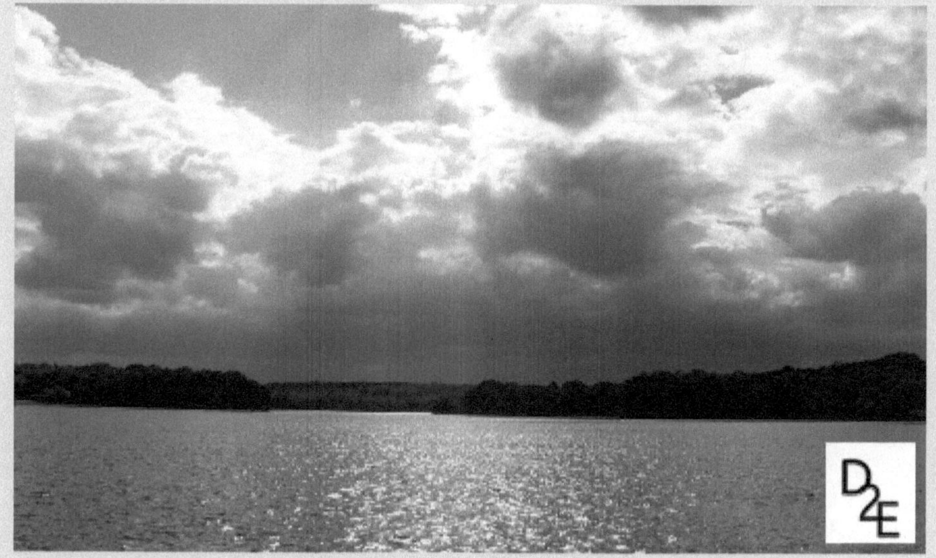
D2E

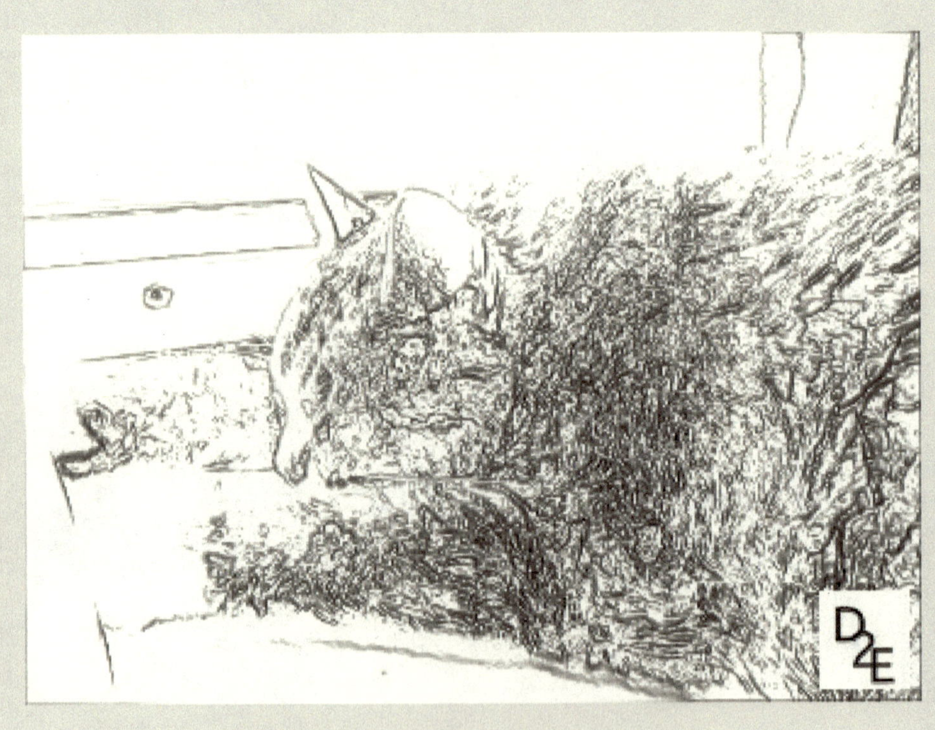
D2E

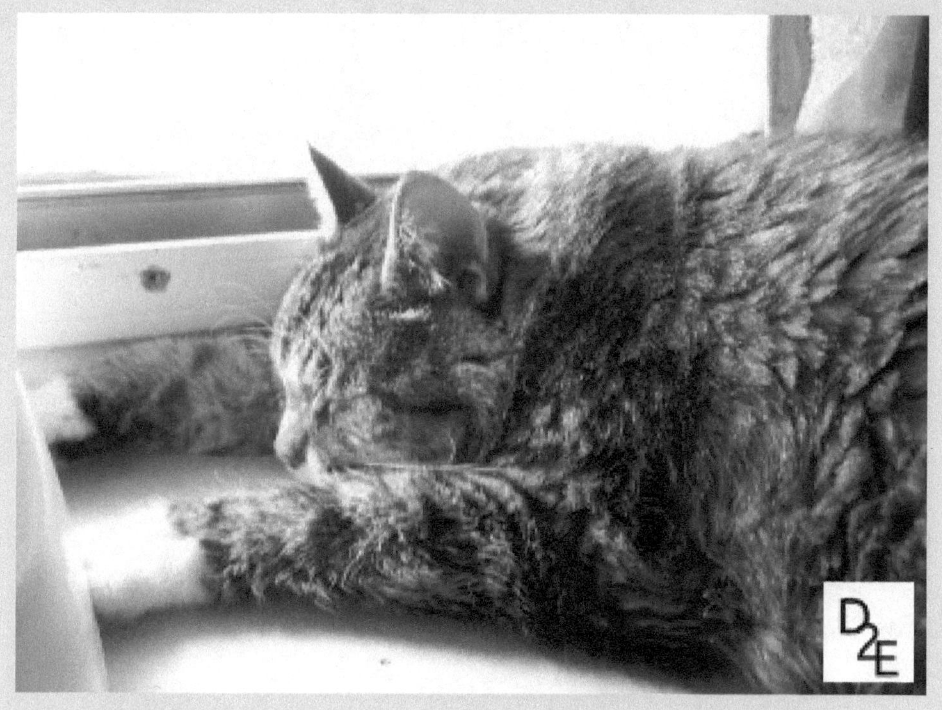
D2E

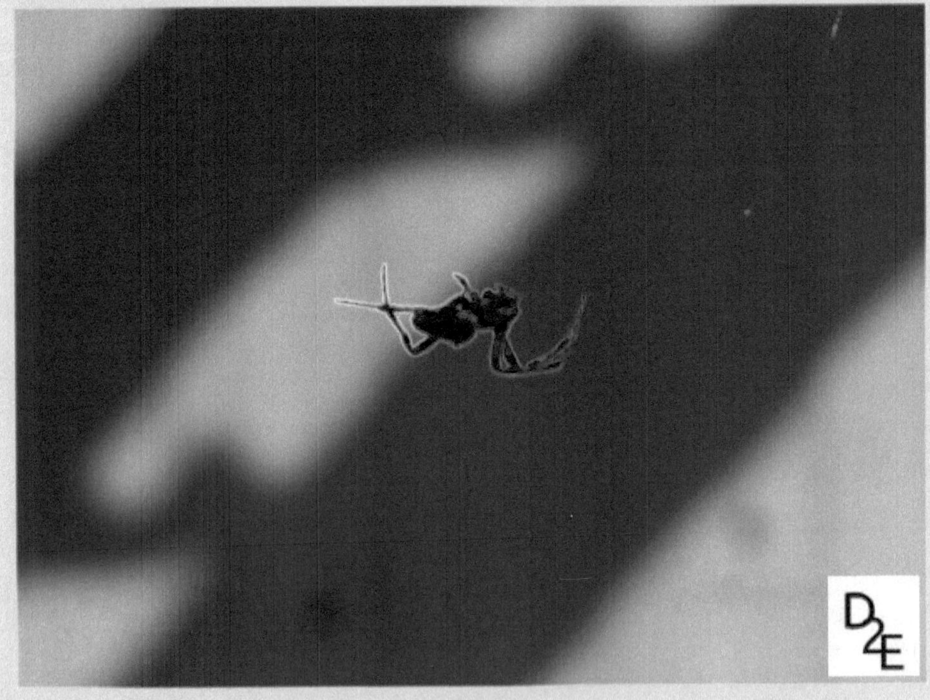
D2E

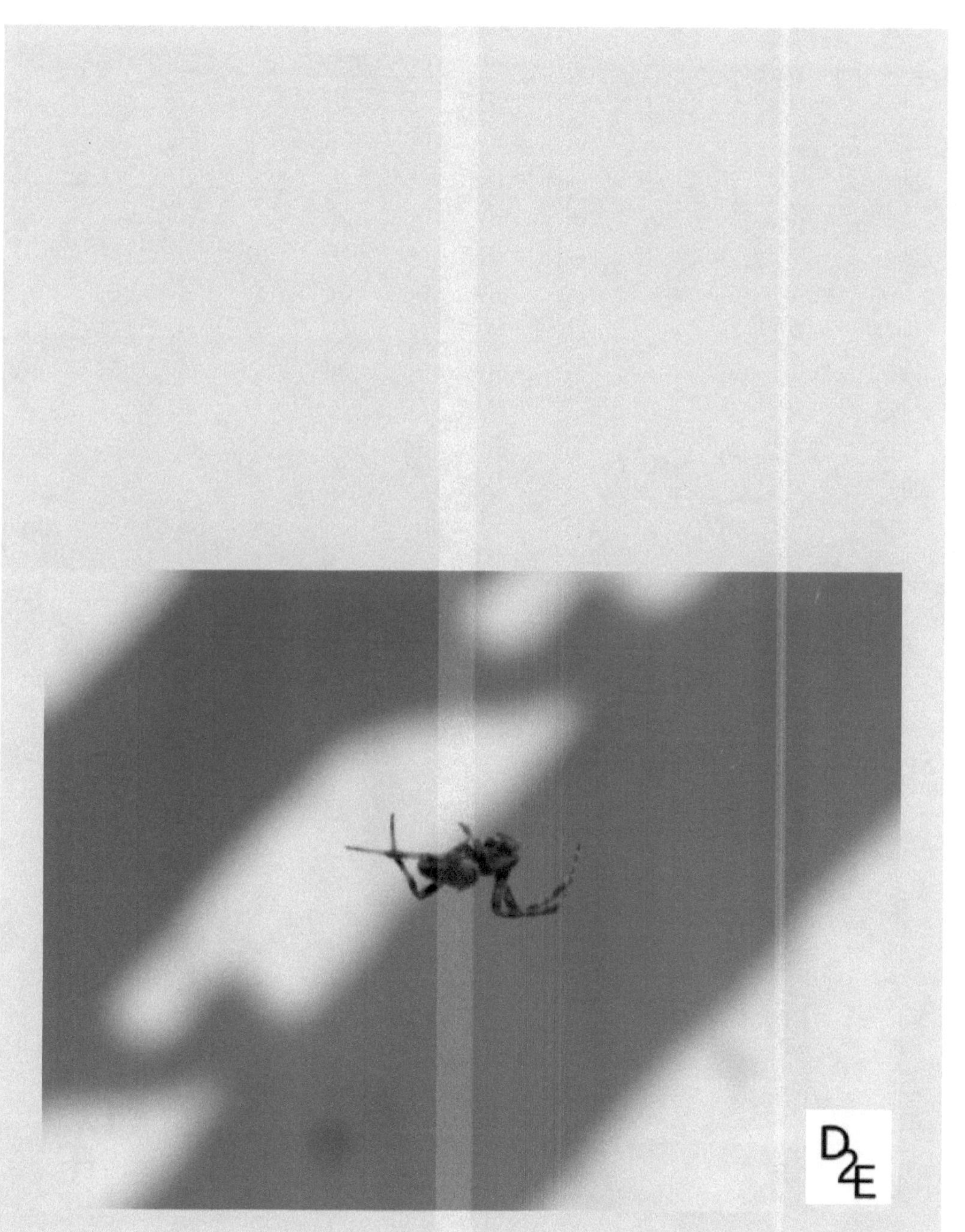
D2E

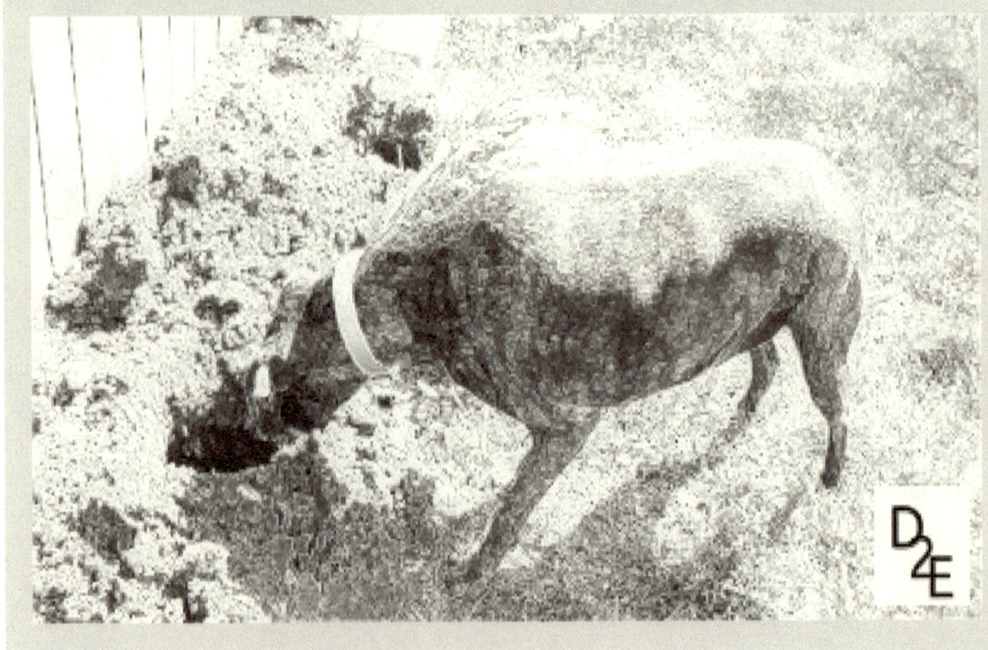
D2E

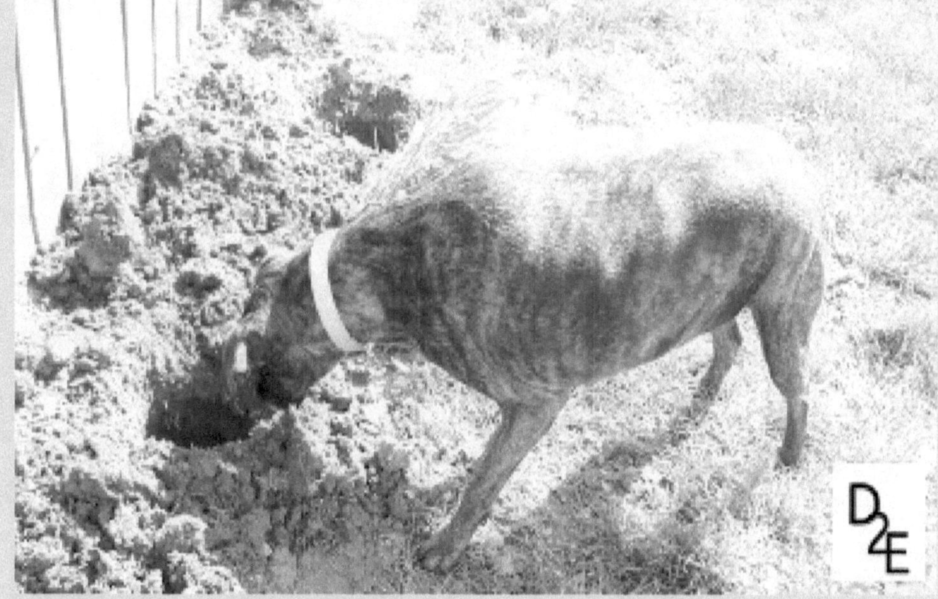
D2E

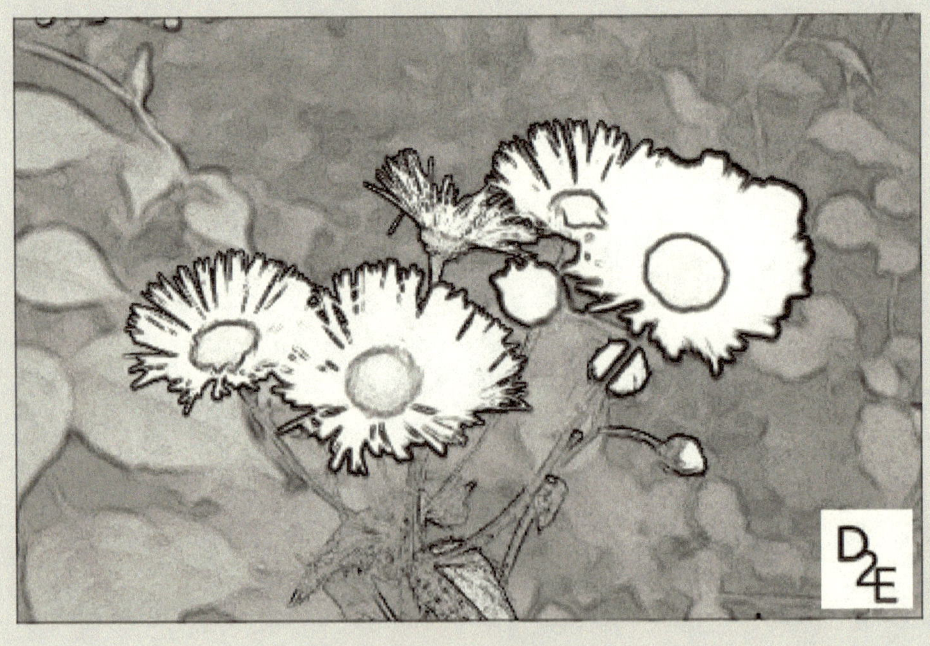
D2E

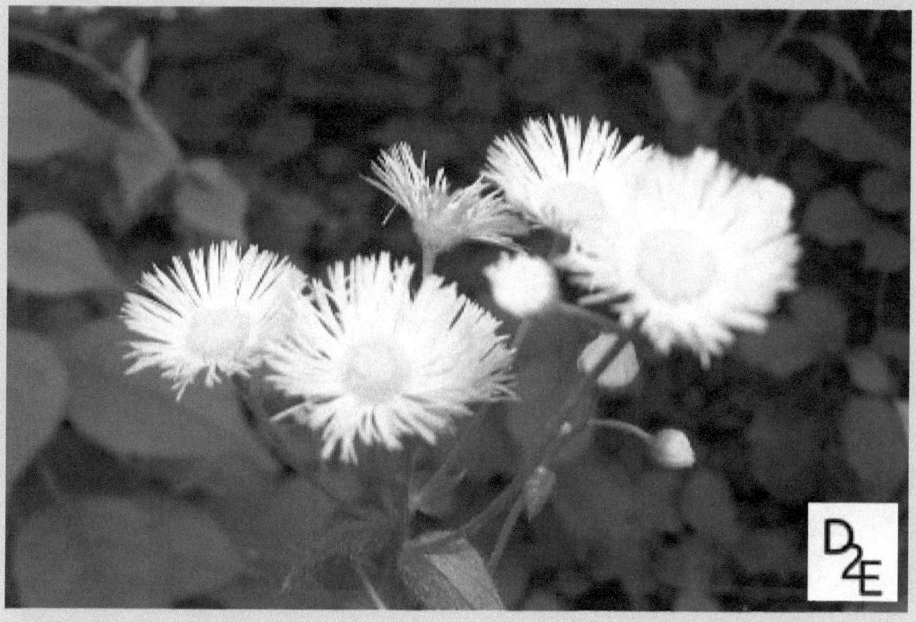
D2E

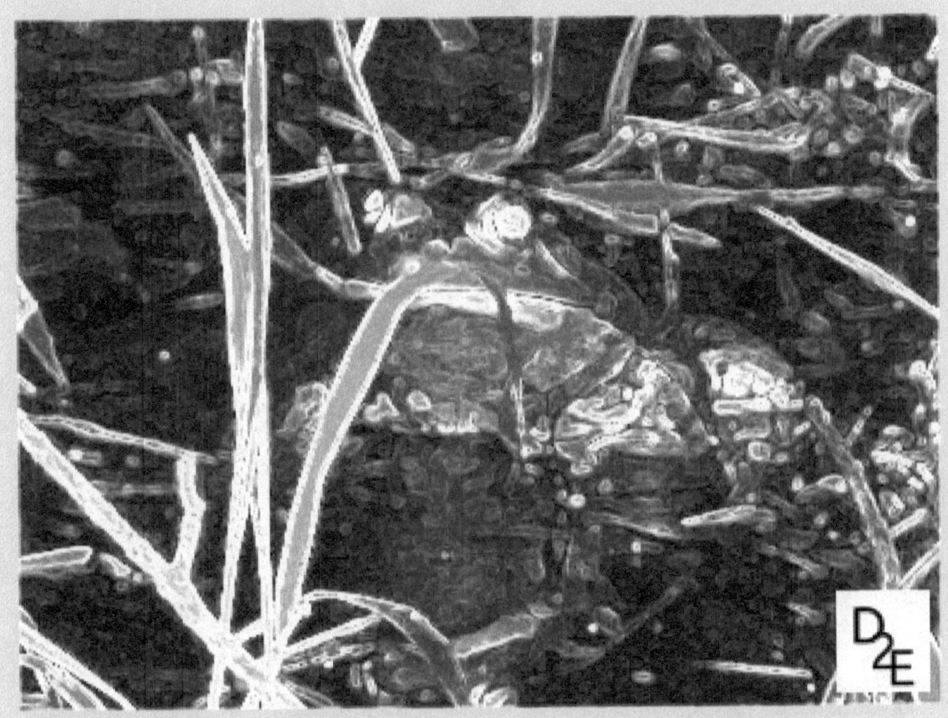

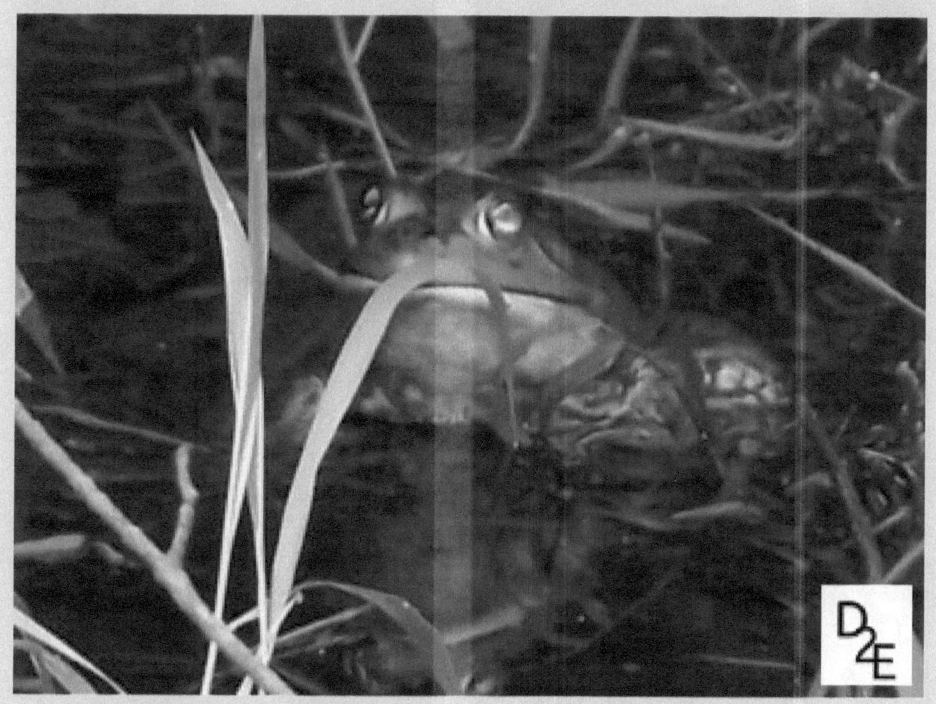
D2E

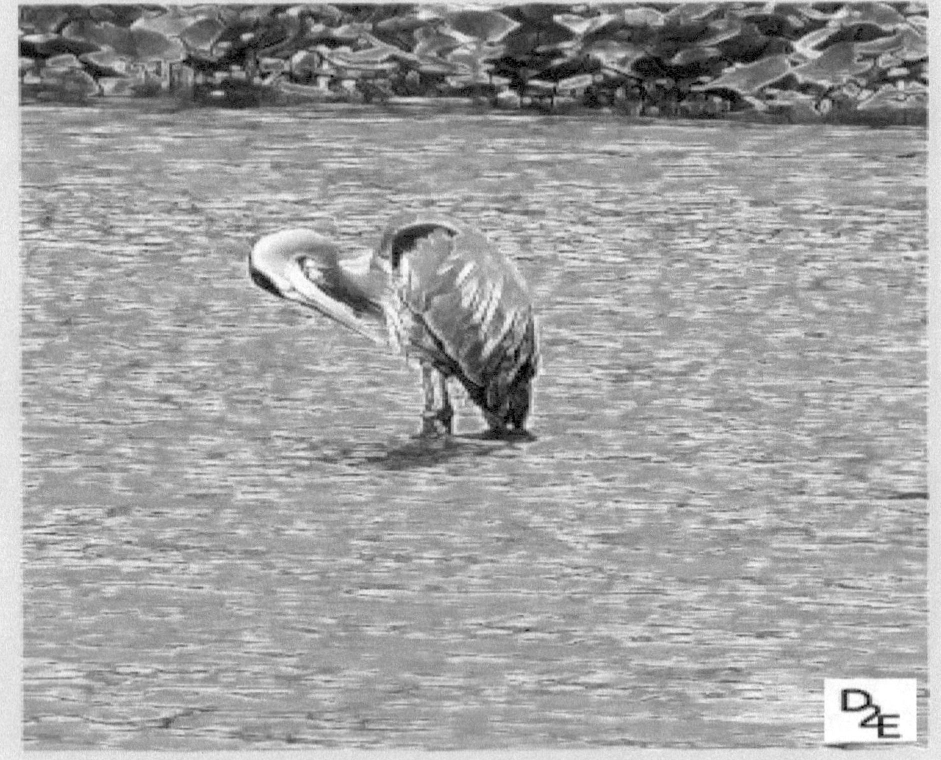
D2E

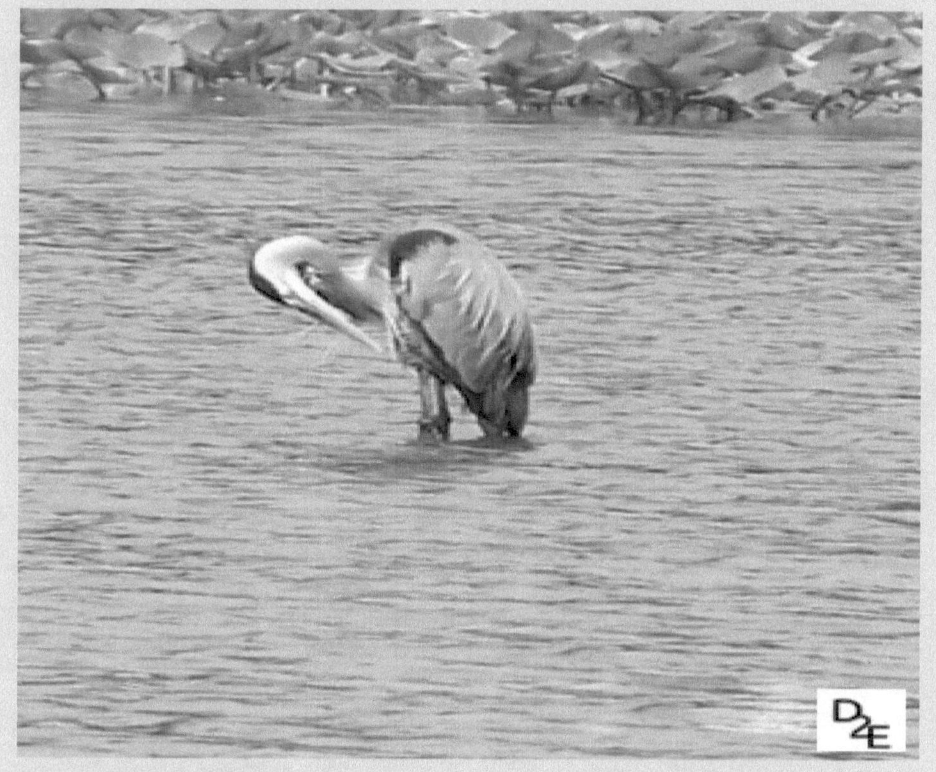

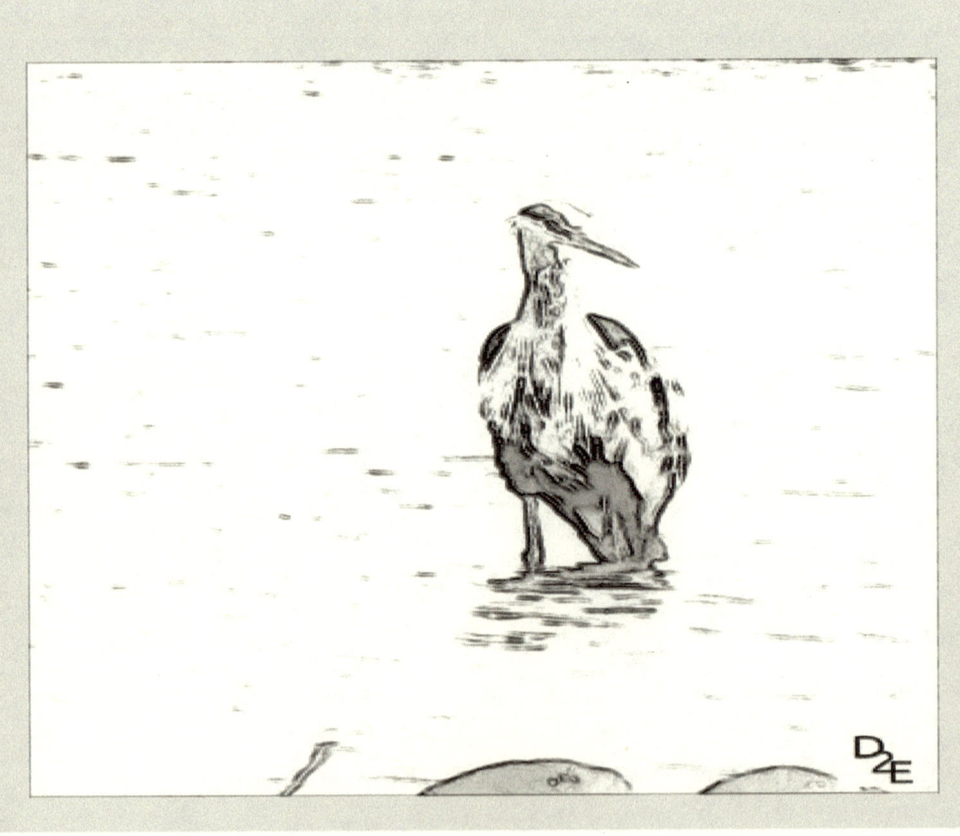
D2E

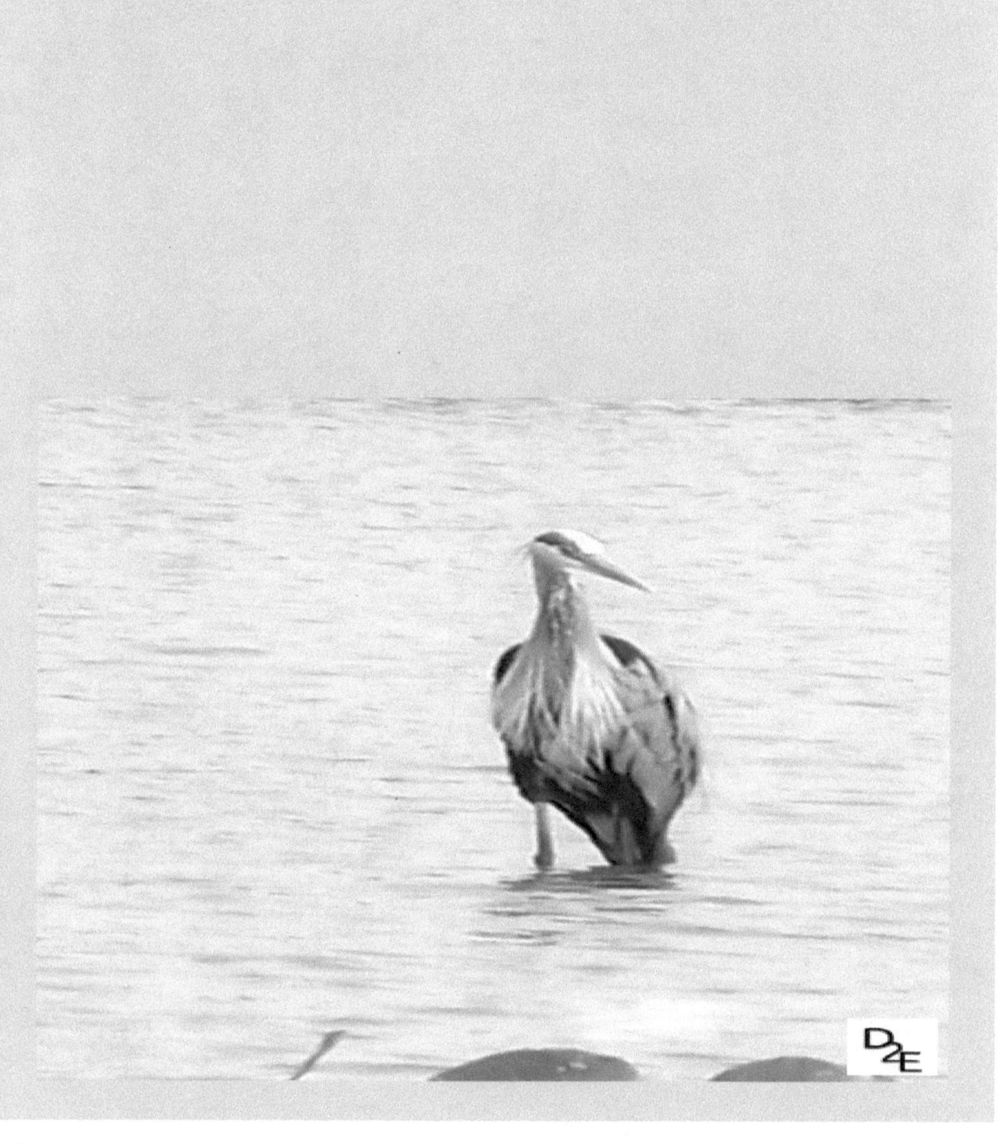
D2E

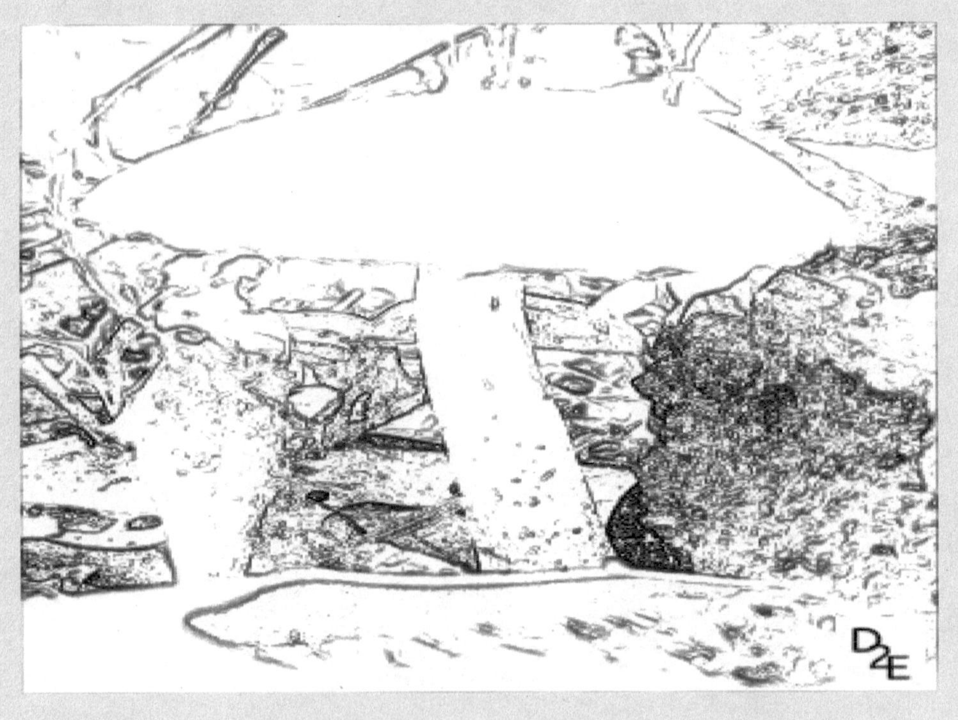
D2E

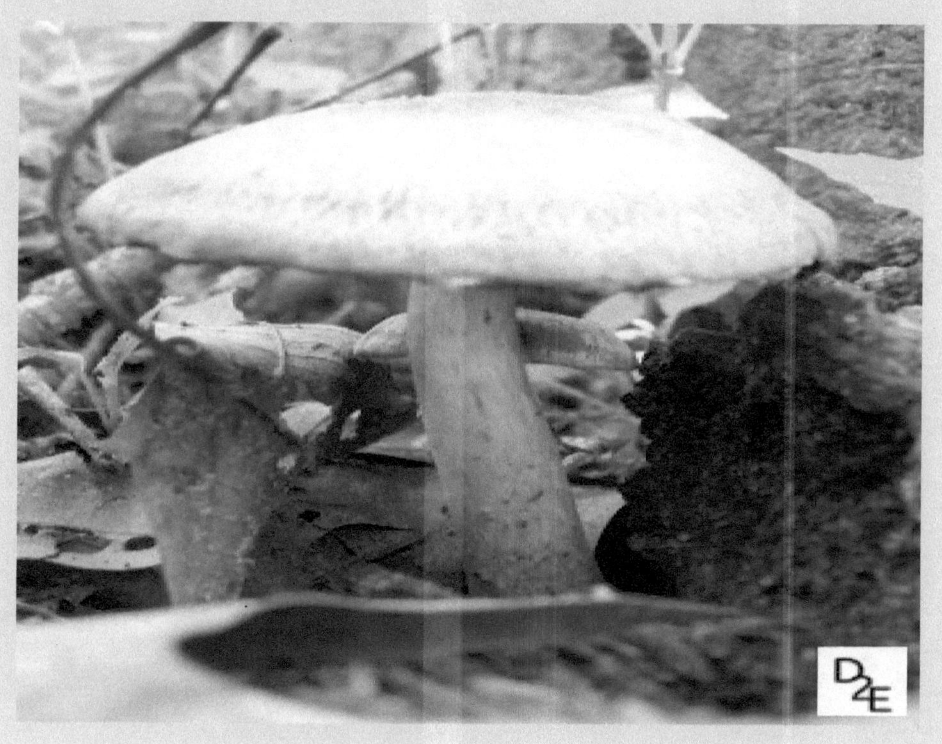

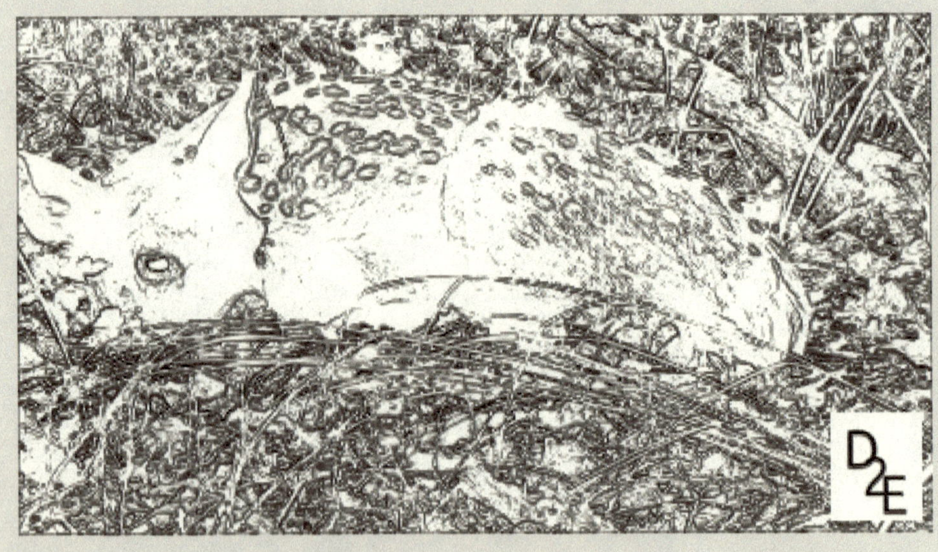
D2E

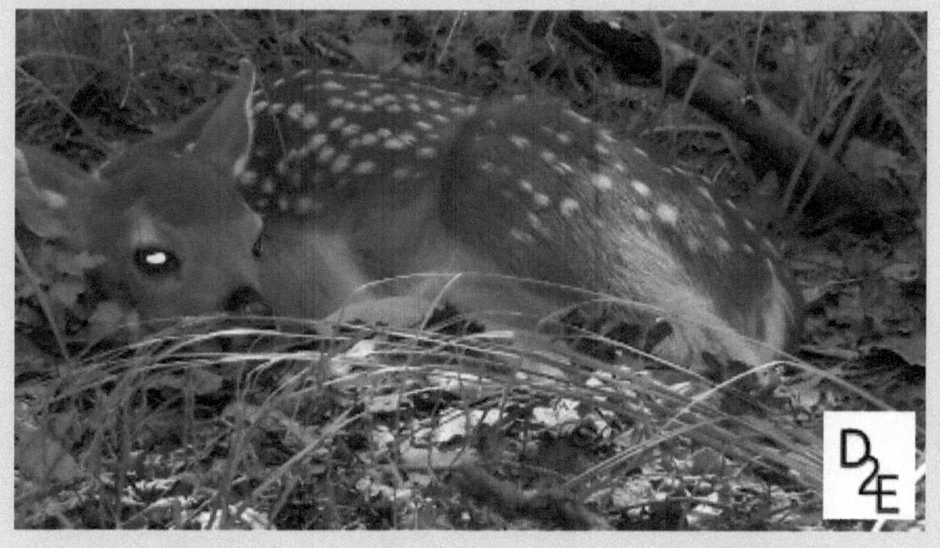
D2E

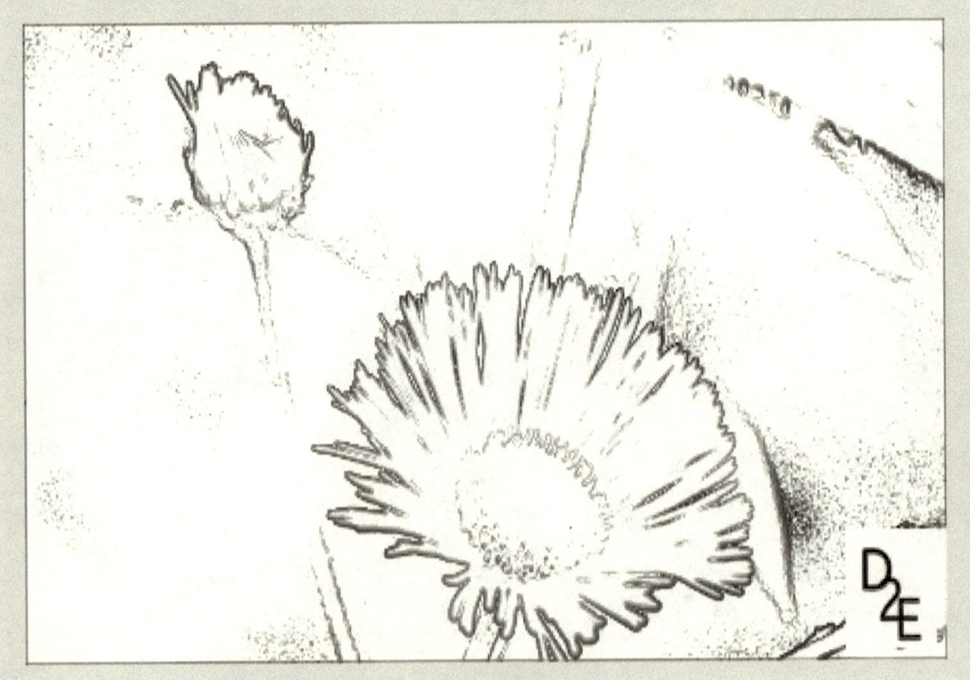

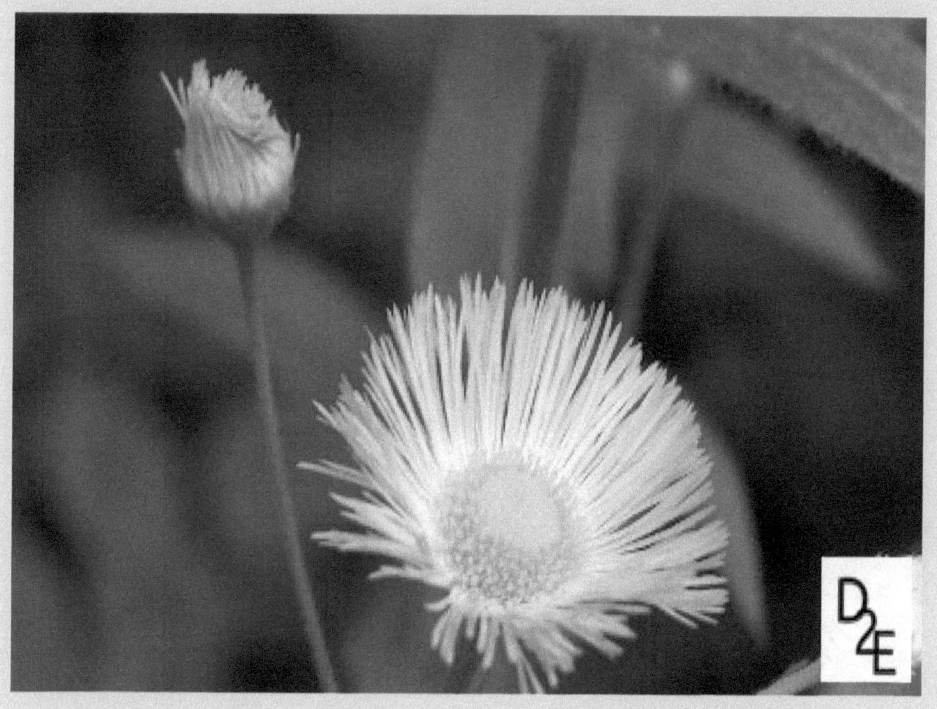

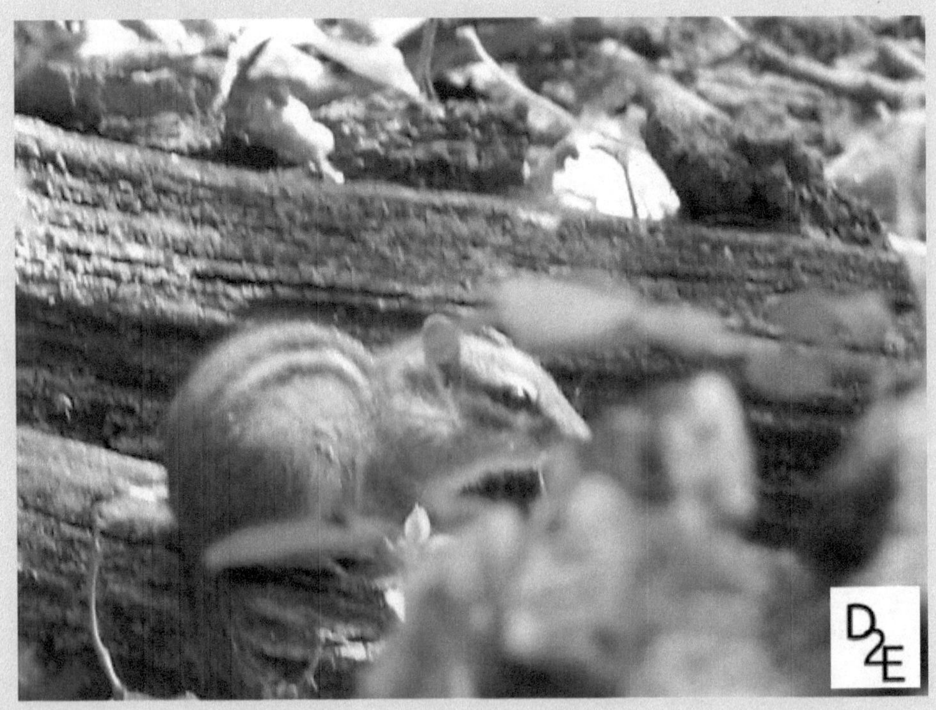

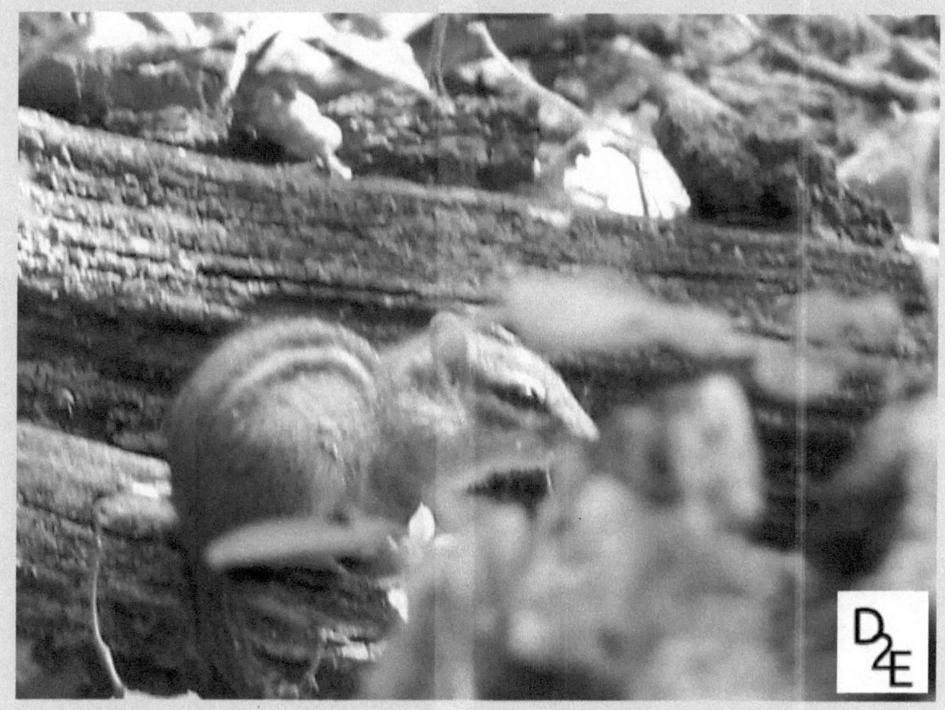

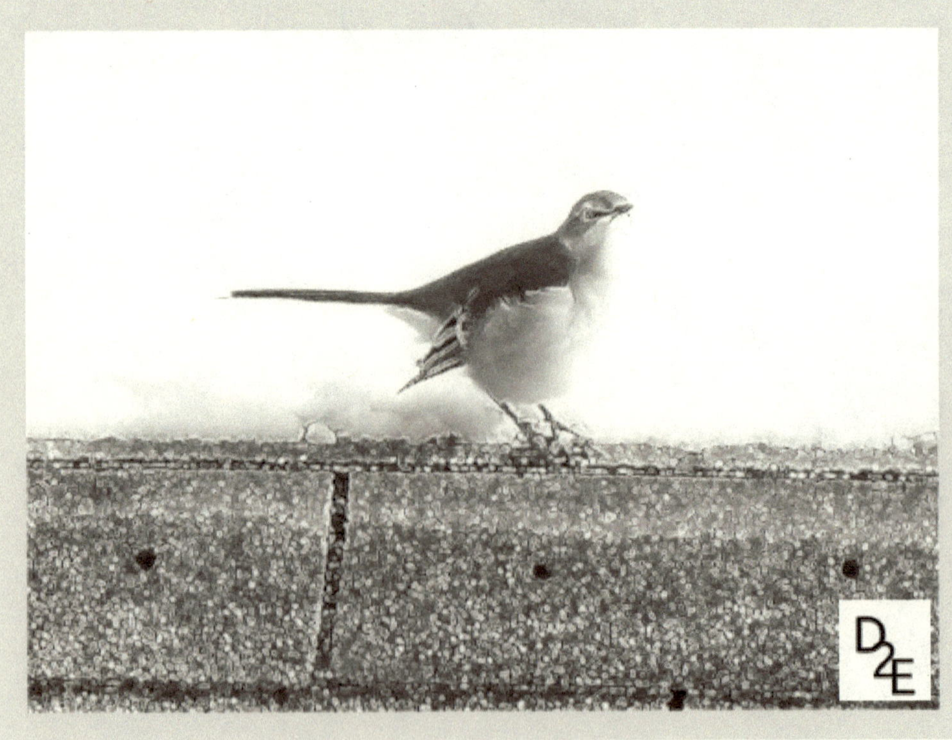
D2E

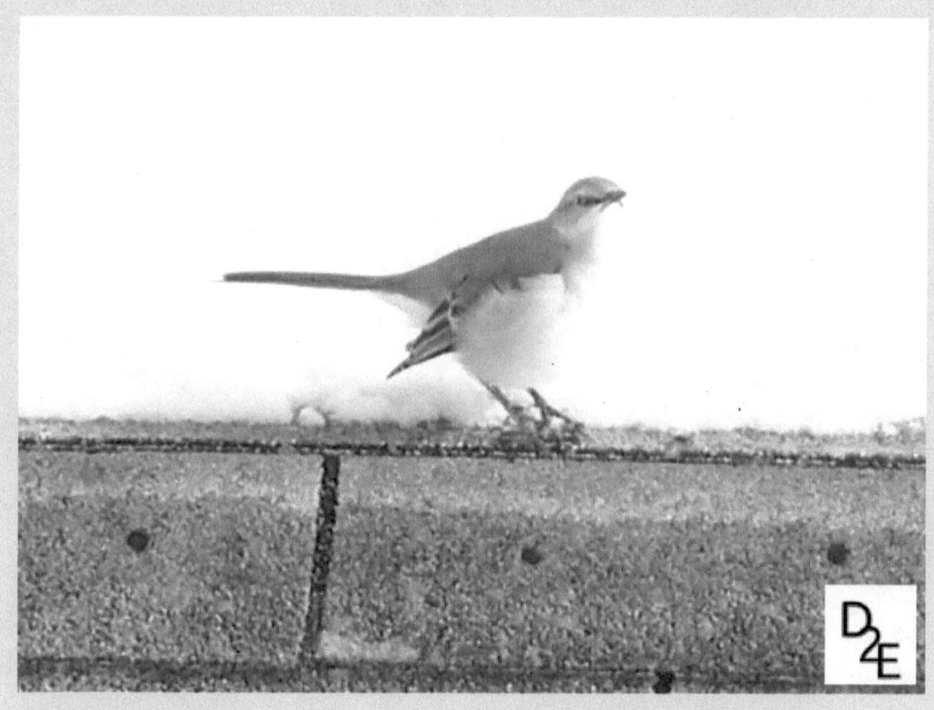
D2E

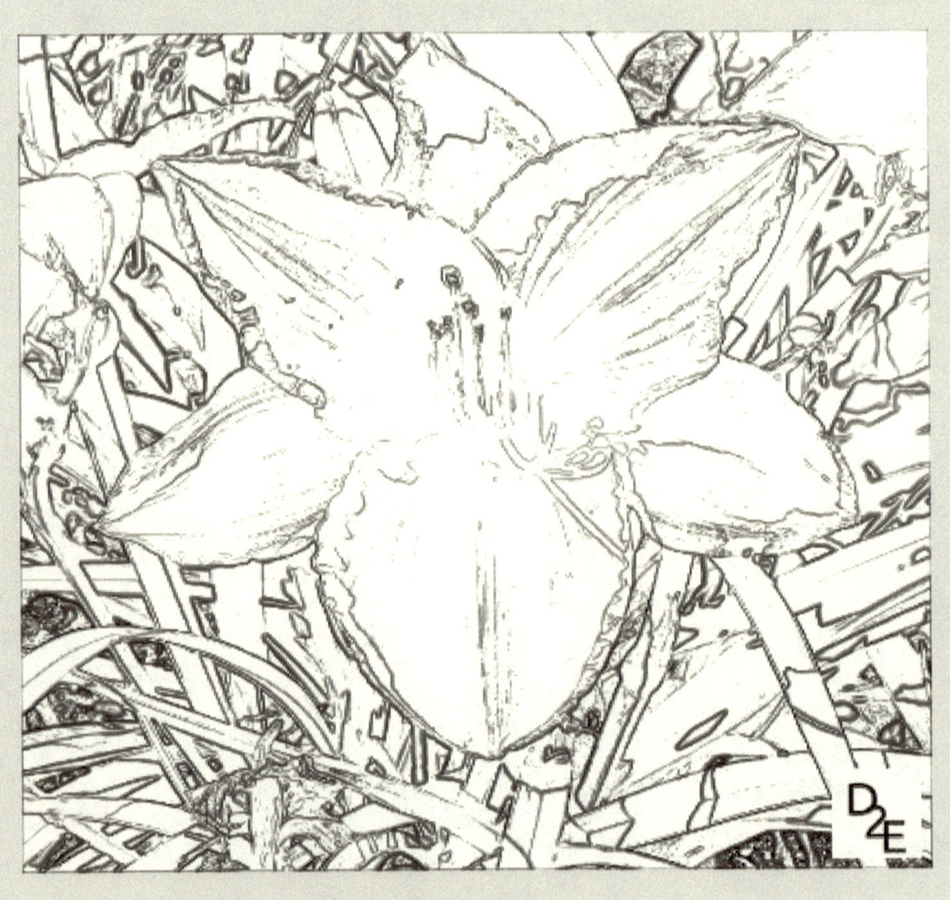
D2E

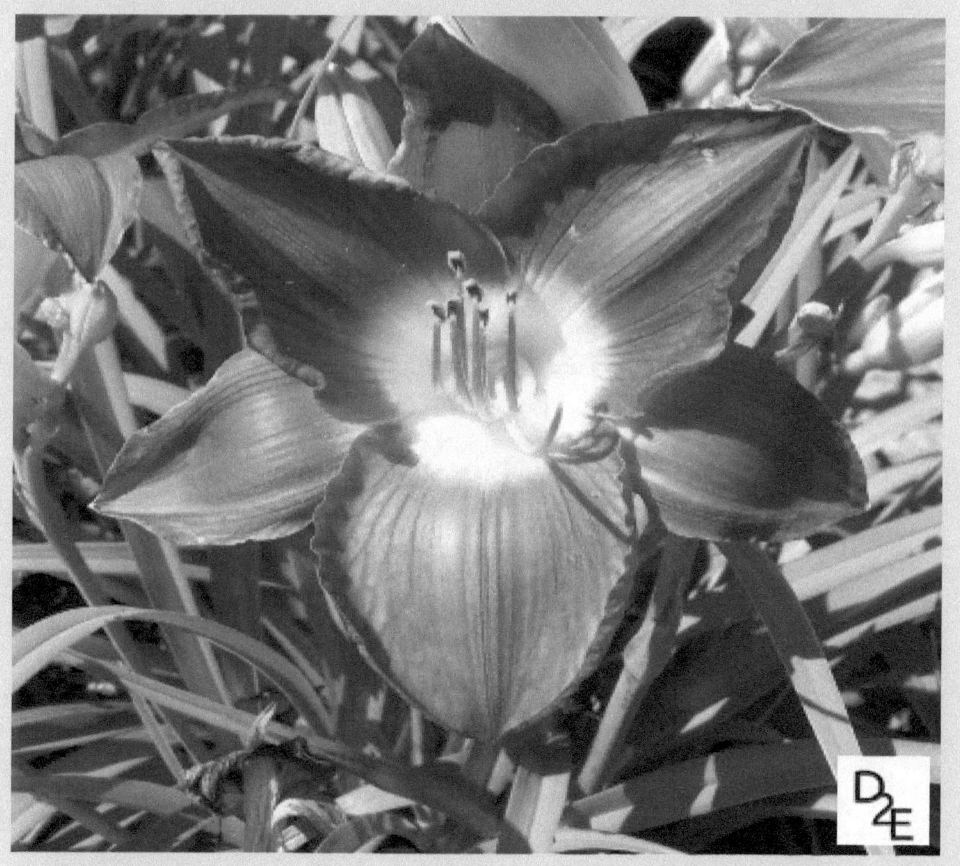
D2E

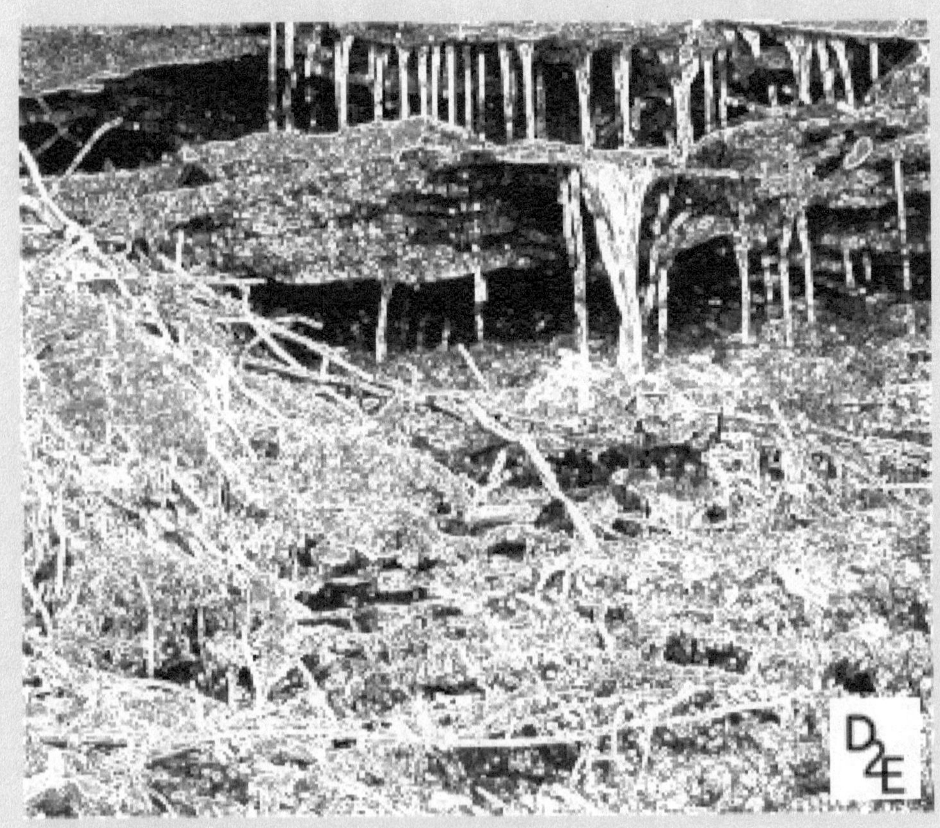
D2E

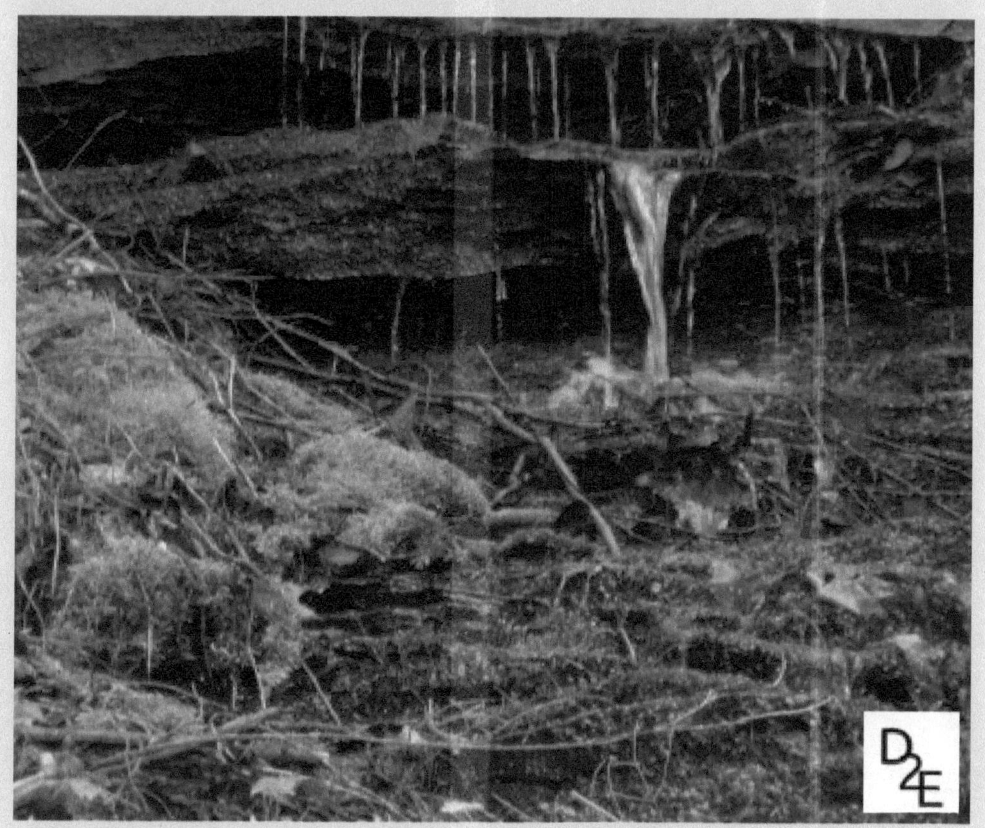

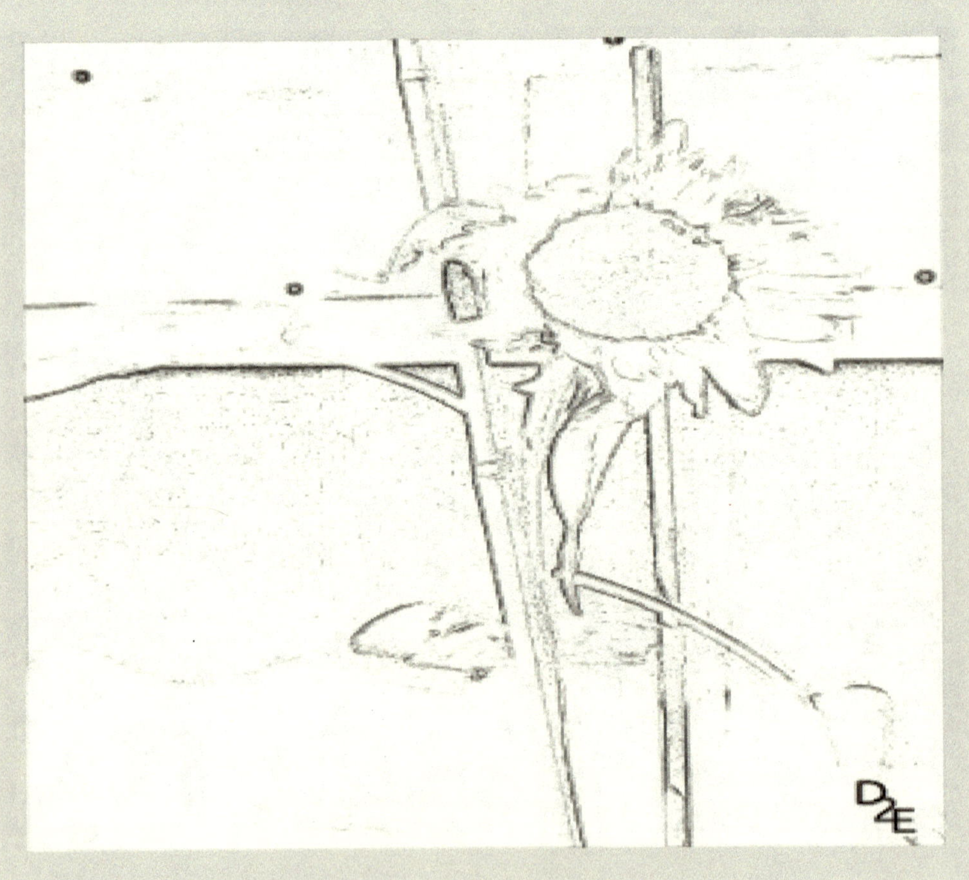

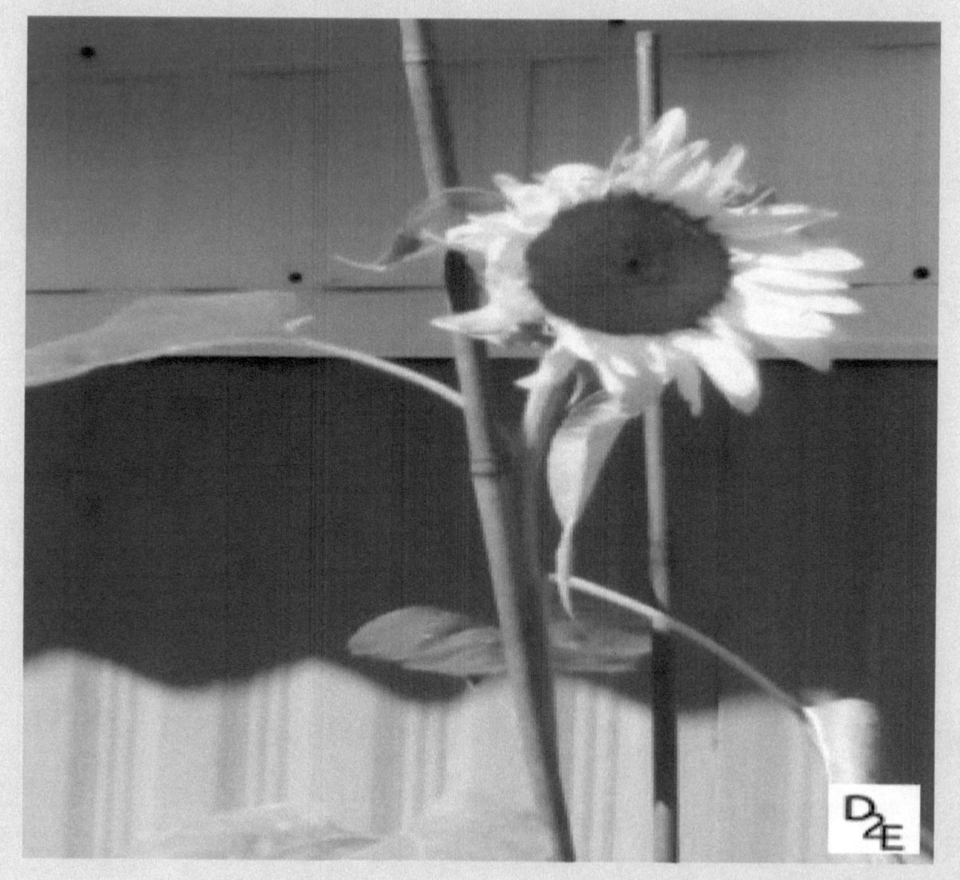
D2E

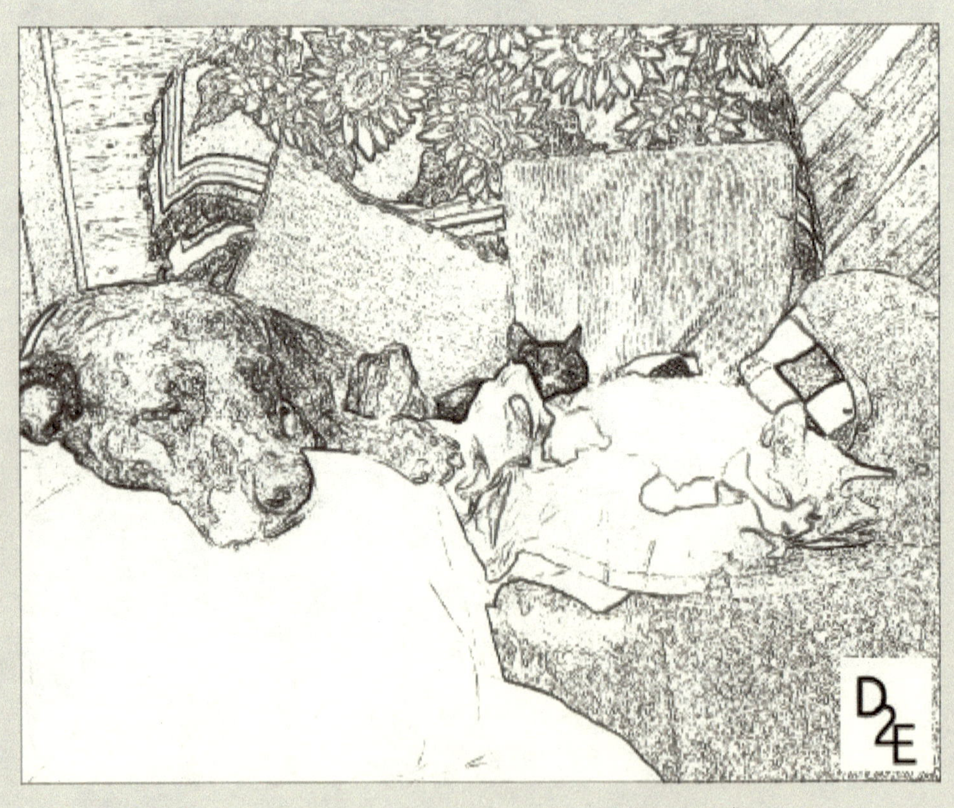
D2E

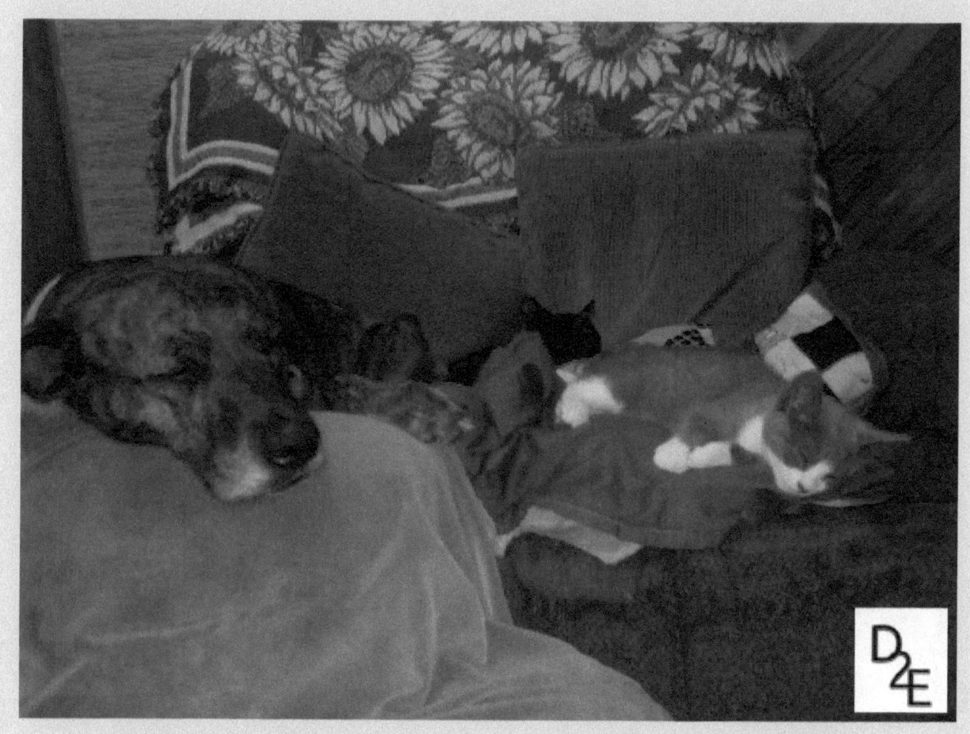
D2E

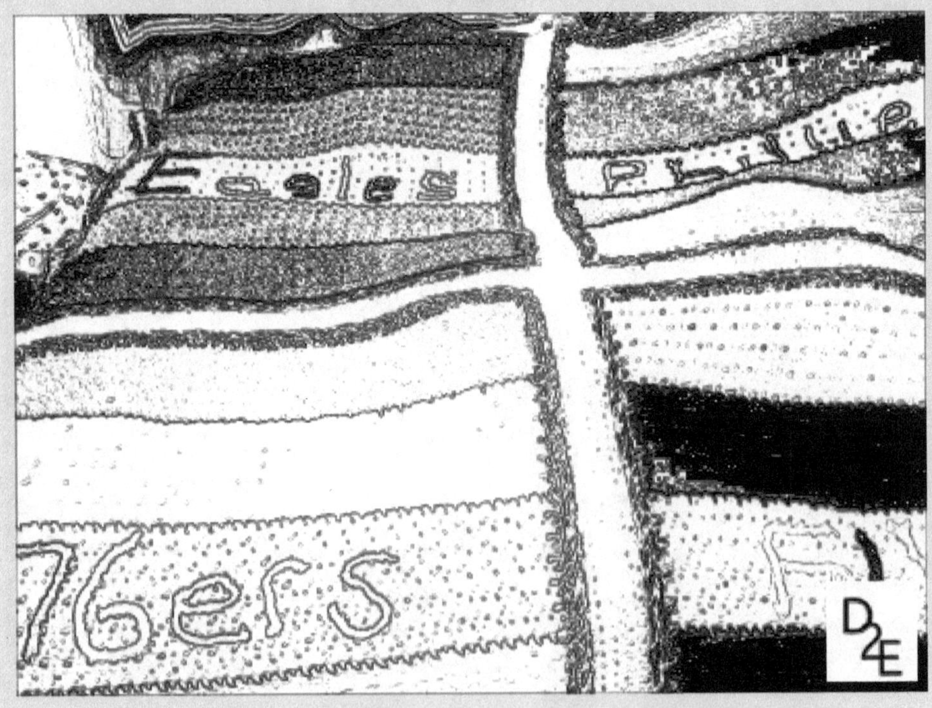
Eagles
76ers
D2E

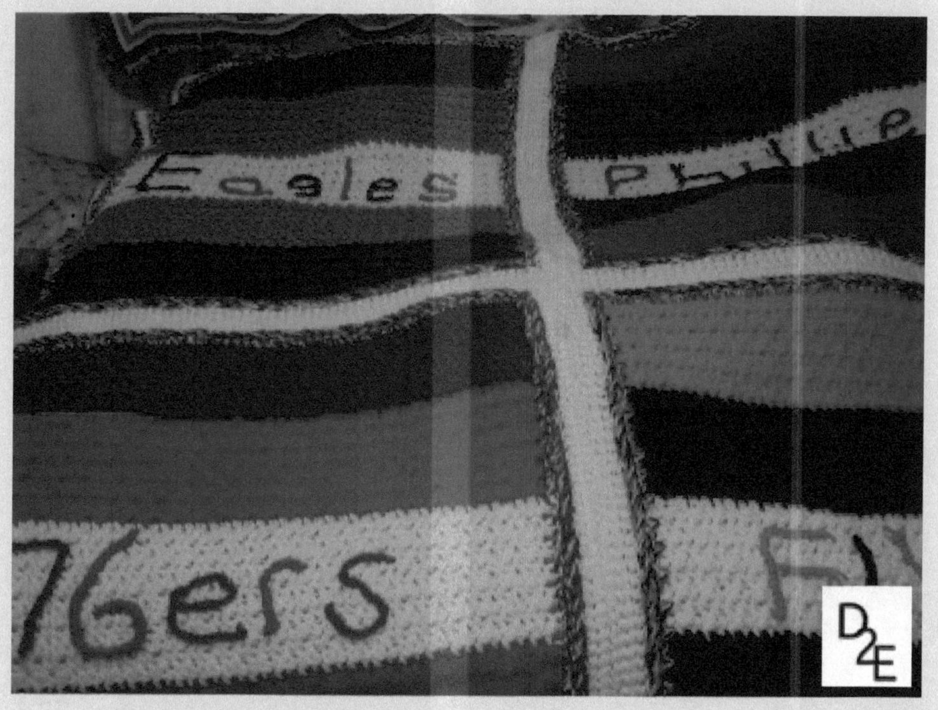
Eagles
76ers
D2E

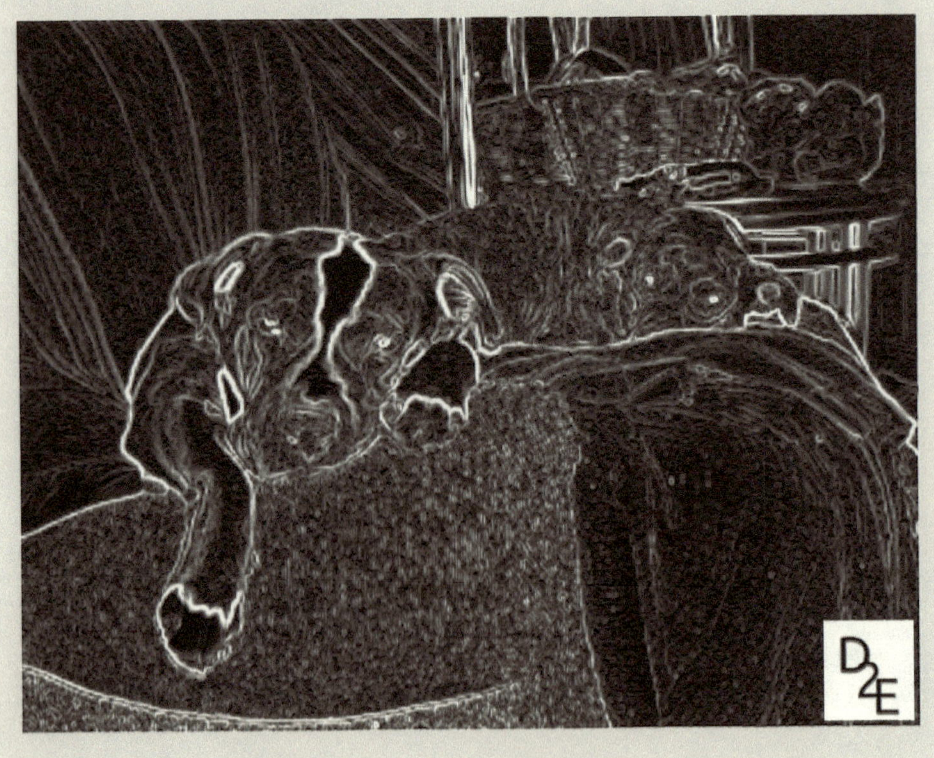
D2E

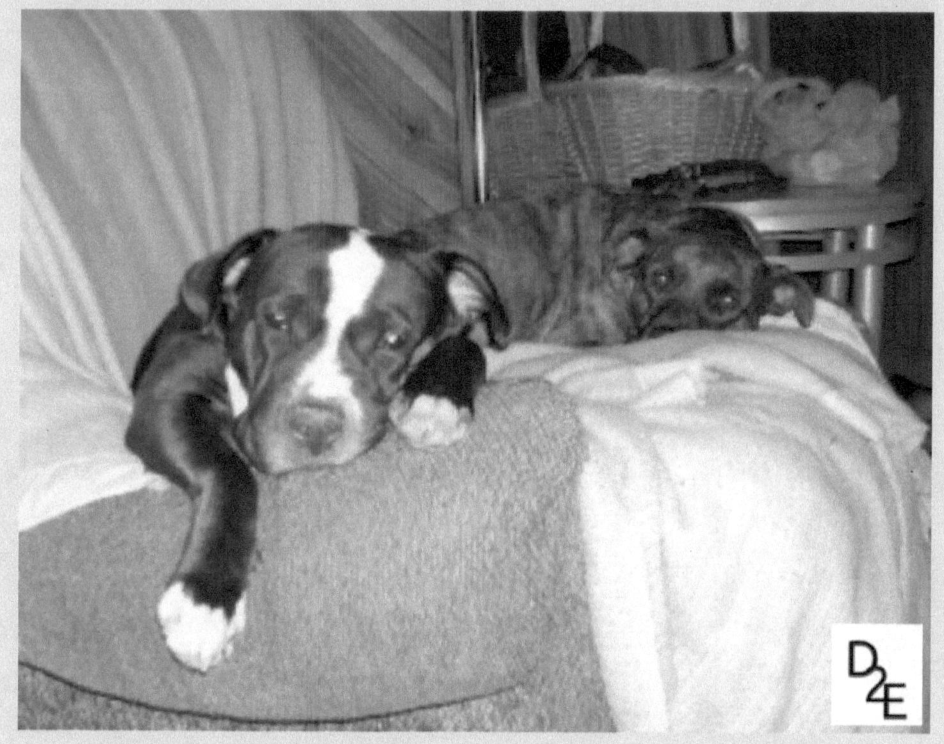
D2E

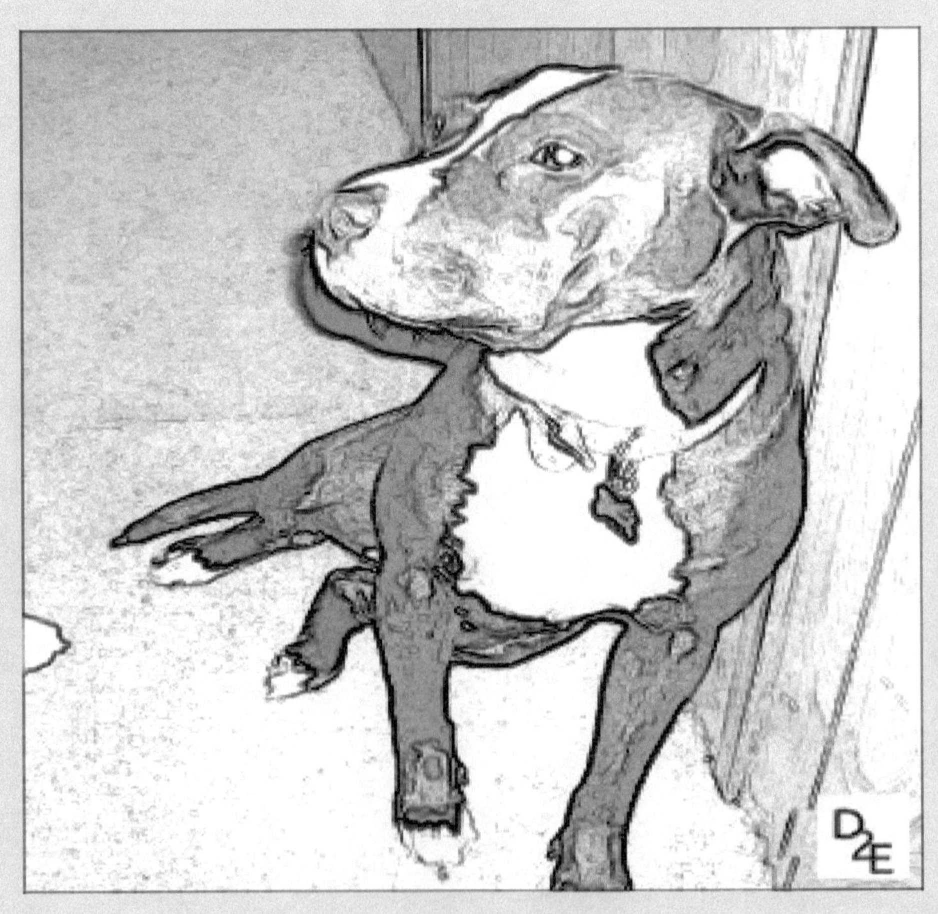
D2E

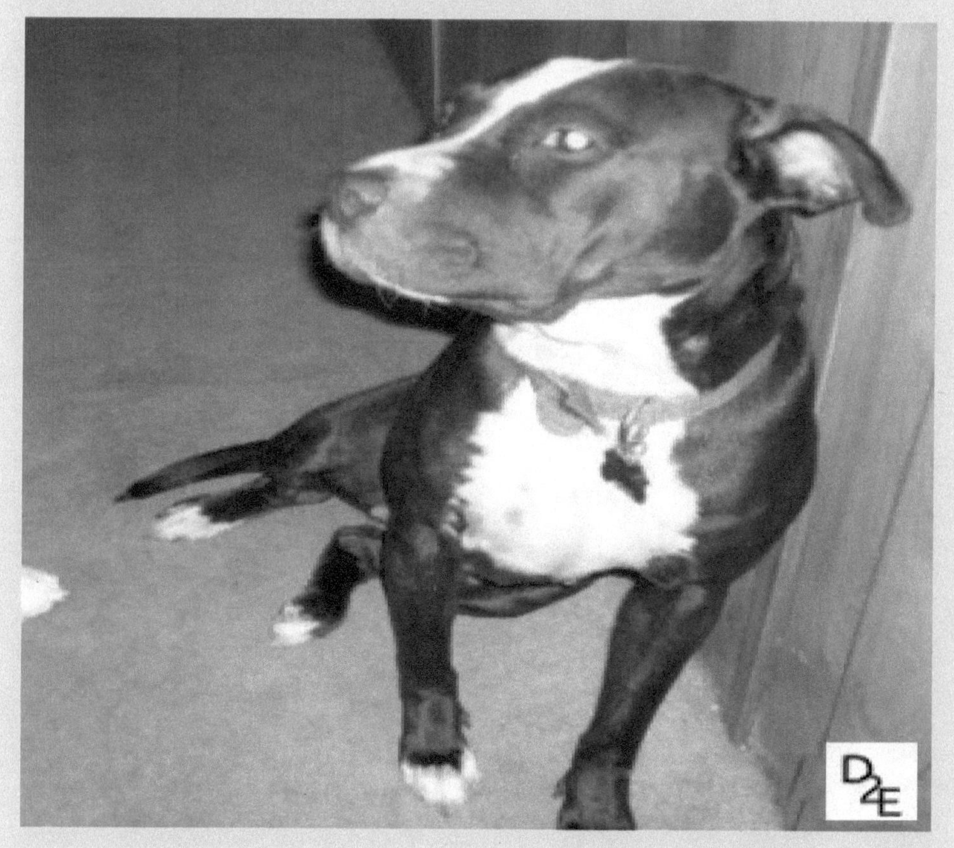

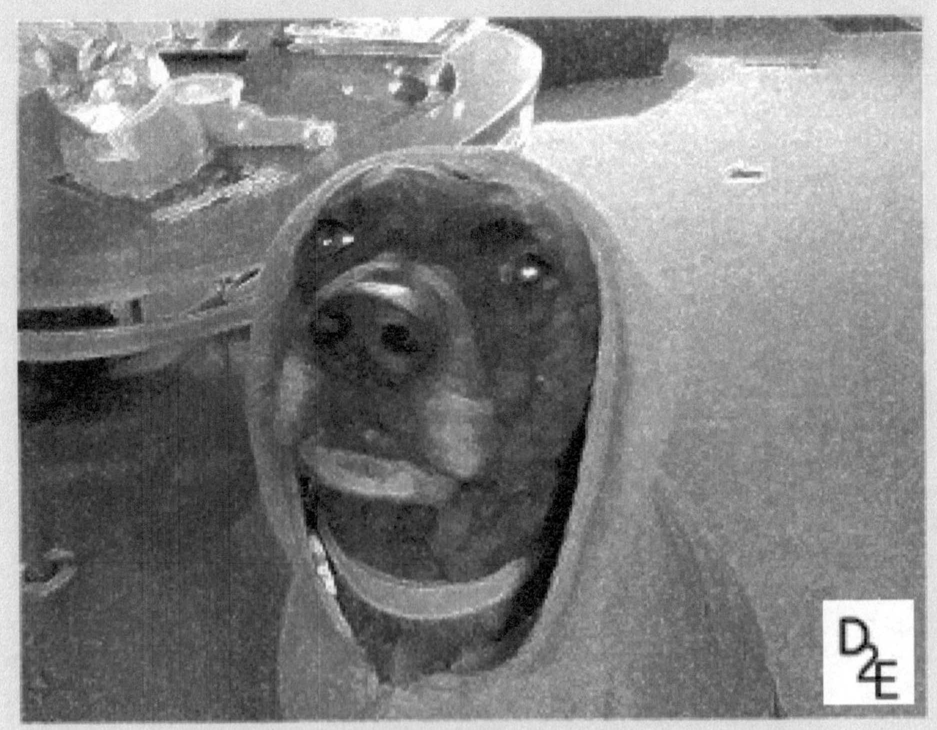
D2E

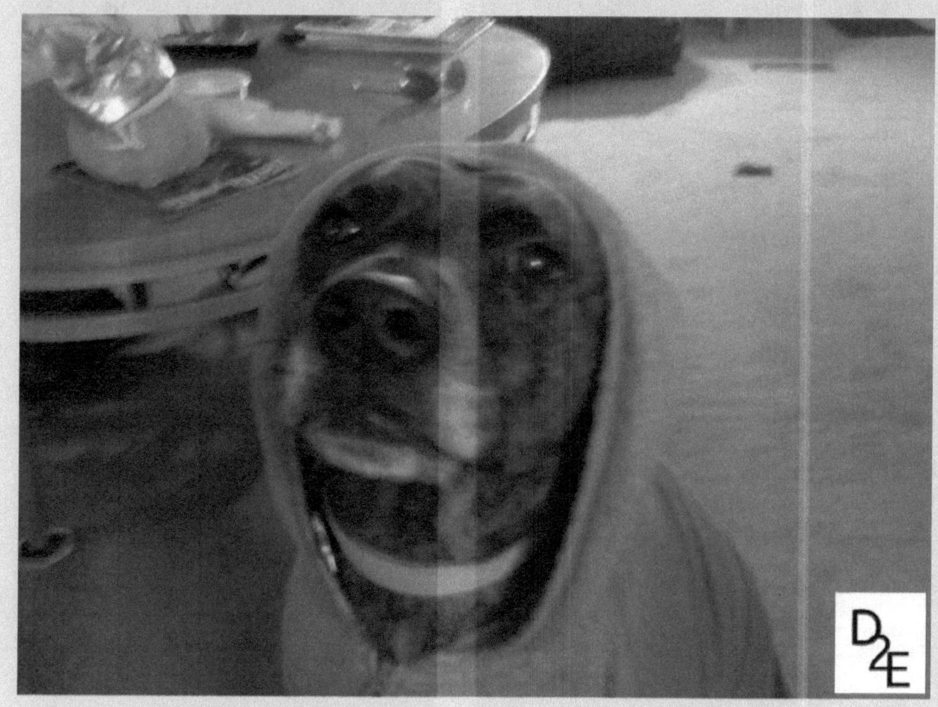
D2E

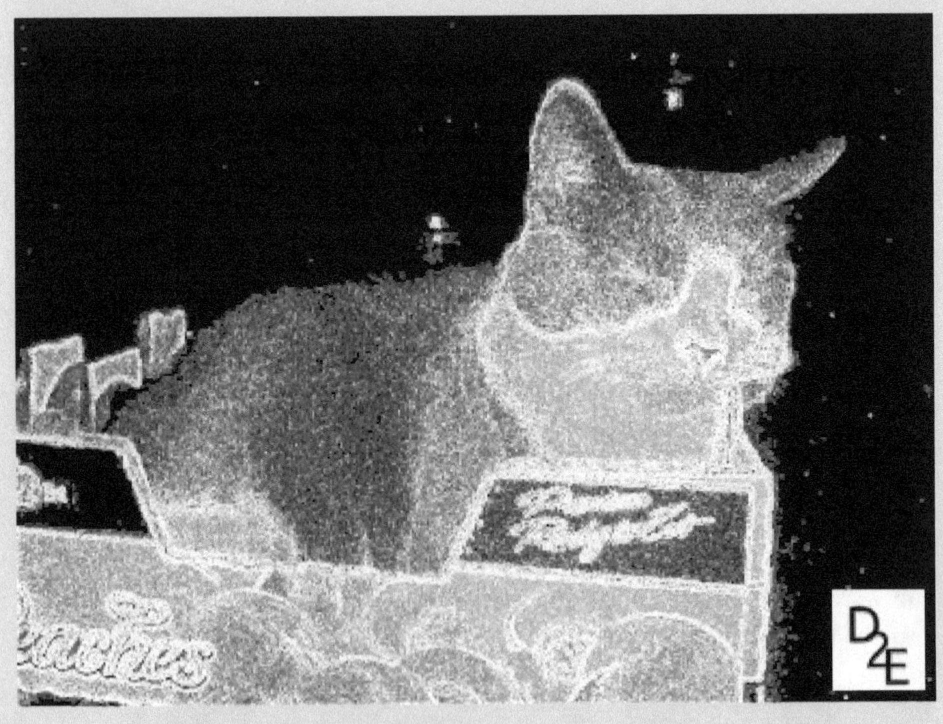
D2E

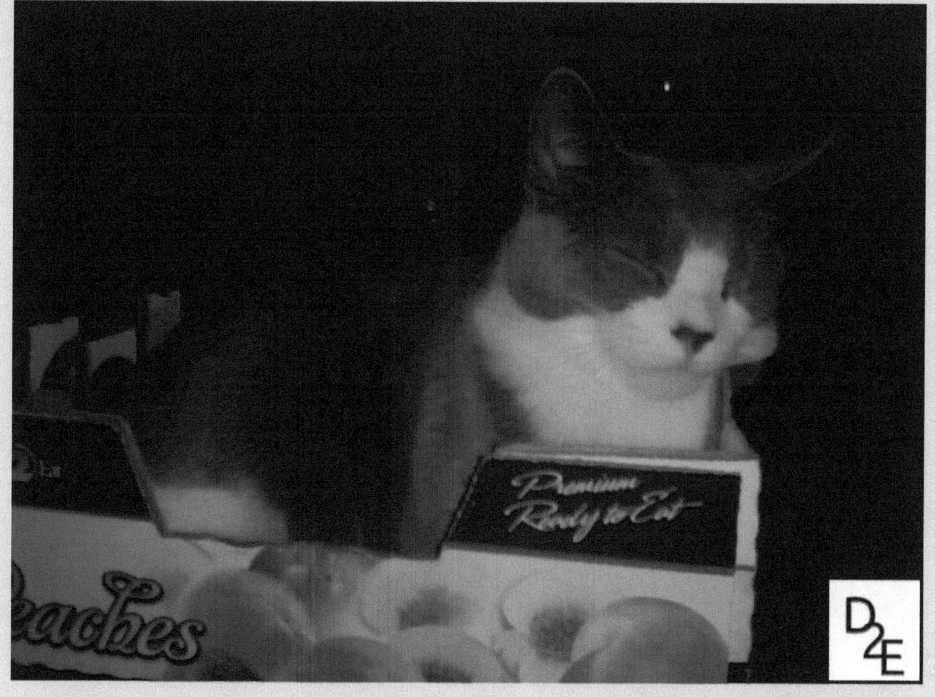
Premium
Ready to Eat
D2E

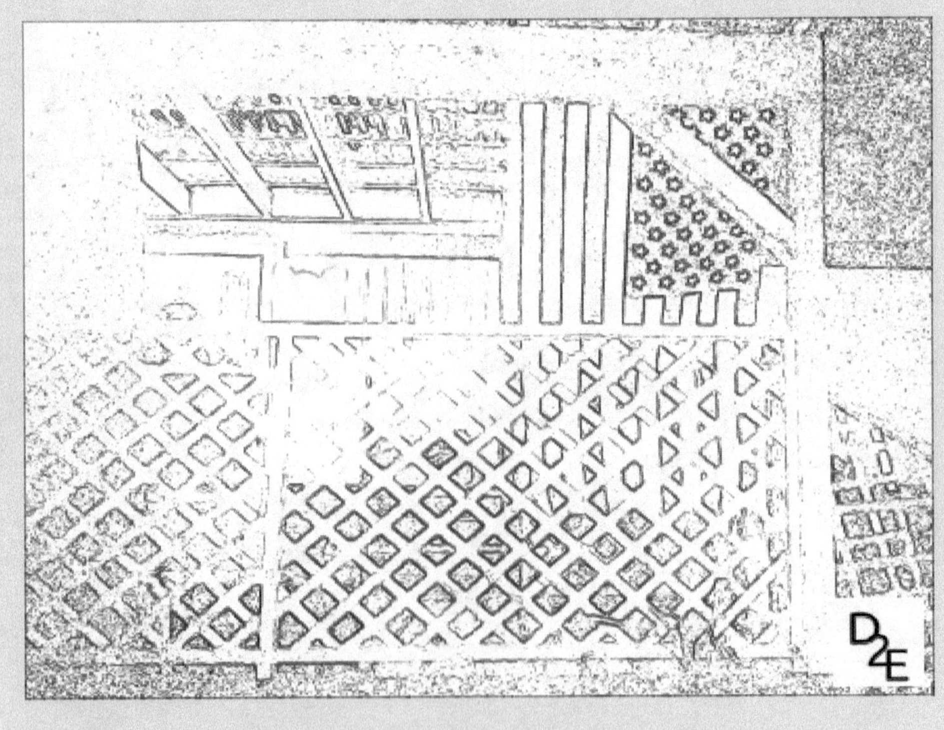
D2E

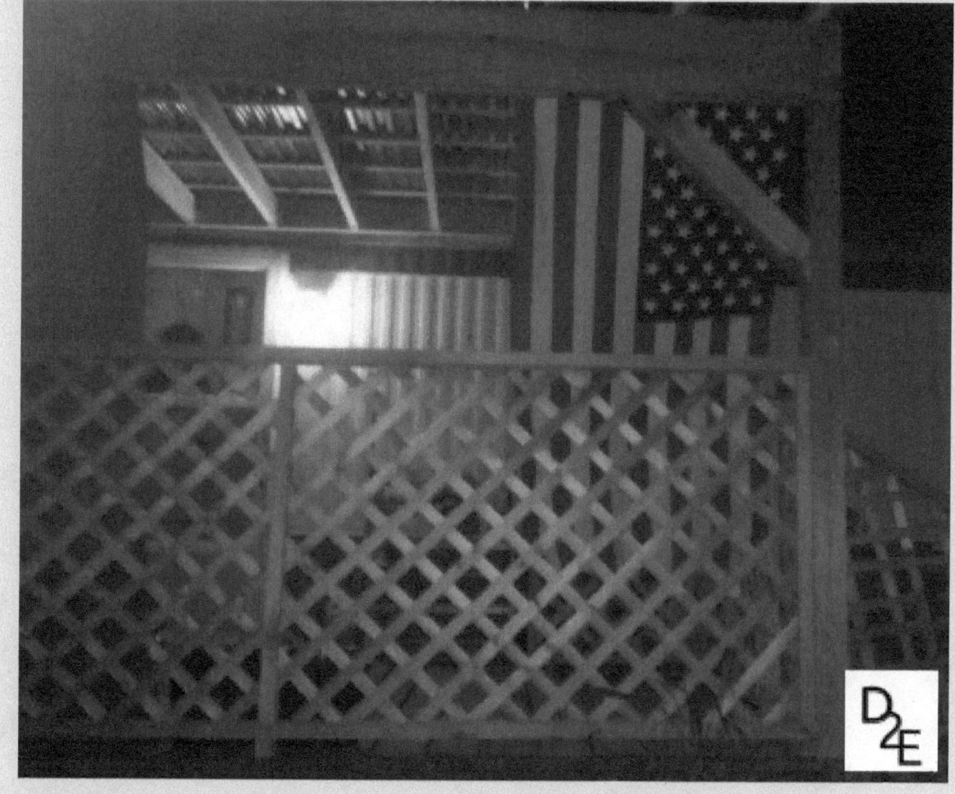

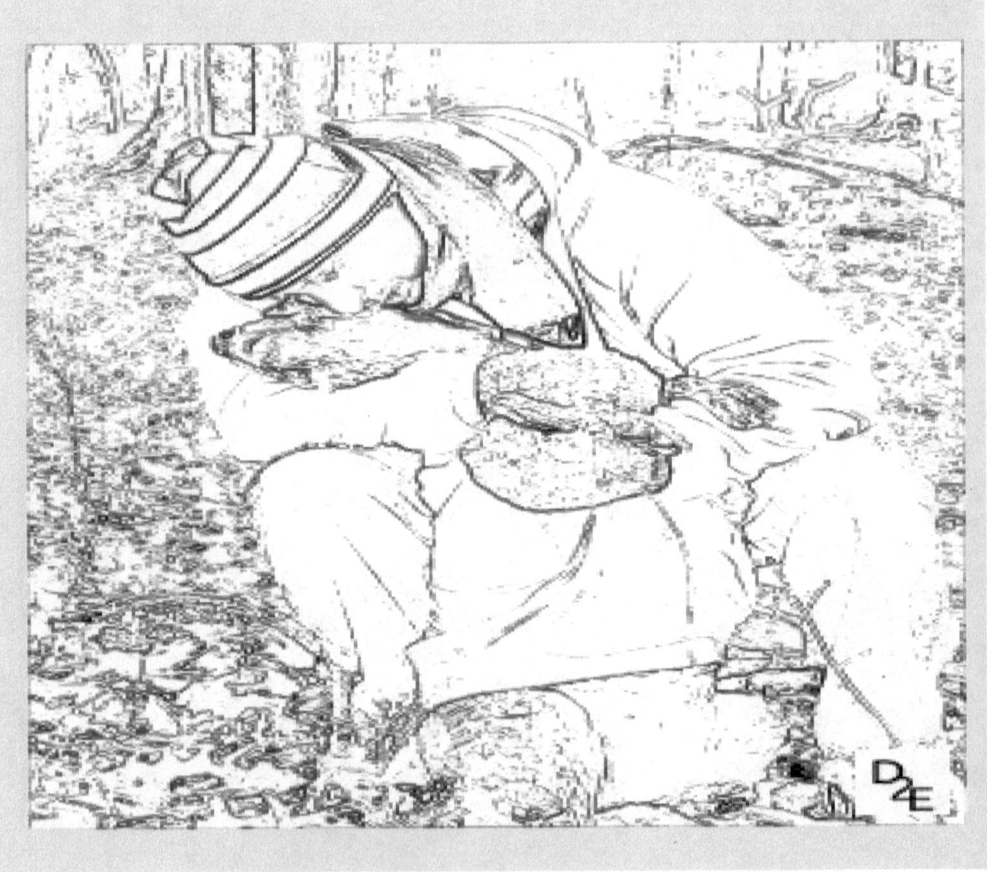

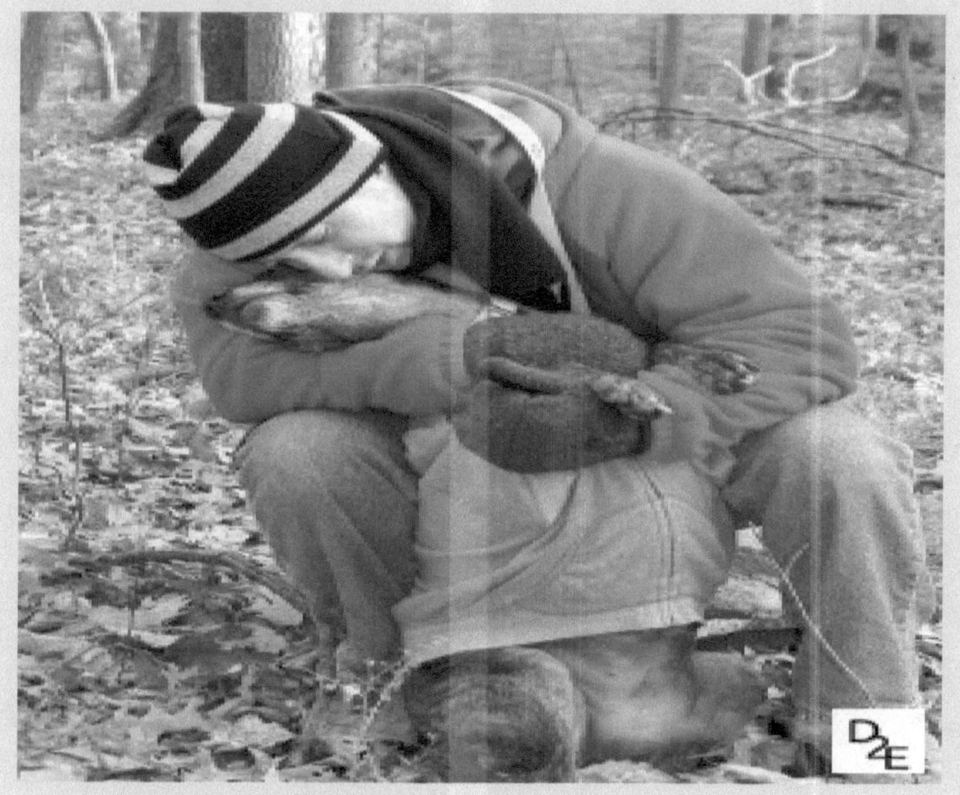
D2E

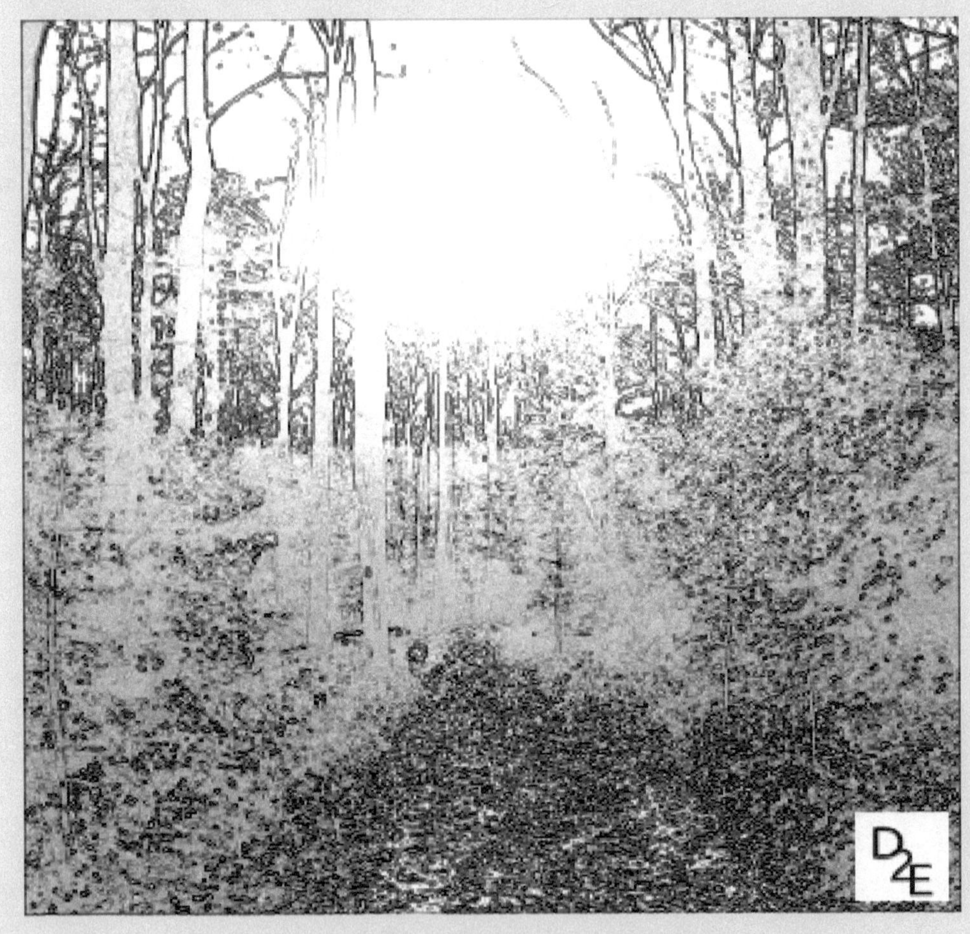
D2E

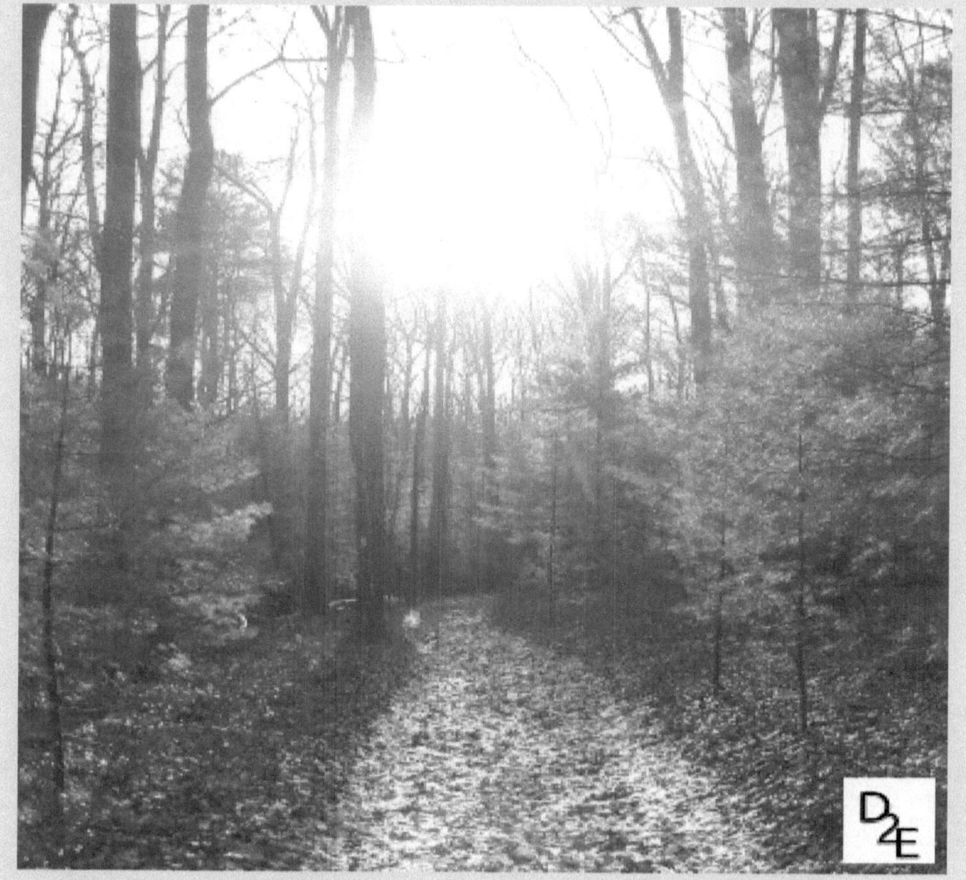

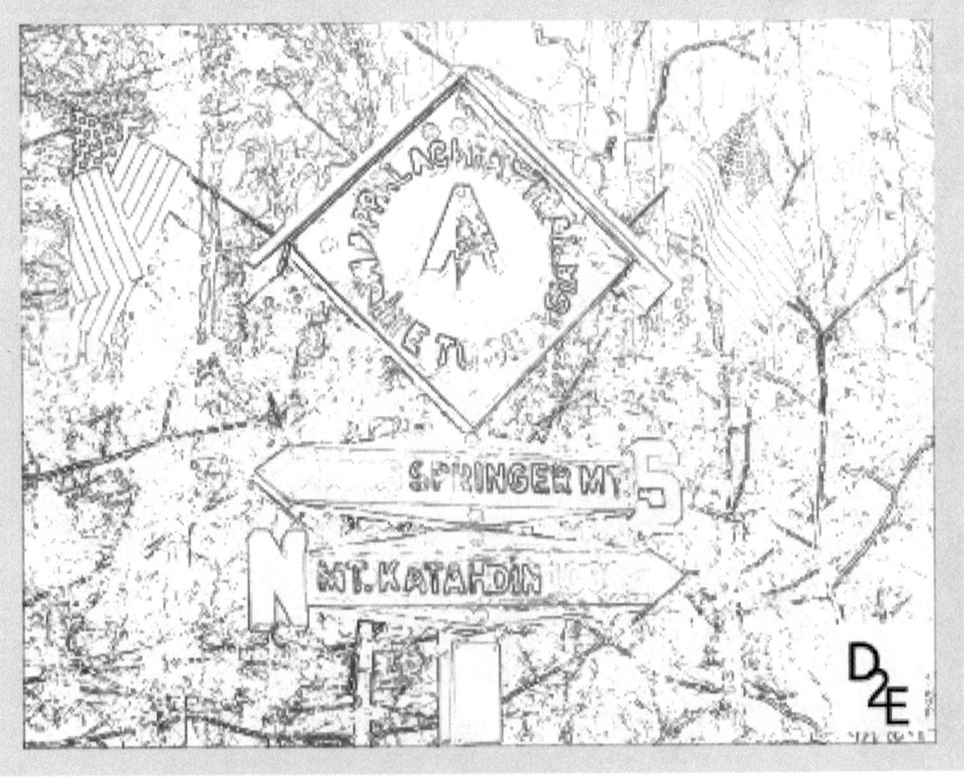
SPRINGER MT
S
N
MT. KATAHDIN
D2E

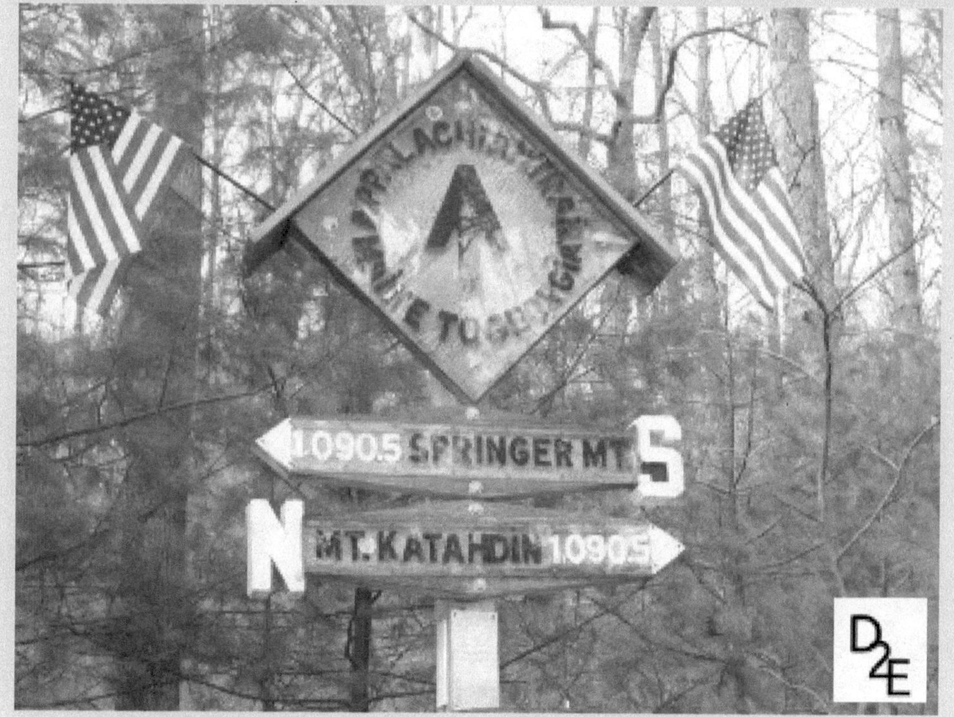
1090.5 SPRINGER MT.
S
N
MT. KATAHDIN 1090.5

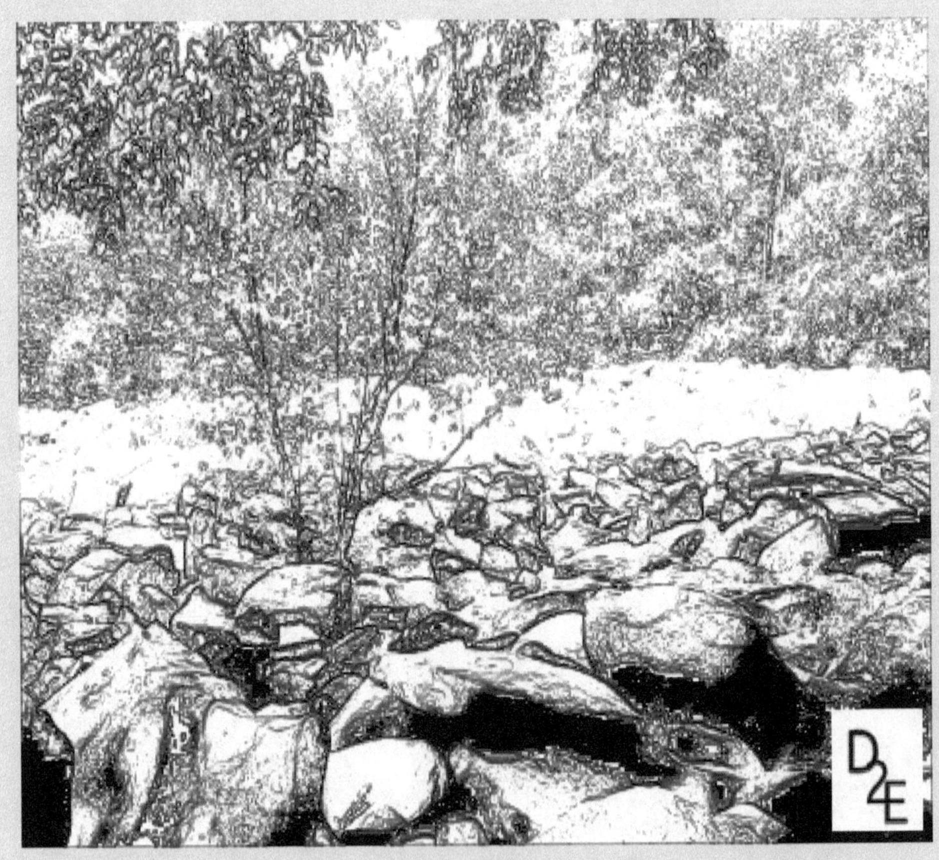

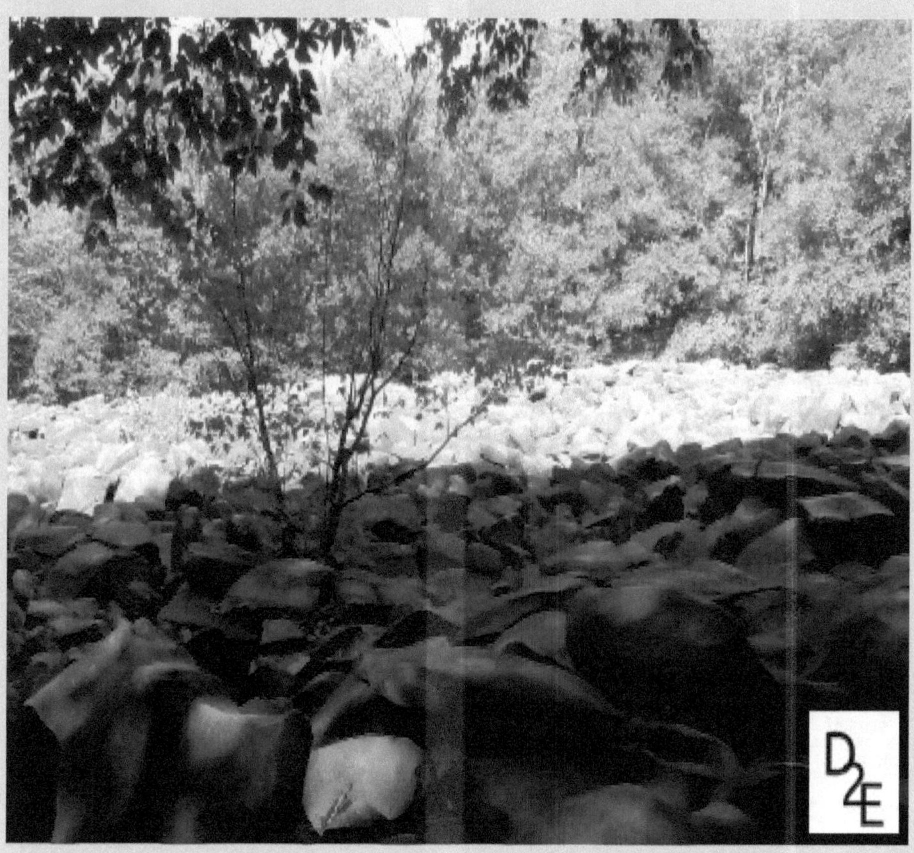
D2E

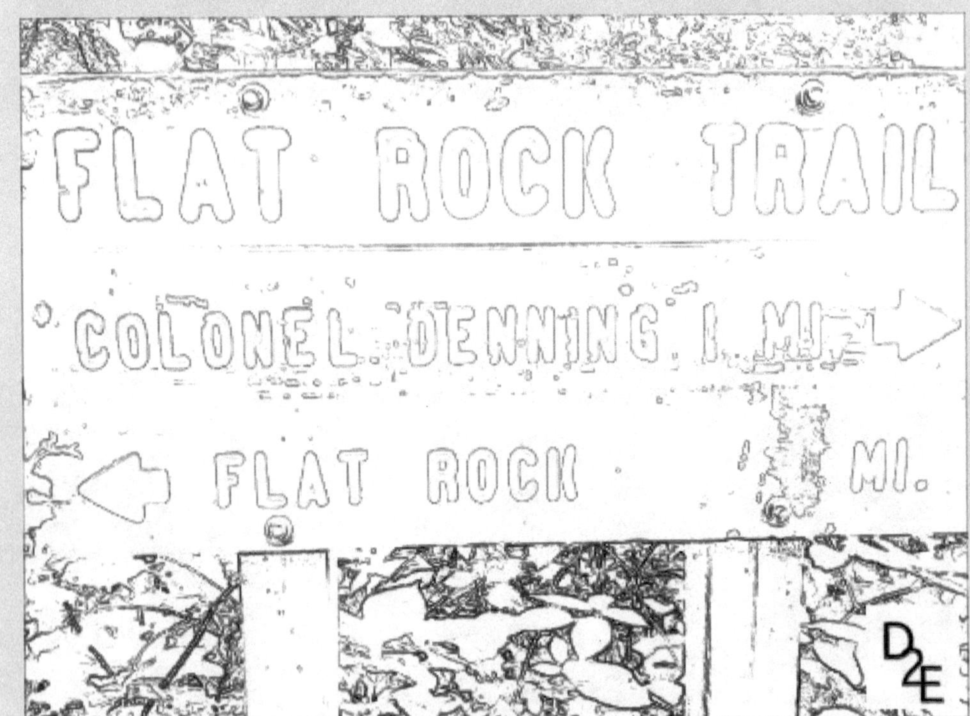
FLAT ROCK TRAIL
COLONEL DENNING 1 MI.
FLAT ROCK
MI.
D2E

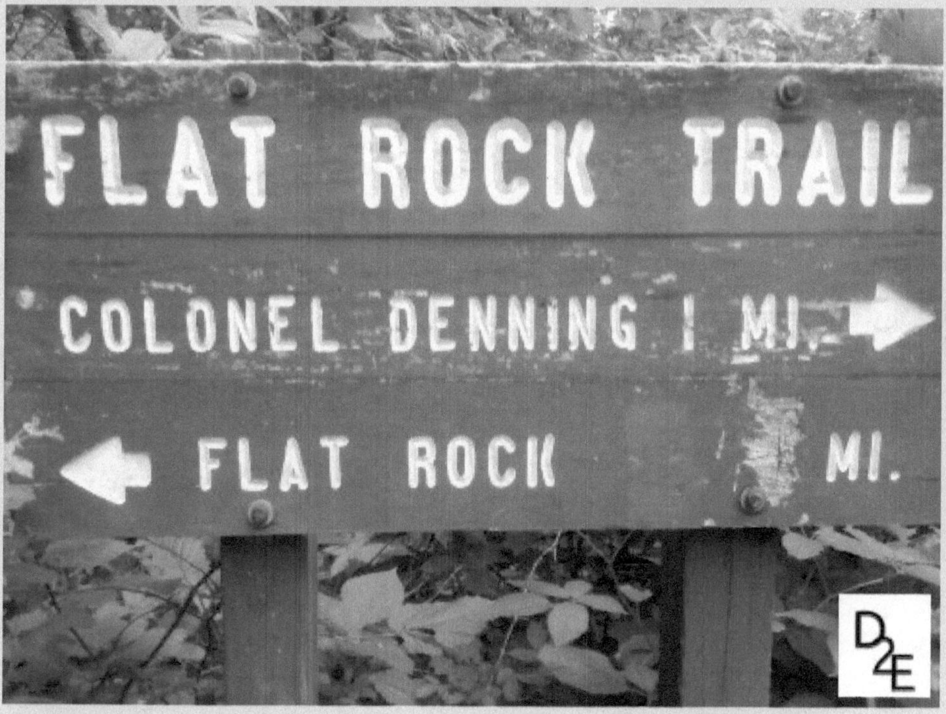

FLAT ROCK TRAIL
COLONEL DENNING 1 MI.
FLAT ROCK MI.
D2E

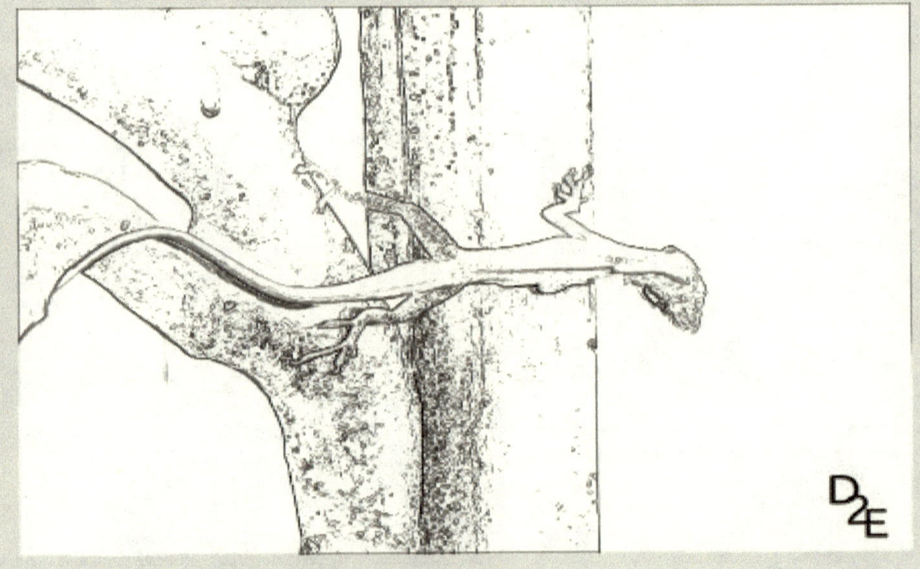
D2E

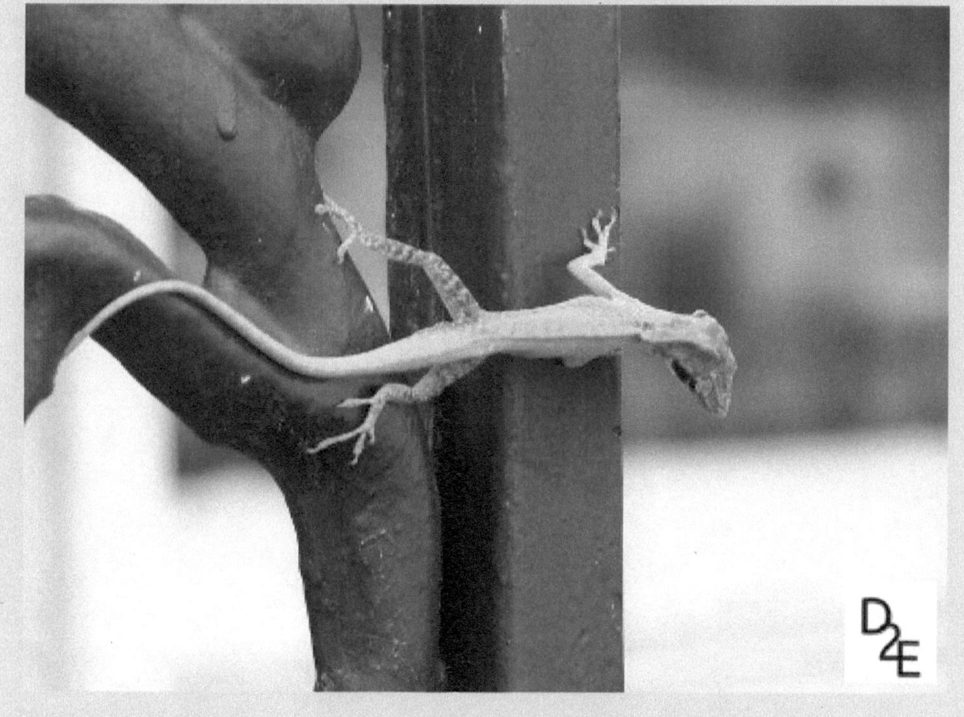
D2E

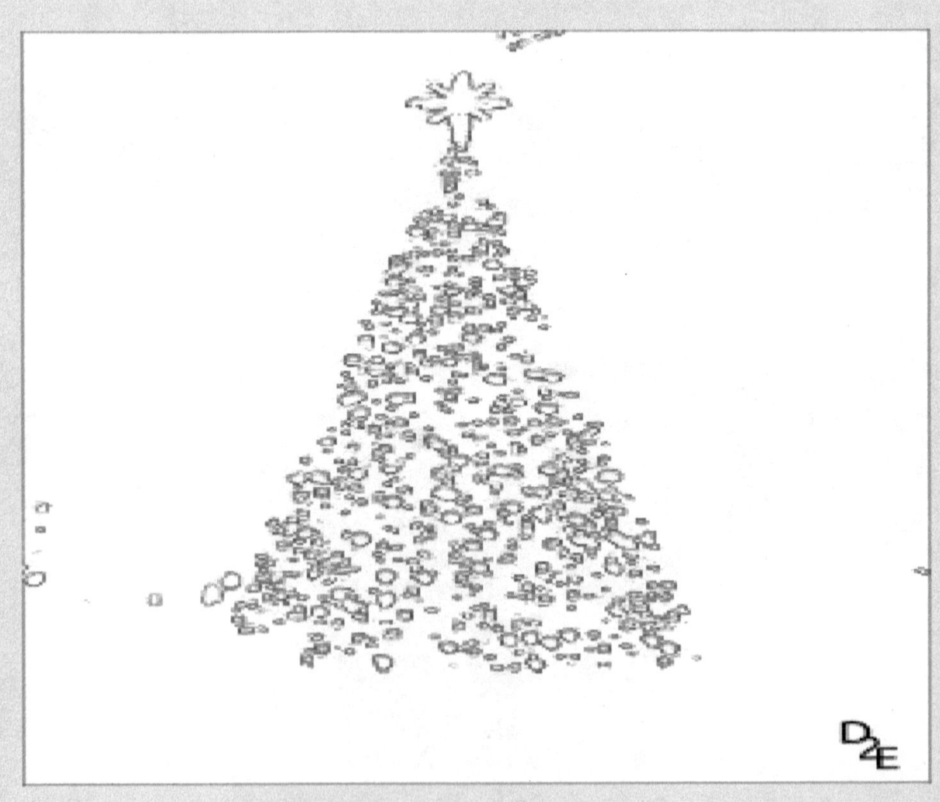

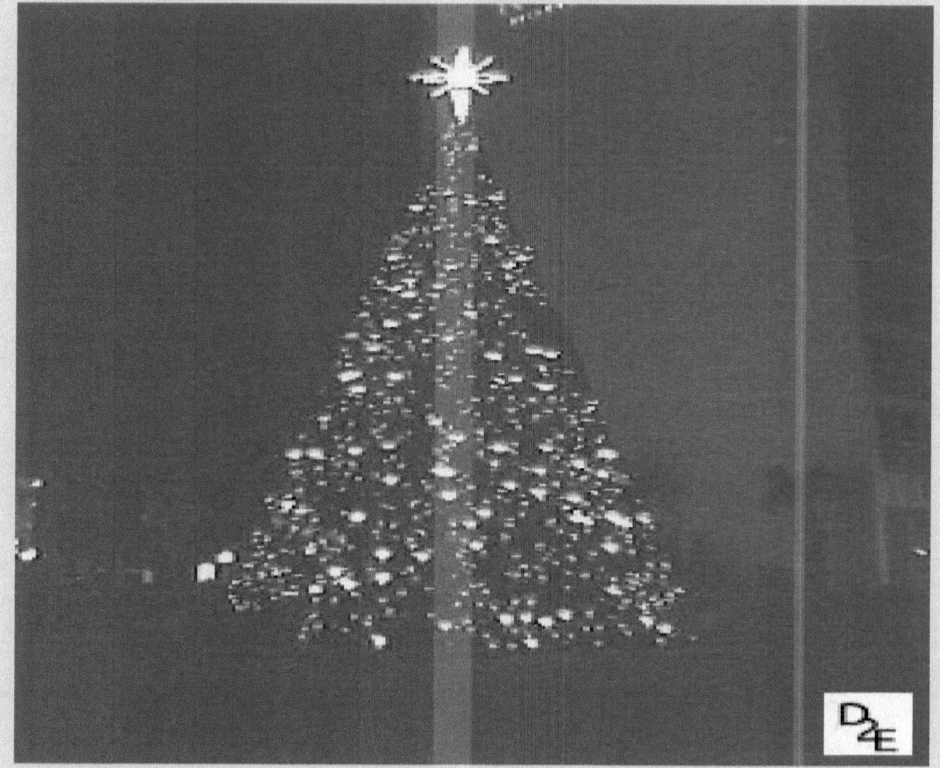
D4E

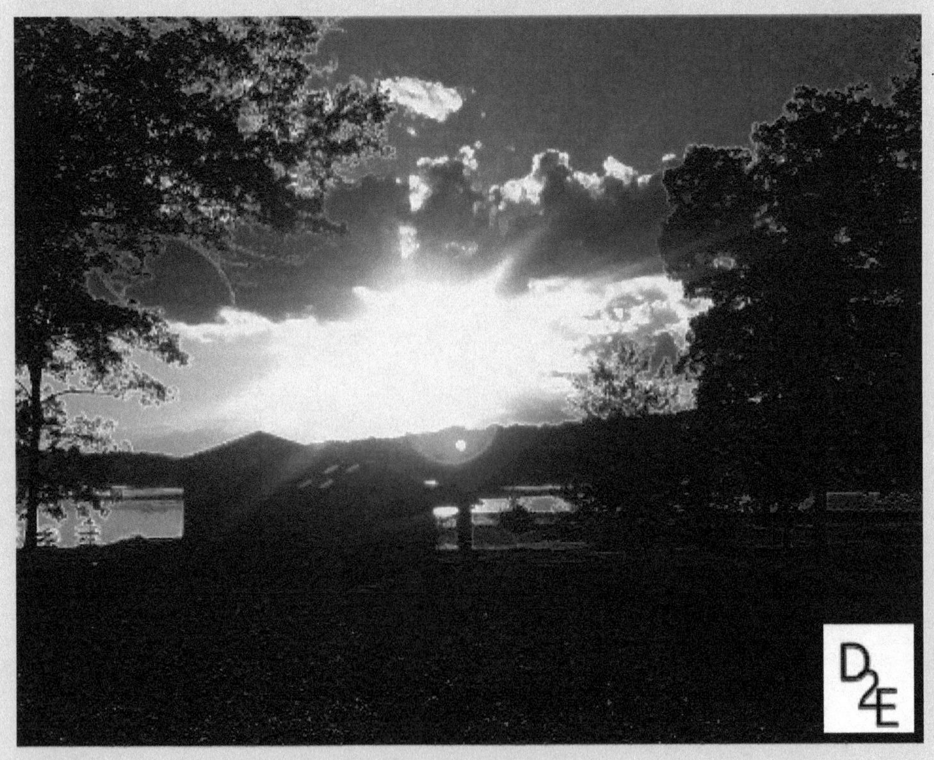
D2E

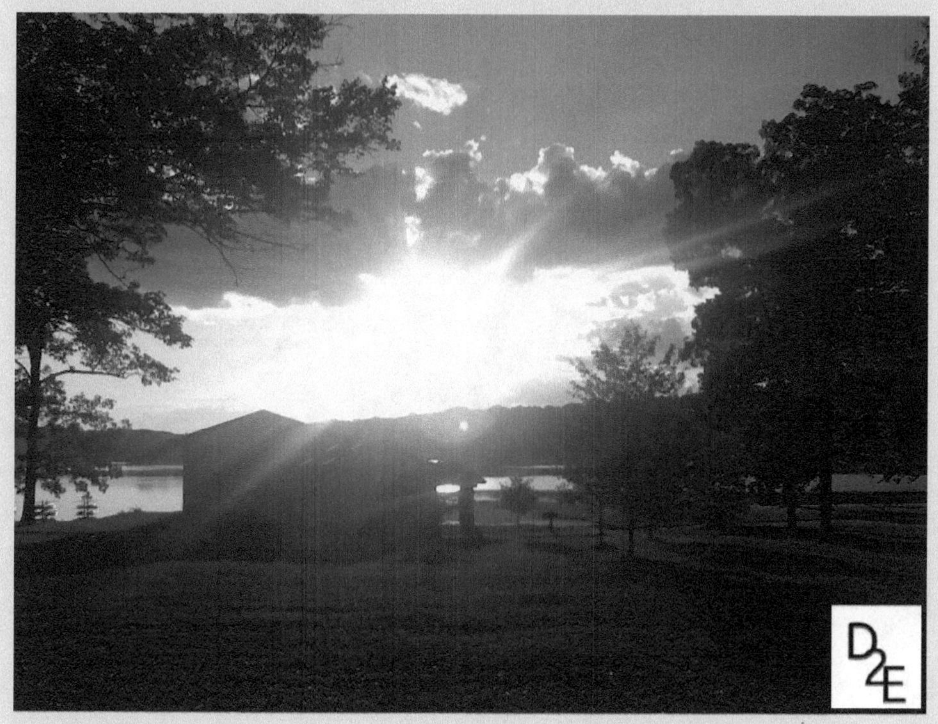
D2E

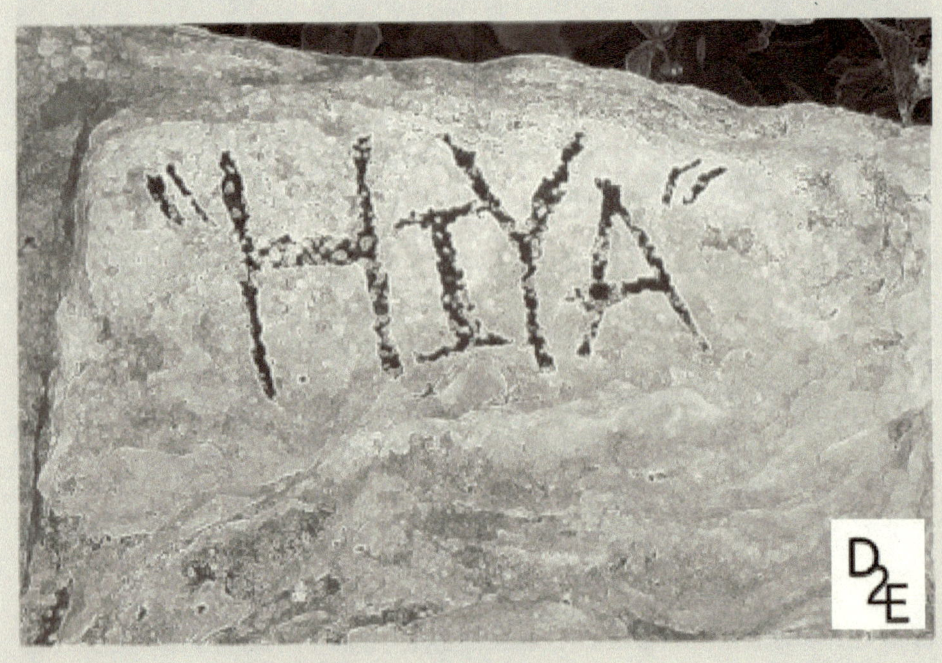
"HIYA"
D4E

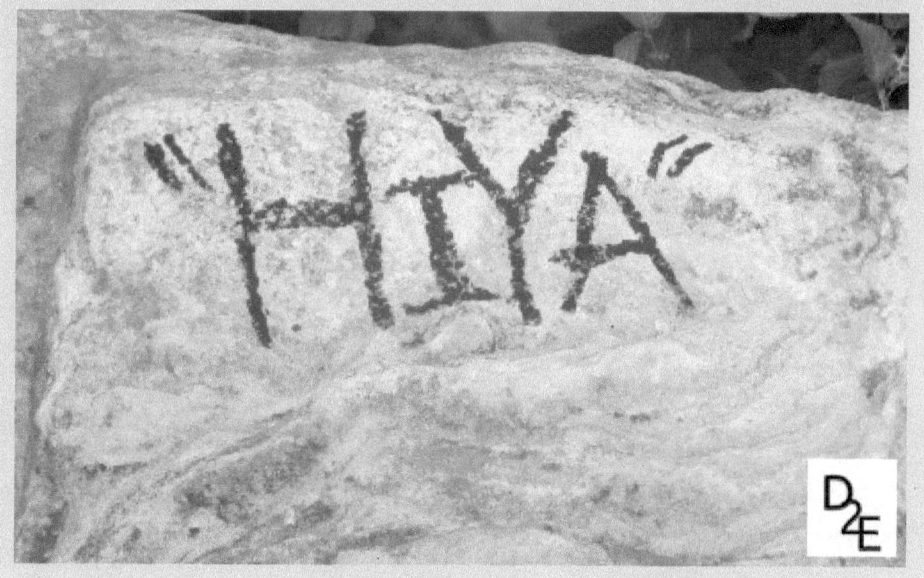
"HIYA"
D2E

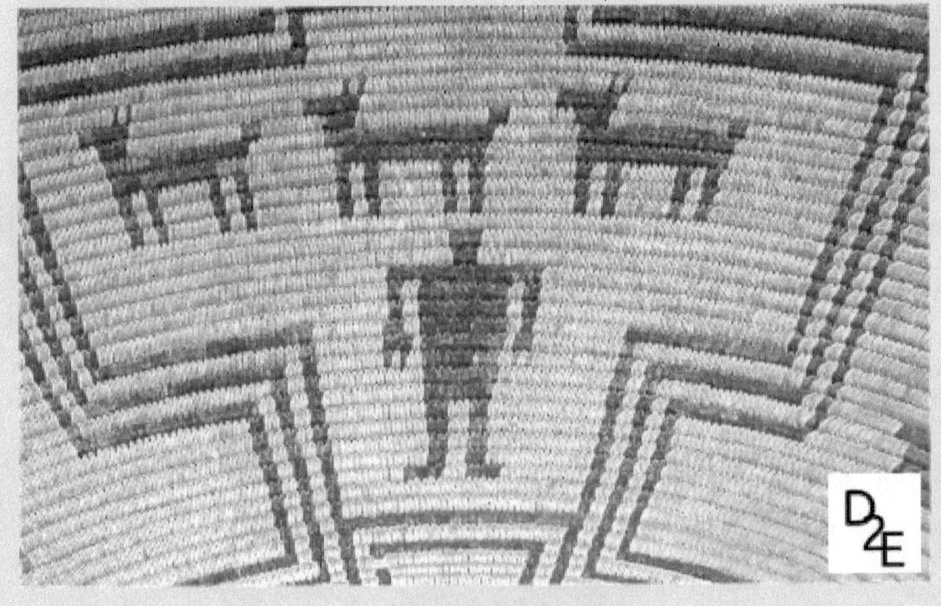
D2E

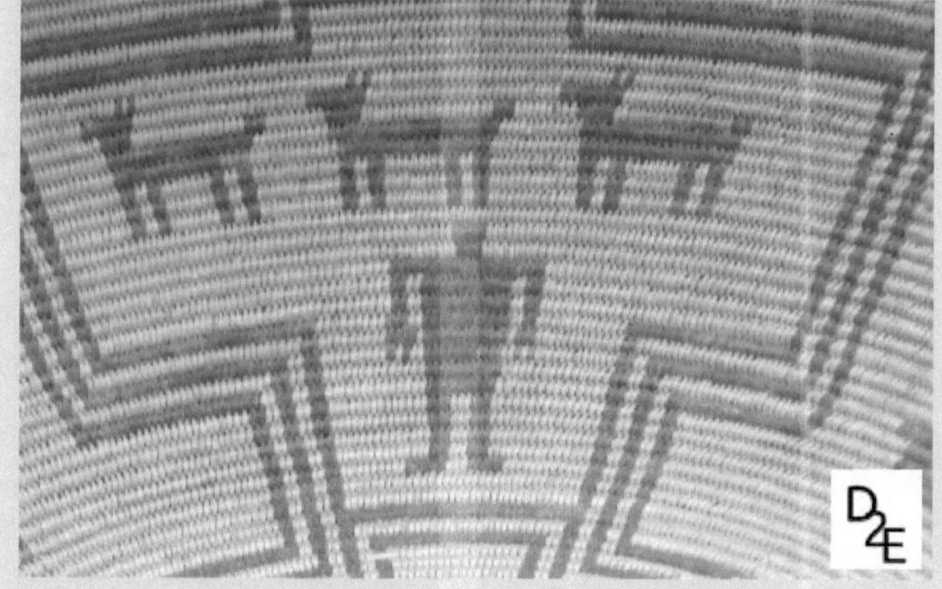
D2E

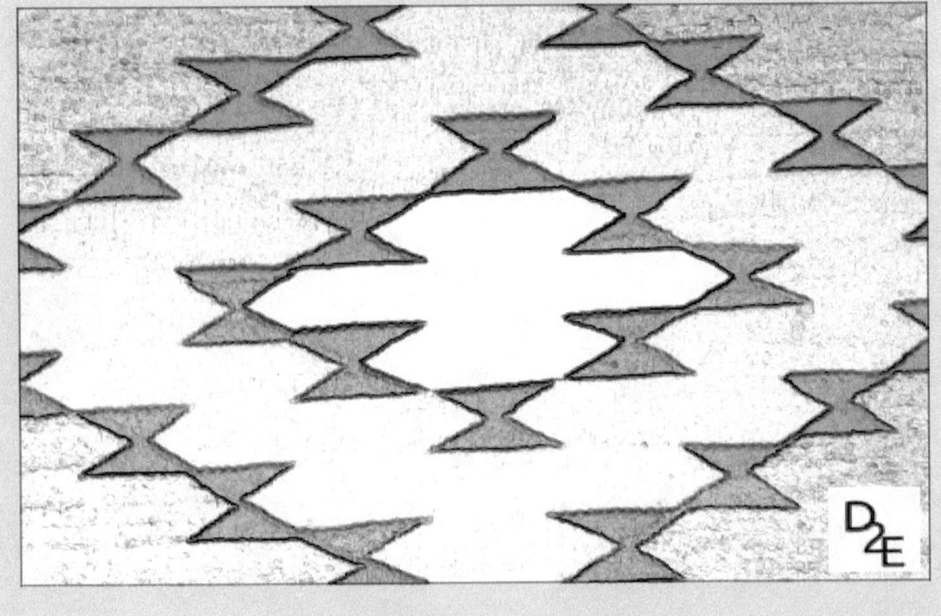
D2E

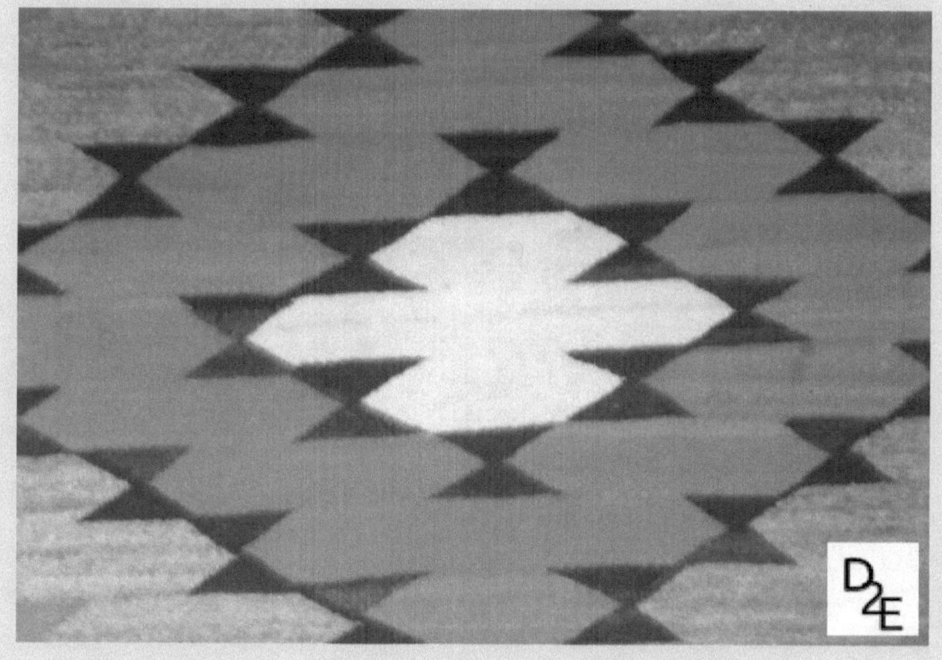
D2E

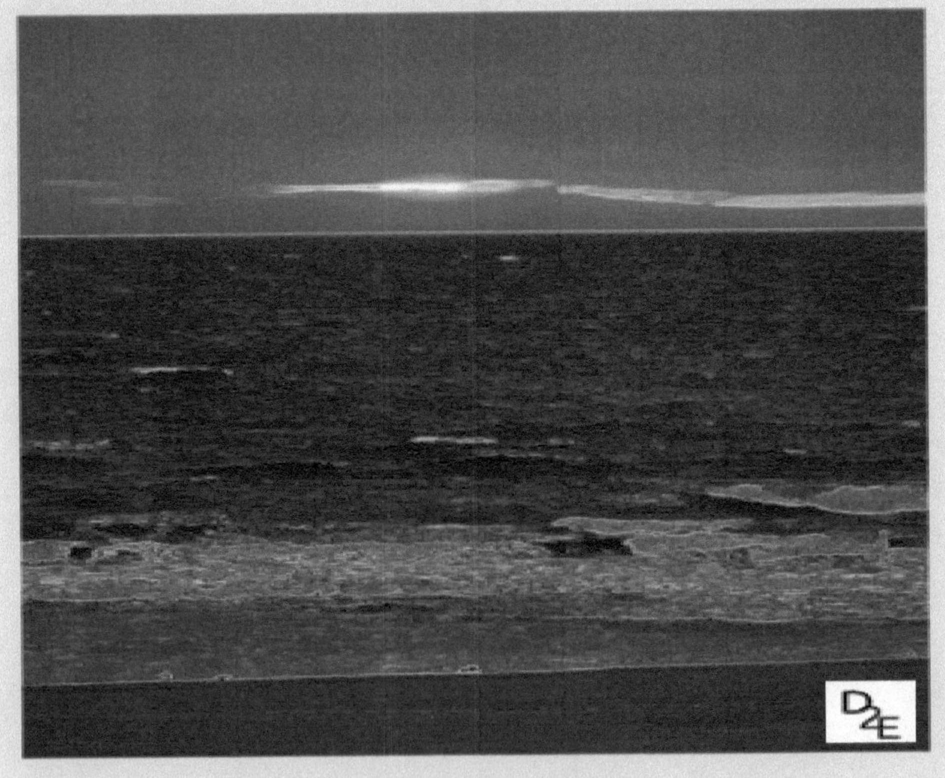
D2E

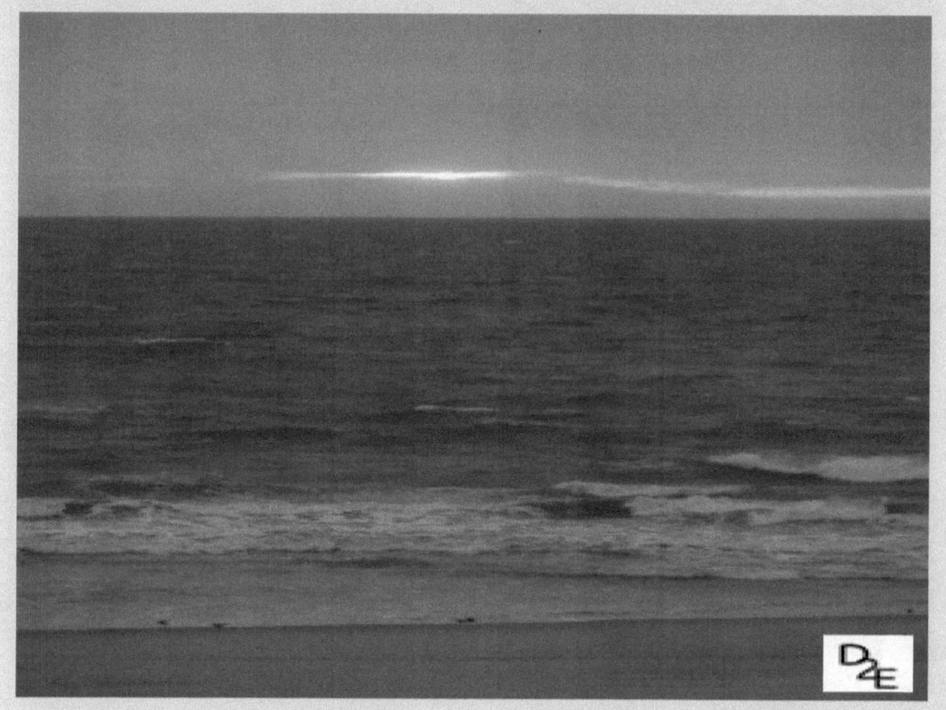
D2E

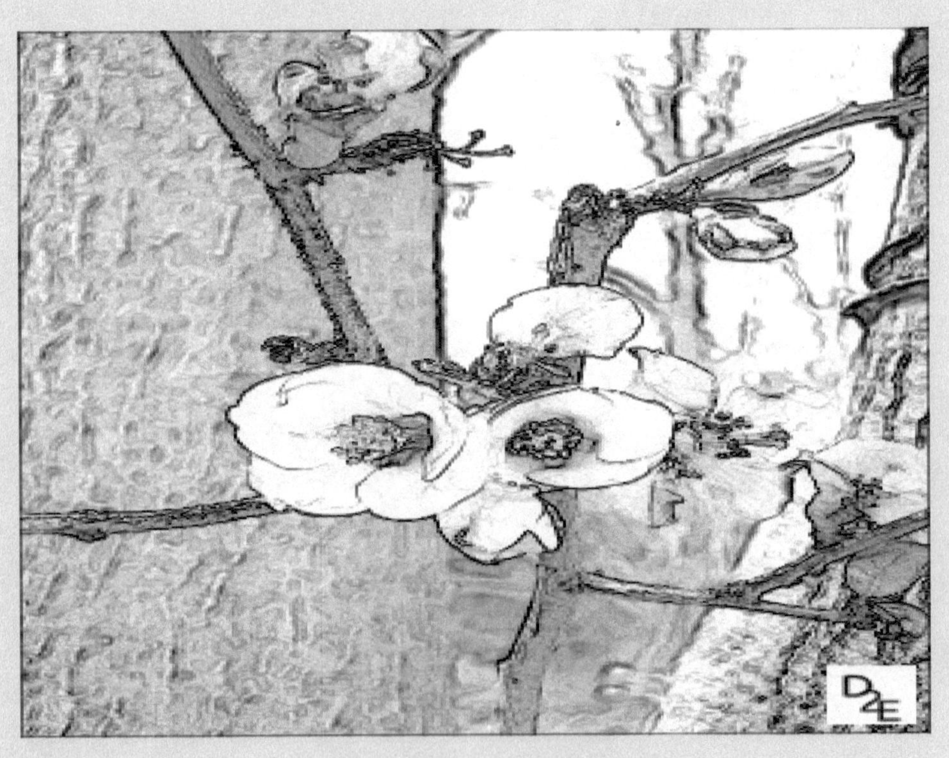

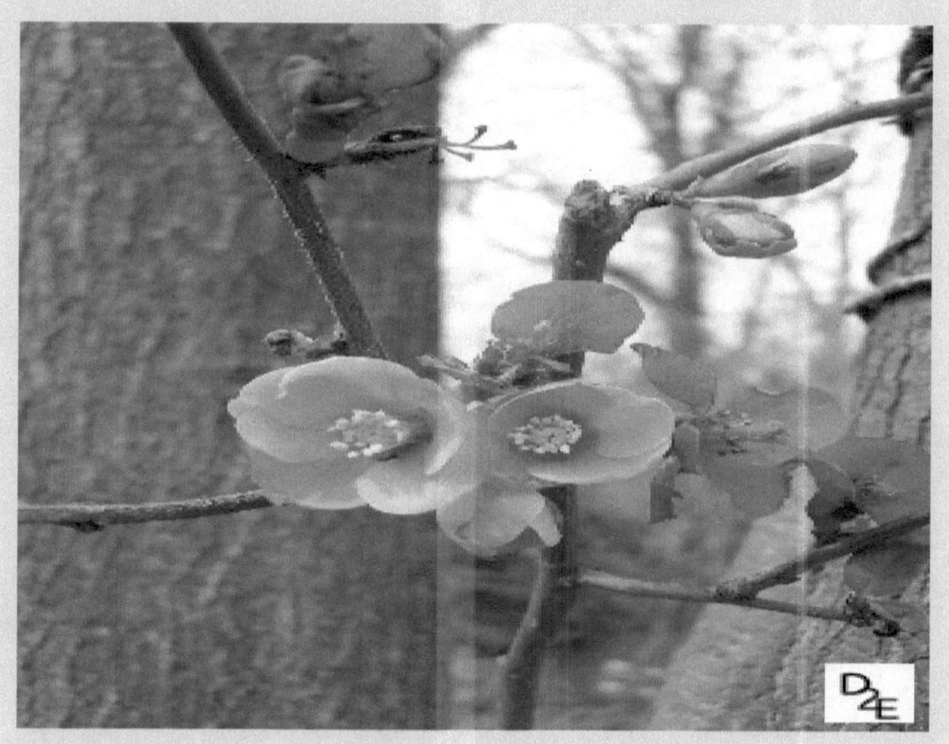

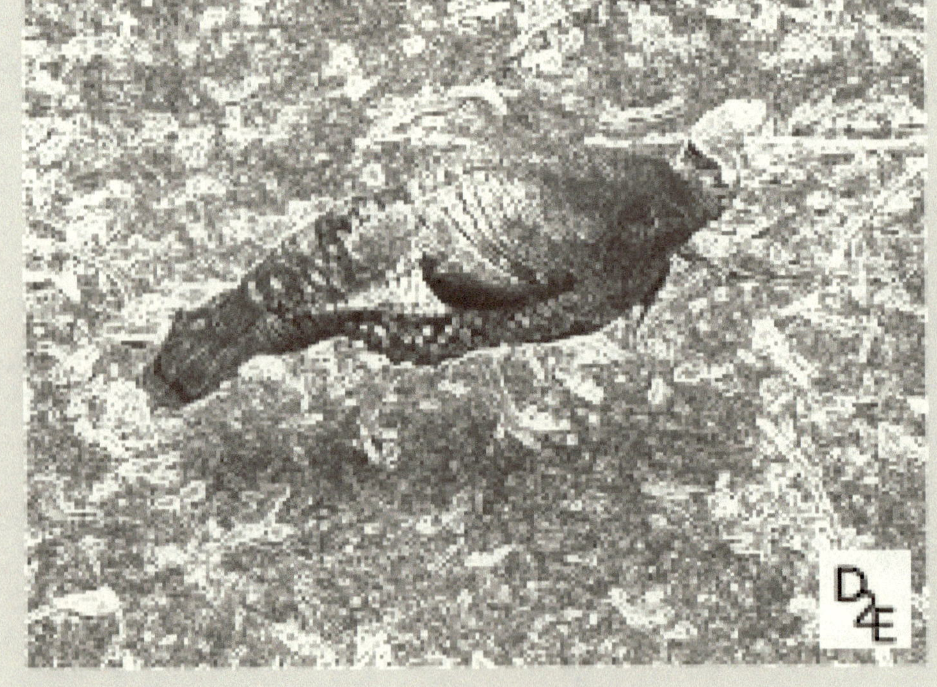

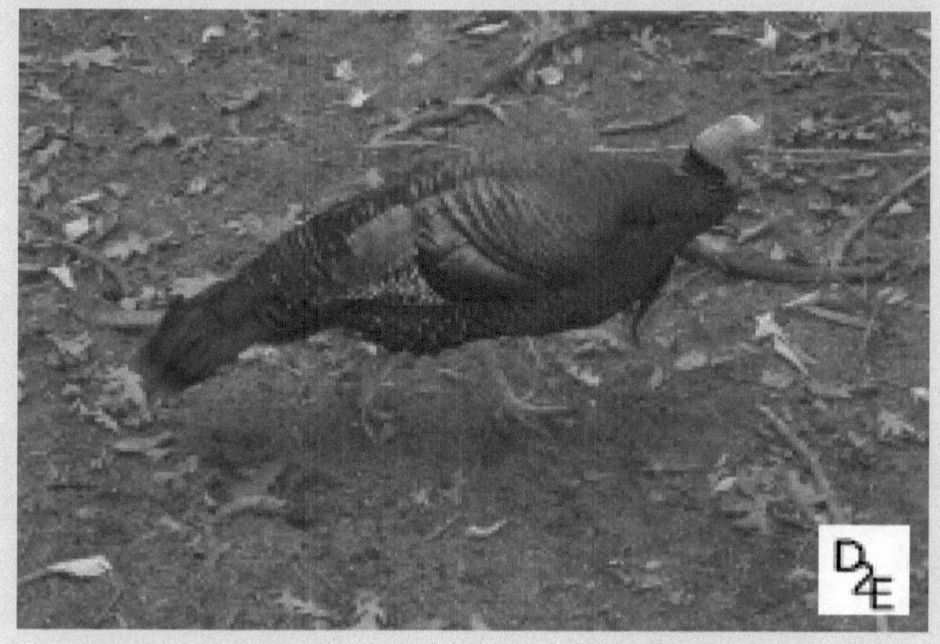

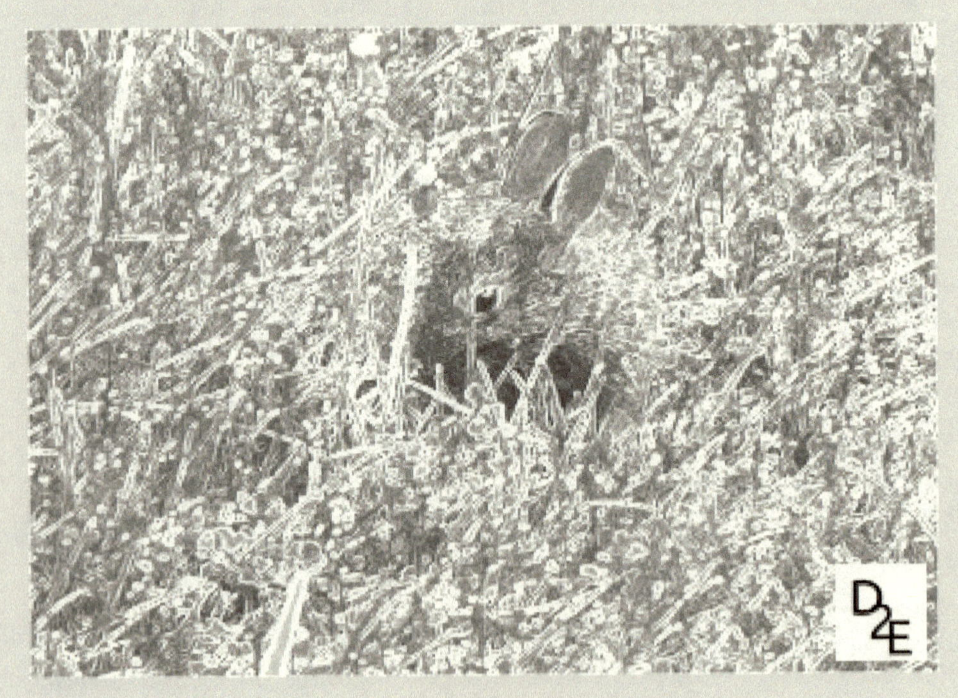
D2E

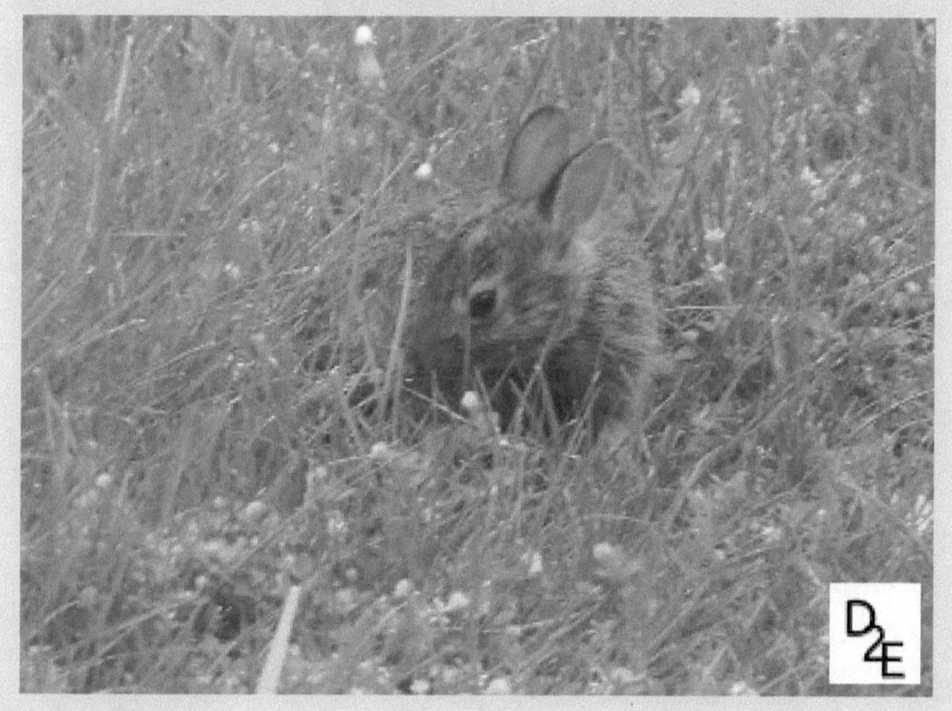
D2E

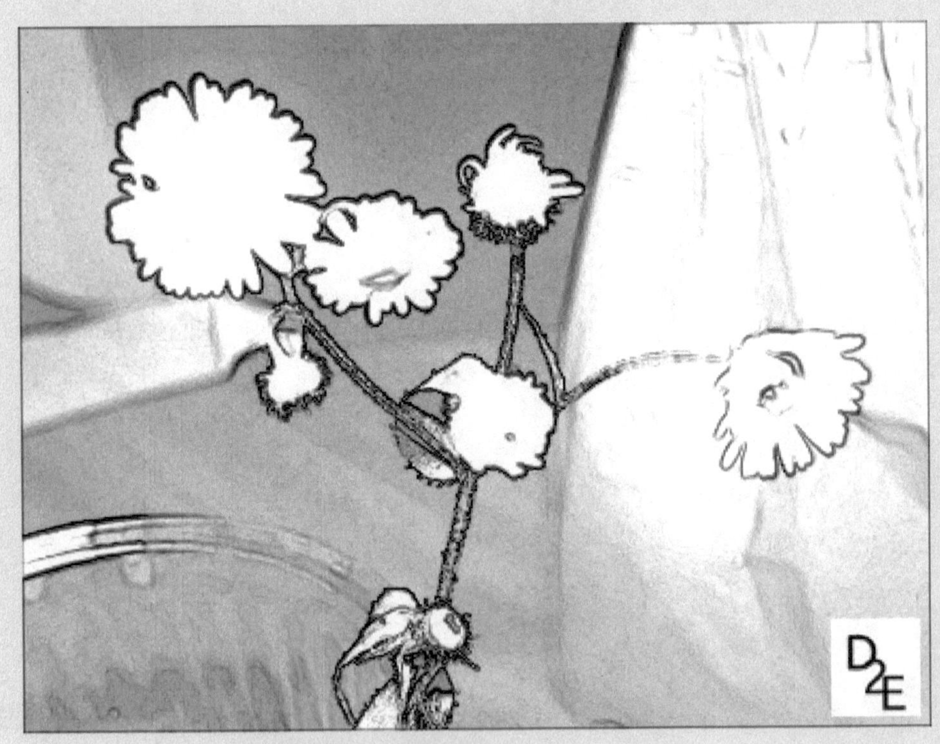
D2E

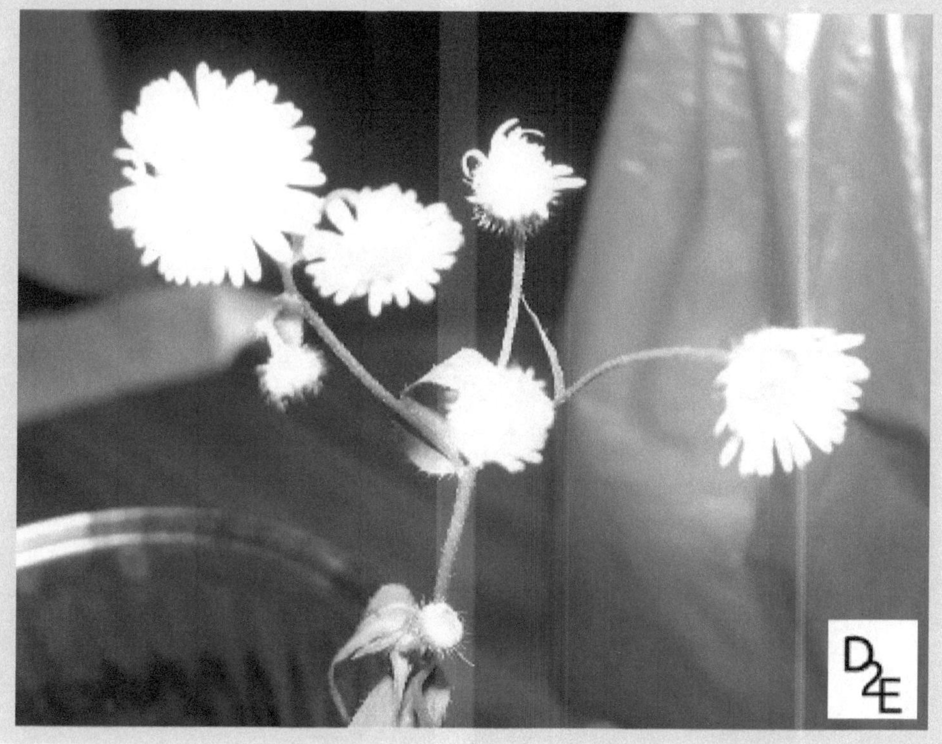

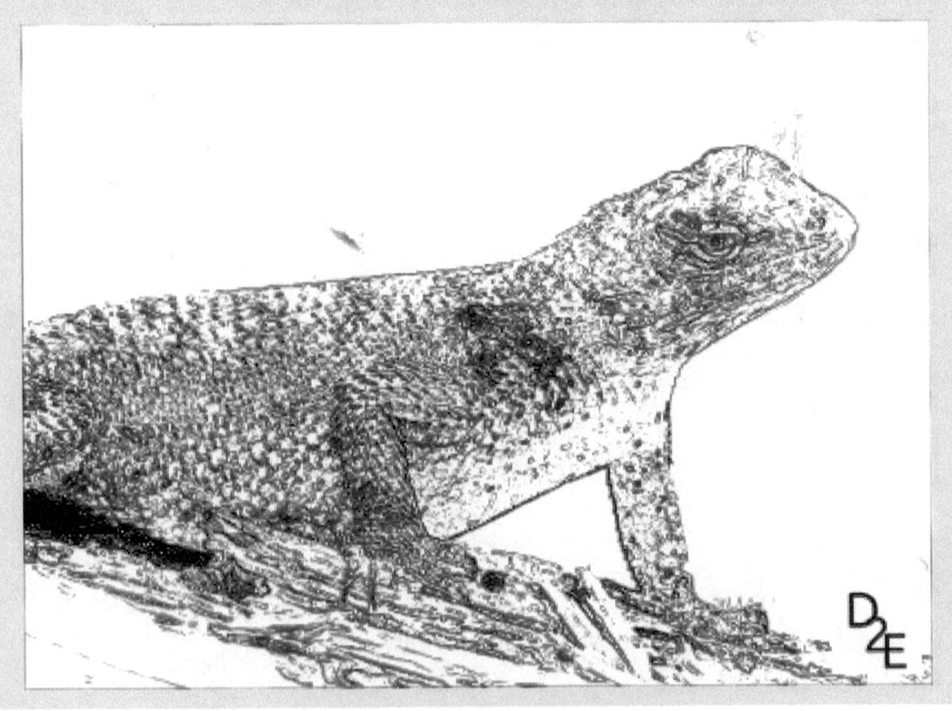
D2E

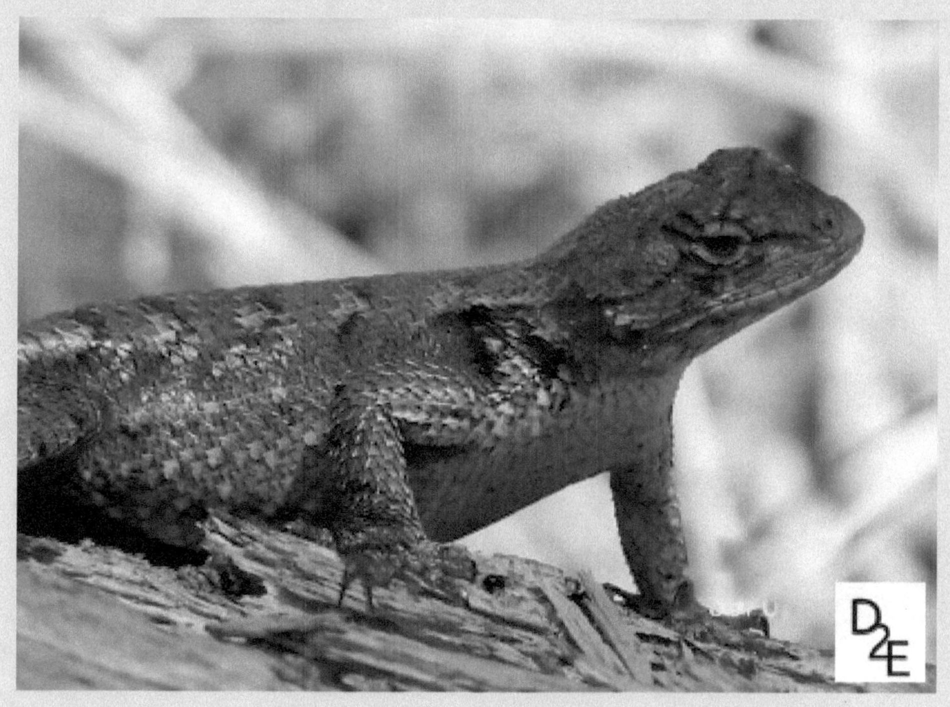

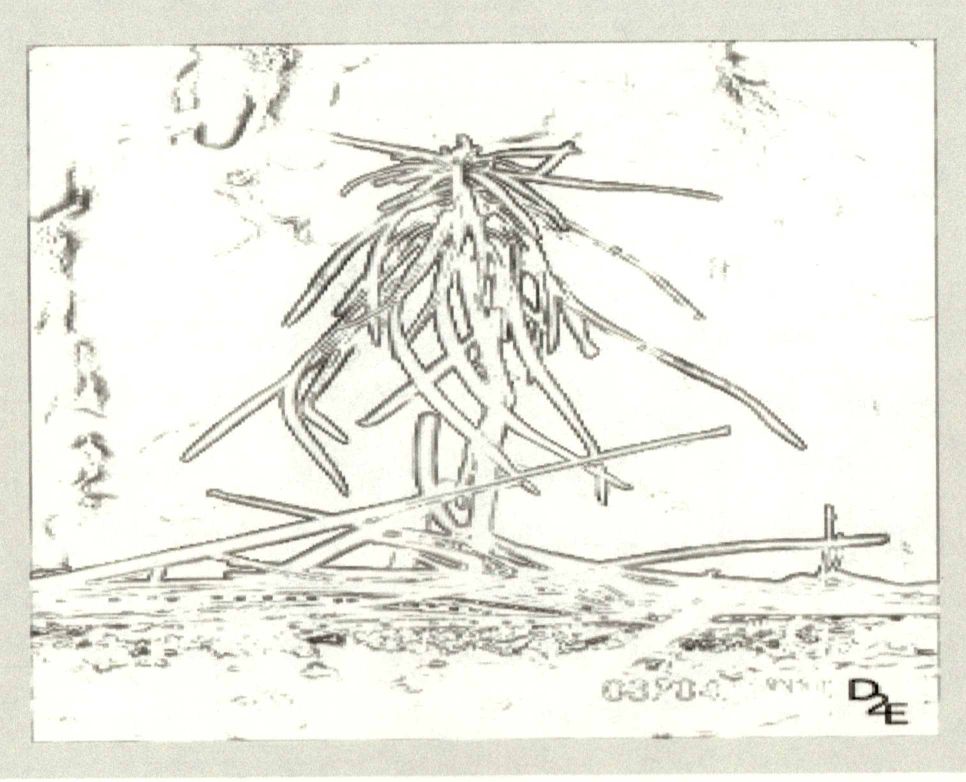

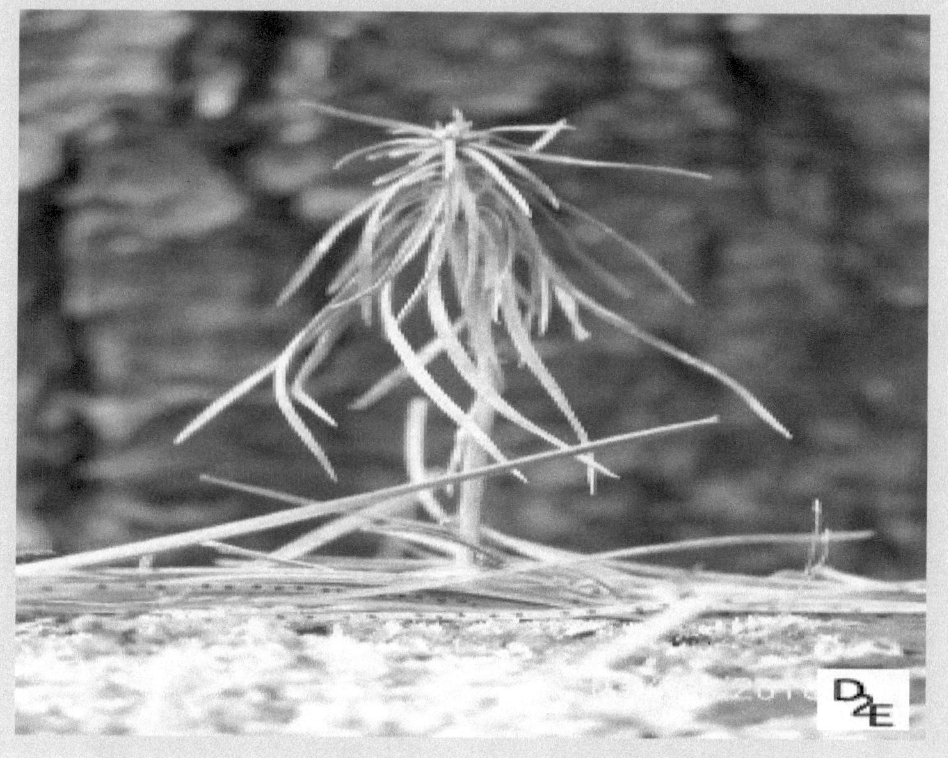
D2E

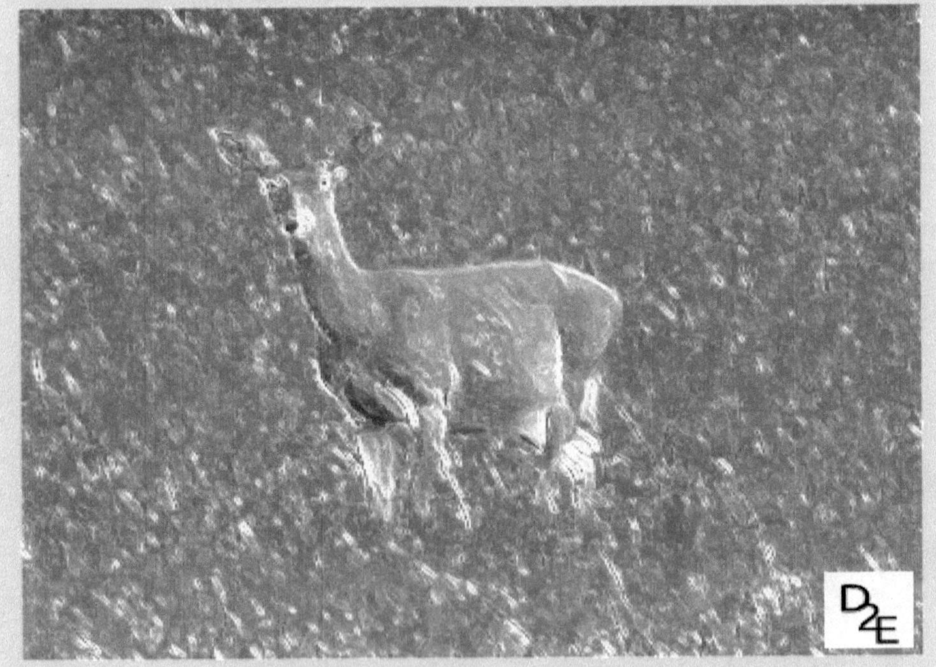
D2E

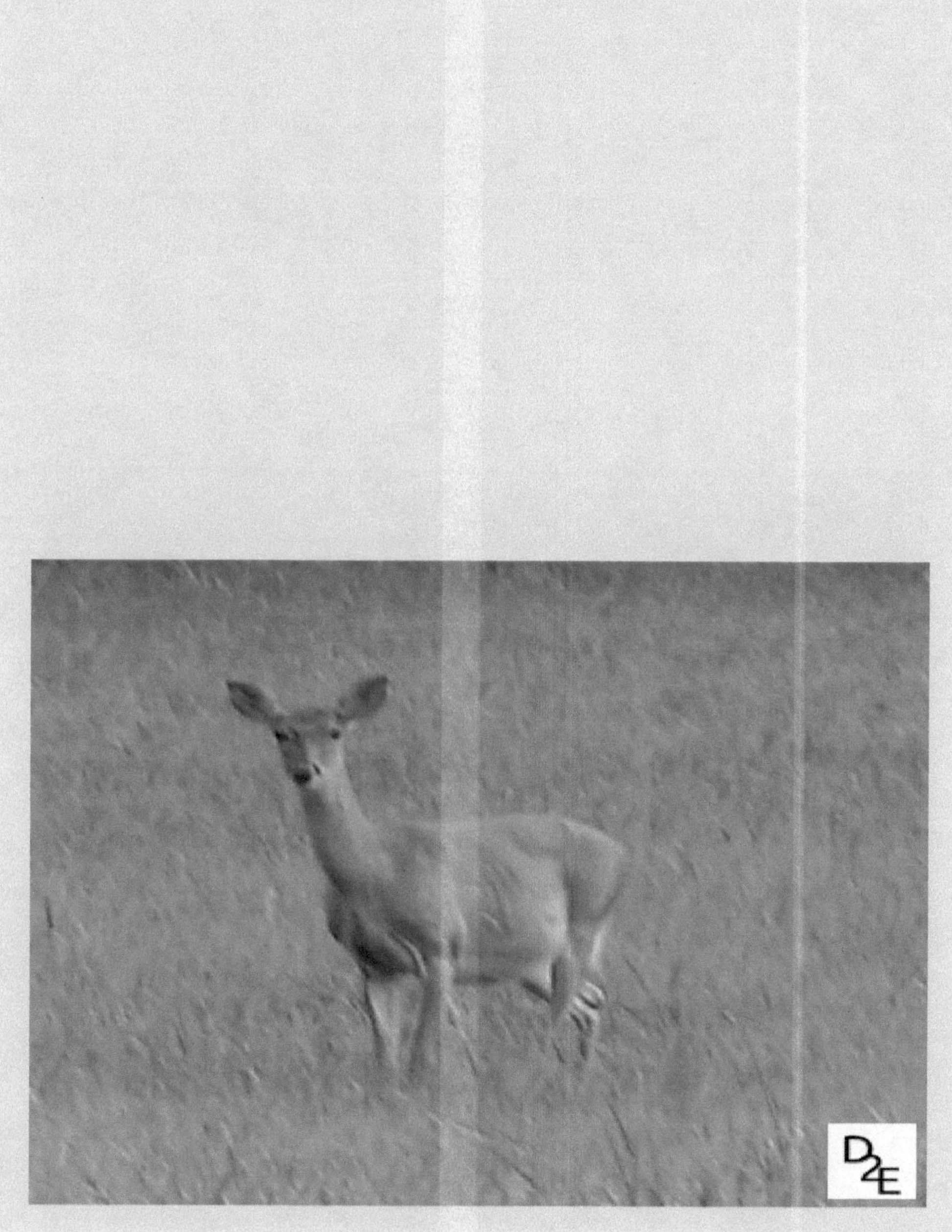
D2E

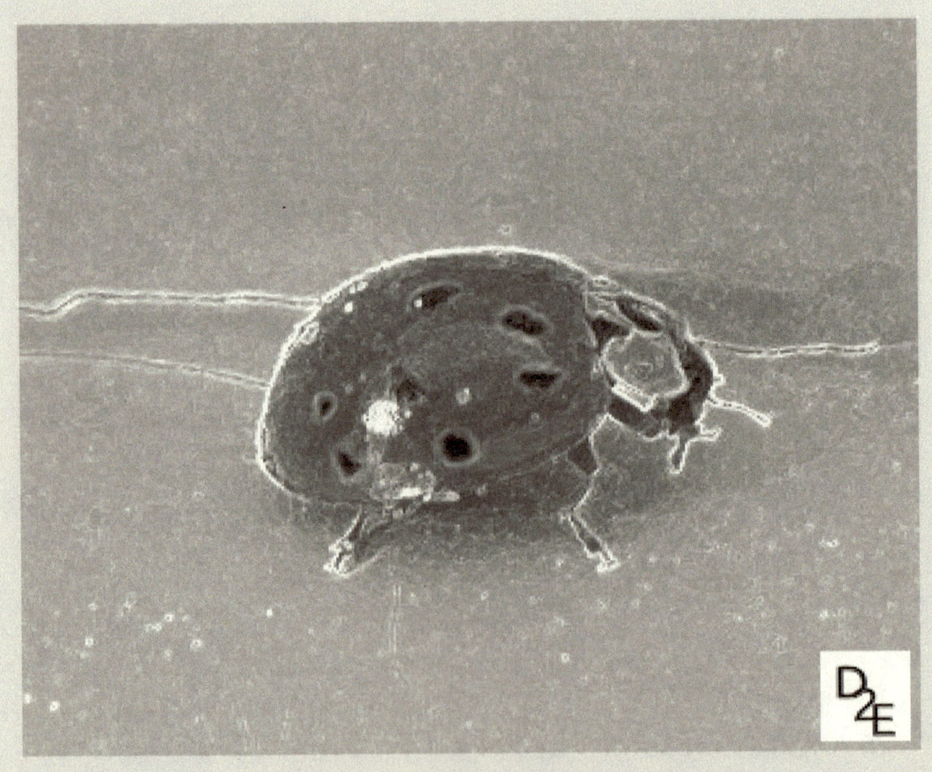
D2E

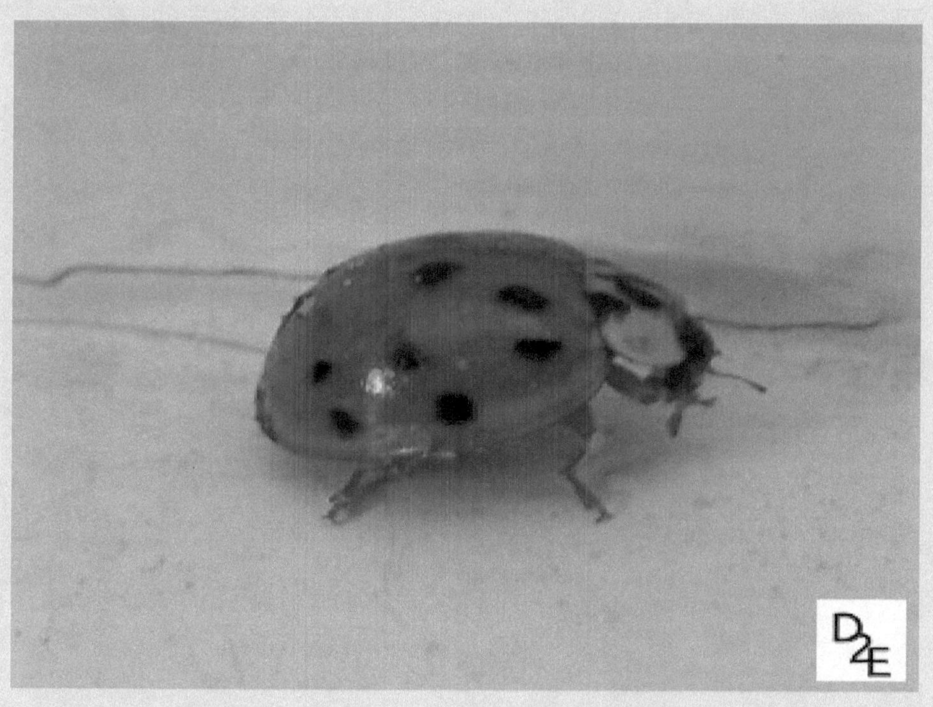
D2E

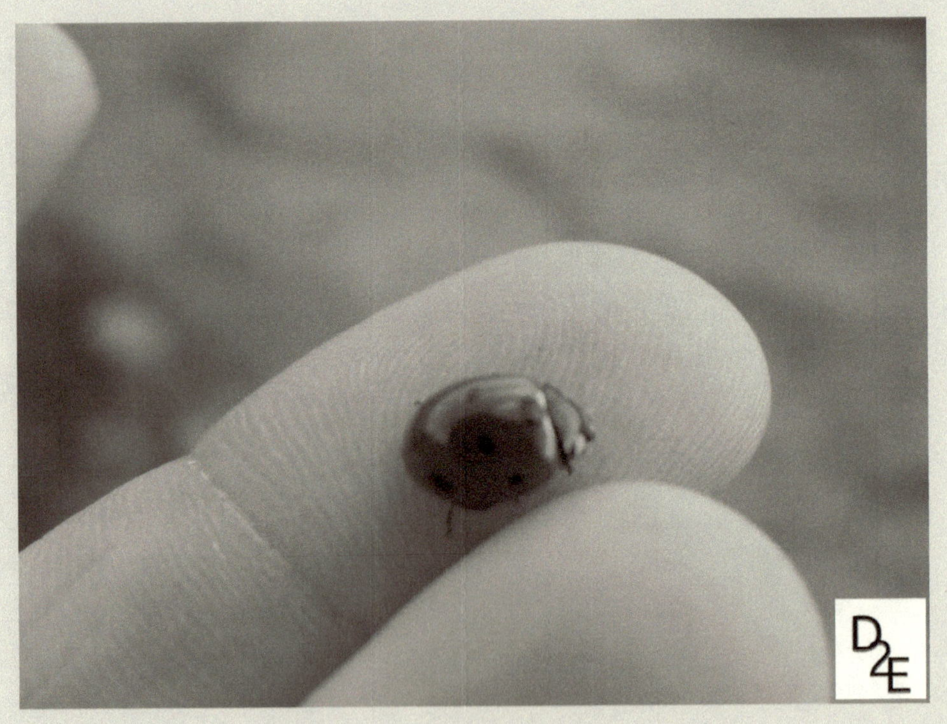
D2E

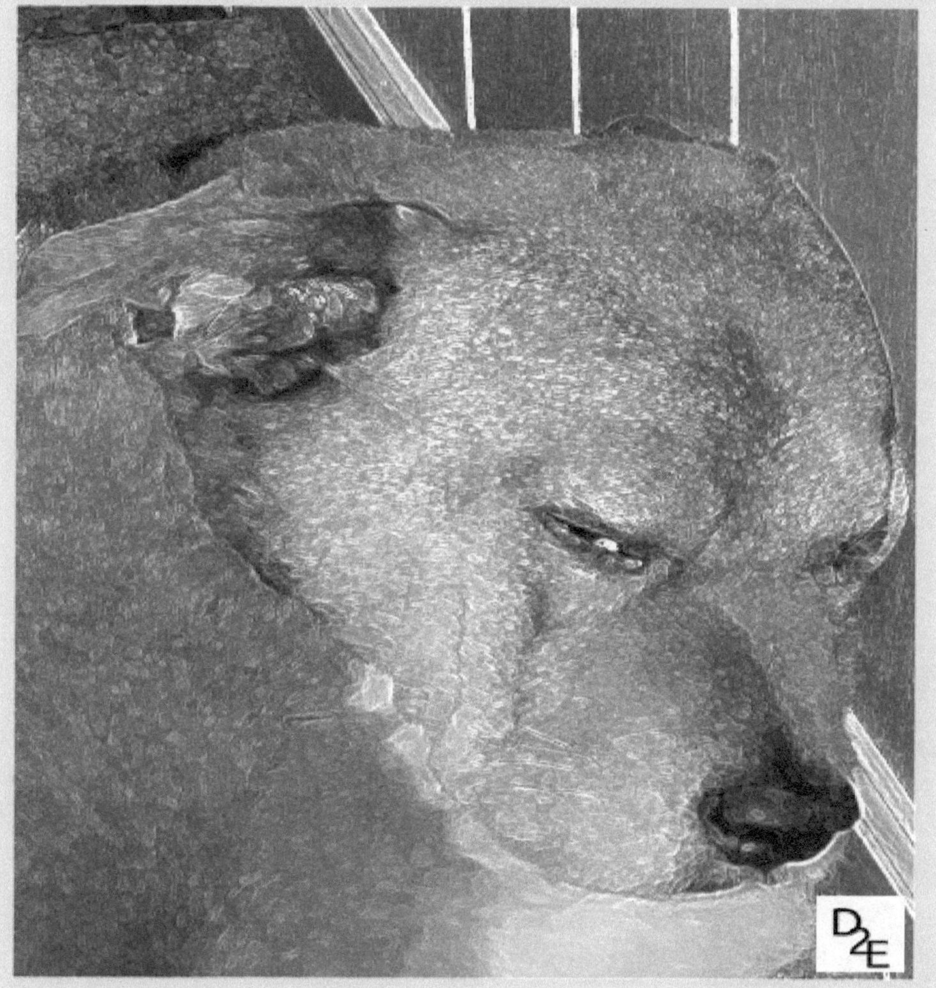
D2E

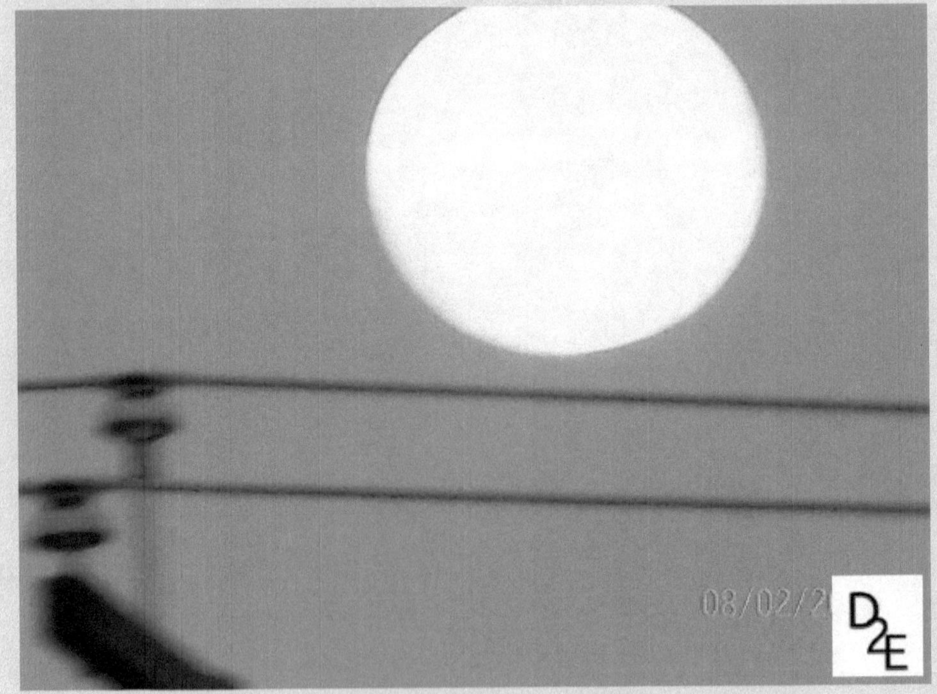

About the Author:

Brian's Bio:

Brian D. Satterfield's the founder of "Brians Trauma Project". A global movement promoting healing to dealing with any of life's horrific events. He's an author, (working) certified peer specialist, advocate, speaker, group facilitator, and a trauma recovery aid. To date, he's written four books, while presenting keynote speaking and wellness workshops. Regarding holistic health, trauma informed care, and trauma recovery.

Since 2002, Brian's motivation to serve his global community stems from his high ACE (Adverse Childhood Experiences) Score. Stemming from: spinal scoliosis, parental neglect/verbal & emotional abuse, nine years childhood sexual abuse via an adult family member. That developed into life long chronic pain, chronic fatigue and numerous persistent treatable medical conditions. In 2009, opportunities presented themselves to Brian where he found himself experiencing peace and contentment for the first time, ever. He wanted more of it! He implemented a strict trauma recovery-oriented treatment plan he uses on a daily basis.

Brian lives in South-Central Pennsylvania, USA with his pets and partner. He likes: writing, educating (on trauma recovery), weekly workouts, all Philadelphia professional sports teams, concerts, rock-N-roll, cinema-movies, gardening, tattoos, day hikes, black coffee and peanut butter. He also finds humor in any situation...

Brian volunteers with: Pennsylvania Office of Victim Advocate (PAOVA), National Alliance (on) Mental Illness (NAMI) [board member], US Pain Foundation, Disabilities Rights PA (DRP) [mental health advisory council], and Male Survivor [board member]....

Free Legal & Free Health Resources:

www.brianstraumaproject.org/resources

www.ingramcontent.com/pod-product-compliance
Lightning Source LLC
LaVergne TN
LVHW091126080826
845145LV00008B/2063

* 9 7 8 0 9 9 9 4 7 1 7 3 9 *